"*Beginnings* meets a precise need in patristic studies and in the history of early Christian biblical interpretation: the need for a historically astute, theologically sympathetic, and hermeneutically sophisticated analysis of the fathers' reading of Genesis 1–3. Here at last is a work that truly sets in relief the many layers of meaning that patristic commentators saw in these rich and evocative opening chapters of the Bible. Rather than dismissing their work as premodern, prescientific groping for a valid explanation of the stories of creation and fall, Bouteneff definitively demonstrates the profound theological contextualization at work in early Christian exegesis of the Genesis cosmogony. This is a superb monograph."

—Paul Blowers, Dean E. Walker Professor of Church History, Emmanuel School of Religion

"I hope this remarkable study will be widely read and appreciated. From the start, the reader is obliged to grapple with questions about how a text is to be read when it can be demonstrated that layers of subsequent interpretation have had as much, if not more, influence than the text itself. And what more crucial text is there than Genesis 1–3, which has shaped Christian understanding of both creation and fall in ways that are now controversial, both within the churches and in the public domain? Though not always agreeing with the analyses presented here, I can guarantee that hardly anyone, whatever their starting point, will come away from this book without having found some new insight."

—Frances M. Young, Edward Cadbury Professor of Theology, retired, University of Birmingham

BEGINNINGS

BEGINNINGS

Ancient Christian Readings
of the Biblical Creation Narratives

Peter C. Bouteneff

Ｂ
Baker Academic
a division of Baker Publishing Group
Grand Rapids, Michigan

Published by Baker Academic
a division of Baker Publishing Group
P.O. Box 6287, Grand Rapids, MI 49516-6287
www.bakeracademic.com

Printed in the United States of America

Library of Congress Cataloging-in-Publication Data

Bouteneff, Peter.

    Beginnings : ancient Christian readings of the biblical creation narratives / Peter C. Bouteneff.

      p. cm.

    Includes bibliographical references and index.

    ISBN 978-0-8010-3233-2 (pbk.)

    1. Creation—History of doctrines. 2. Creation—Biblical teaching. 3. Creationism—History of doctrines. 4. Creationism—Biblical teaching. I. Title.

BT695.B63 2008

222'.110609015—dc22   2008016926

Contents

And There Was Evening

A Preface

The biblical creation narratives are evocative, authoritative, and important to people of several great religious traditions, and yet—like much of Scripture—there are debates and disputes among members of the same tradition and between members of different traditions about how they are to be read and what their narrative details mean. It is all the more difficult to understand them or even to take them seriously in our day, given how much baggage has been laid on them over the centuries by both high art and popular culture—from the Sistine Chapel ceiling to *National Lampoon's Adam and Eve*. Then there are the politicized debates that pit "evolution" against "creation," categories that an increasing number of people consider simplistic. Theological discourse, too, looks to the creation narratives for answers to more questions than they can possibly bear—questions about the cosmos, humanity, gender, theodicy. It would be useful to see how they were read before the accretion of so many layers of interpretation.

Within the Christian tradition alone, the exegesis of Genesis 1–3 has a long and varied history. It is worth inquiring how the creation narratives were read when they were first beginning to be considered authoritative foundational texts, particularly by those instrumental in shaping Christian theology. Although this question may be relevant to anyone studying the history of ideas, it is of particular concern to traditions that vest authority in patristic witness. But the evolution of the early Christian interpretation of Genesis 1–3 is of more than antiquarian interest: like all good history, it has the potential to illuminate the present. In this regard, one feature becomes clear from even a cursory study of this period: we do not find a univocal reading or a single method (which might confound those who would impose a single fixed framework on these narratives). We do, however, find a consistent and coherent pattern of reading, whose theological character is considerably different from the modern mainstream. And even if this pattern cannot be adopted wholesale by contemporary readers of all predilections, it may at least point them to something more substantive, constructive, and meaningful than the results of either atheological modern criticism or overwrought theological analysis.

The Authors under Review

What do we mean by "ancient Christian" thought or interpretation? A narrow definition of "Christian" in the first centuries after Christ no longer suffices. Recent scholars have made a compelling case for expanding the definition of what properly constitutes early Christian theology and practice and for blurring the lines between orthodoxy and heresy. Yet at least for the purposes and scope of the present study, I am mindful of the undeniable divide between the first- and second-century authors who read the Genesis narratives in terms of the God who sent his Son into the world as its unique Savior and those who took Paul's spiritualization of the law as license to construct parascriptural accounts of cosmic origins. The lines that separate Irenaeus and Valentinus are not especially blurry, nor are those between Tertullian and Marcion. The tendency of "orthodox" writers to exaggerate or distort the positions of their "heretical" challengers is equally undeniable and significant, but it does not obliterate those categories. Although the study of the totality of the ancient literature is both necessary and fascinating, and although neither mainstream nor marginalized theologies ought to be ignored or short-changed in research, the two still ought to be studied as separate categories. And they generally are: any responsible study of theology in the early Christian centuries will be concerned with hermeneutical questions, their polemical context, and their political and ecclesiastical influences, but we still end up with books on "lost Christianities," on different stripes of gnostic and Manichaean writers, as well as on the church fathers.

This book focuses on the last group. After looking selectively at the period when the Genesis creation narratives first resurfaced among hellenized Jewish writers and LXX translators, it surveys Paul and the NT. It then primarily explores the early Christian writers who wrote in Greek during the first four Christian centuries. Tertullian—the sole Western author—is included there as well because of the seminal importance of his contribution.[1] These authors— whether through a patriarchal conspiracy or the guidance of the Holy Spirit (or some combination thereof)—were responsible for the early formation of Christian theology and still resonate among contemporary Christians, in

---

1. Jerome and Augustine are outside our time frame, and Ambrose's *Hexaemeron* relies so heavily on Basil's that he does not require separate treatment in this study.

particular those who take early patristic voices seriously: Orthodox, Roman Catholics, and sectors of all the mainline Protestant denominations, Anglicans, free churches, and many evangelicals. Our study ends with the Cappadocian fathers, who represent the first sustained harvest of Origen's exegetical ideas.

So this book covers about four centuries of early Greek patristic reflection. With regret, we must leave for another study the great Antiochene exegetes and rhetoricians who came later, the glorious Syrians Aphrahat and Ephrem (themselves contemporaries of the Cappadocians), and Augustine, whose rich and diverse study of the creation narratives was so influential in the Christian West.

The Questions We Pose

In our time, the text of Genesis 1–3—the six-day creation, God's seventh-day rest, and the drama of Adam and Eve in paradise—is brought to bear on questions about the relationship between God and creation; the origin and logic of evil; death, sin, and the relationship between the two; the nature and vocation of the human person, including human sexuality; the relationship between human and nonhuman creation; and the process and chronology of creation. These and others constitute *our* questions, and the way in which we moderns frame them does not always overlap with how the ancient writers did. Furthermore, each ancient author explores particular facets of the creation narratives that may have nothing to do with original sin, image and likeness, creation out of nothing, the evolution/creation debate, human personhood, marriage, sex, and gender. We must read them in terms of what interested them, or what their context, their readers, oppressors, or ideological challengers elicited from them. Some authors do speak about creation out of nothing, about sin, and about gender, but not all do. This book will take each author on his own terms, which means that the subjects treated will necessarily vary.

In this book I pose one overarching question to the writers I treat: how literally did they read the creation narratives? This question may seem anachronistic since it implies categories like "history," "myth," "parable," and "allegory," whose meanings have evolved over time and moreover at no point acquired a commonly agreed-on meaning. Ancient sensibilities about the relationship between "history" and "story" were different from ours. But how different? Reading the ancients, we find that during any single era perceptions of and concerns about historicity and its relationship to truth vary among contemporaries at least as much as they do across the millennial divides. Some of the ancient authors indeed treat the question explicitly. Not dissimilarly, we witness today a potent and widespread concern as to whether Genesis 1–3 records events that occurred in the physical universe as they are described. Among and within traditions, and even outside fixed religious traditions, the debate simmers. In my own Orthodox tradition I can testify to different microclimates: some writers insist on the historicity of the narratives (with some variation as to the age of the Earth, the nature of the six "days," etc.); others insist that they are essentially etiological stories (but are no less true for being so); others hold positions that somehow occupy an intermediate stance; others fail even to be bothered with the question.

When we consider our contemporary situation, it is almost inappropriate to speak of a debate between these views, for scholars tend to talk only to their respective camps. Indeed, one of the main reasons that I will dwell on the question of historicity is that so few studies even bother to address it outright. People are generally so convinced of their own position—and so sure that those who consider otherwise are intellectually or spiritually depraved—that they see no need to argue for it. The other factor muting the debate is more positive: the sacramental and liturgical life of the church does not depend on where one stands on this issue. The language and ethos of worship subsume these questions in a way that is profoundly unifying and affirmative so that all may stand side by side hearing the same Scripture readings, singing the same hymns about them.

But there remains a divide. It has to do with the question of how Scripture works and what it means to say that it is inspired by God. But it also has to do with the question of whether "truth" and "historical facticity" are inextricably interdependent. Some say that if Scripture is inspired by God and Genesis 1–3 does not describe physical history in a literal way, then God lied. Others maintain that God is speaking the truth here through story. Both would agree that a parable or a fable can be true. But can the dynamics that apply to a parable or a fable apply to these narratives also?

I have alluded to the perception that questions about truth and historicity are unique to the modern era, that they were irrelevant to the scriptural authors. The following passage, from an explanation of OT storytelling, is a good example of that attitude:

> Twentieth-century Western audiences are at a major disadvantage when approaching biblical narratives. Our philosophical presuppositions demand that a story produce its historical credentials before it is allowed to speak; we impose modern historical methods on traditional narrative and imagine that our questionable reconstruction of events is more meaningful than the value-laden form in which our community has enshrined its vision. In many of the sciences, we are geniuses when compared to the generations gone by; in the area of traditional narrative, however, we have become unappreciative philistines.[2]

2. McCarthy and Riley, *Old Testament Short Story*, 53. I cited this paragraph in Bouteneff, *Sweeter Than Honey*, 79.

We are thus reminded, very appropriately, that some or most of the biblical authors did not experience cognitive dissonance between truth and story or, in any case, that Scripture neither features nor reflects any expressly literary-critical thinking. But this absence did not extend equally through antiquity and the Middle Ages. It was not universal in the time of the scriptural authors either. Herodotus and Thucydides, for example, indicate their critical consciousness when they assert the *necessity* of historiographic embellishment and the deliberate recasting of accounts to suit the needs of the present. More to the point, the early Christian writers were also concerned with historicity or the relationships between history, story, and truth. In fact several of our writers address the very basic question "Did this actually happen in the physical world?" They pose it of Scripture as a whole but specifically of the Genesis creation narratives.

A study such as ours inherently concerns three broad stages in the history and interpretation of Genesis 1–3. One stage is its composition and redaction. The second (which is our subject here) reads and interprets this text at the outset of Christian reflection. The third is the interpretation of the texts today. Stages two and three are not as far apart as they may seem: both in antiquity and in the present we find a coexistence—albeit a frequently tense one—between critical and precritical readings.[3] I suggest that it is between stages one and two that we find the decisive difference. Were the creation narratives, in the form in which they were told and then codified in writing, intended for analyses by a Theophilus, an Irenaeus, an Origen, a Basil?

But analyzed they certainly were. There were a variety of early Christian approaches, however implicit, to the question of historicity, together with a palpable silence on the matter. But the "critical" questions of history, story, truth, and inspiration exploded onto the scene with Origen, who asked them directly. Origen's brilliance, together with the fierce controversy he ignited, sent wildly uneven shockwaves into the centuries as subsequent generations of theologians grappled with his legacy.

Although "allegory," "typology," "myth," "literal sense," and so on are slippery categories, it is scarcely possible to describe the early church's reading of Scripture without them. For even as these terms require thoughtful definition, they help us map out the breadth of exegetical approaches of the fathers, and the aim and scope of their exegesis. Where these terms appear, they will be accompanied by explanations as necessary, paving the way for a more thorough treatment in the conclusion. But I hope that posing the question of historicity and showing where it is meaningful to the fathers and where it is not will help us discern and explore the patterns of the early fathers' theological and paraenetic reading of the creation narratives, for the

---

3. Here we are not far from Northrop Frye's proposed scheme describing "metaphoric, metonymic, and post-critical" phases: cf. *Great Code*. But note that "critical" with a view to history does not mean the "historical-critical method."

historical-critical method and fundamentalist reading alike often obscure the fruits of their insights.

So, what is the project of this book? It is to listen to what the early Christian tradition has to say about Genesis 1–3. Although it attempts to take the writers on their own terms, it does not pretend to be an entirely disinterested study. Rather it seeks a purposeful discussion that highlights writers selected for their seminal importance in Christian theology and life, in particular within traditions such as my own. Finally, it is impossible to isolate what these authors say about Genesis 1–3 from the question of why and how they arrive at their reading. This study therefore discusses how each author understood and read the Bible—a corpus that was just coming into being during the era here under review. The end result will be the tracing of parallel journeys: generally, the development of early patristic hermeneutics and, specifically, the ways the creation narratives were understood. Although I am convinced that the resulting hermeneutical pattern has much to say to our religious and secular worlds, I will for the most part leave it to the reader to spell out these implications.

A Word about Language

As this book deals with the origins of the world and focuses naturally on the creation and plight of the human person, I have struggled with the question of how best to speak about "humanity" or "man." There is no simple solution how properly to translate the Hebrew 'adam or the Greek ἄνθρωπος. One of the meanings these terms carry refers simultaneously to humankind and human personhood—as collective and generic—but does so in a way that retains a *particular* and *personal* focus. When the fathers spoke of ὁ Αδαμ or even ὁ ἄνθρωπος (rather than ἡ ἀνθρωπότης) to mean "humanity," they retained some of the polyvalence of the Hebrew 'adam. To them it did not mean "humanity" as a collective or abstract term; it somehow had a concrete and particular meaning. With this in mind, were it not for the serious problem of its gender specificity, "man" would be the best word by far to convey this sense of 'adam and ἄνθρωπος. Yet contemporary society, and with it the wider theological community, has simply outgrown it. We cannot but hear the word "man" as referring in the first instance to a male and only by a stretch, at best, as meaning ἄνθρωπος. Respecting this reality, I will use gender-inclusive language in the hope that readers will bear in mind the personal particularity of the Greek and Hebrew original.

Acknowledgments

This book could not have been written without help from friends, colleagues, and family. A research expense grant from the Lilly Foundation helped fund travel, books, and childcare. My colleagues at St. Vladimir's Seminary have encouraged me, primarily by forcing me at gunpoint to write this book and granting me a sabbatical semester in which to do it. Eleana Silk and Karen Jermyn have been of great help to me in the world-class library that they staff here. I could not have asked for a better editor than James Ernest; he and everyone I worked with at Baker Academic have been ideal. I am grateful to Tim Clark, John Barnet, and George Parsenios—Scripture scholars who helped make up for what I lack in that field. I also gained much from conversations with and encouragement from John Behr and Anna Marie Aagaard. My mother, Vera Bouteneff, was of incalculable help in being with my wonderful children while I wrote, and my wife, Patricia Fann Bouteneff, provided unstinting (and unrelenting) support of all kinds, including a copyediting that improved this text beyond words. Among those who reviewed drafts at various stages, I would like to express appreciation to John McGuckin and an anonymous reviewer enjoined by Baker Academic. The mistakes and insufficiencies that remain are mine alone, a fact that does not diminish my gratitude to those named and many not named here.

1

And There Was Morning

An Introduction

As this study is concerned chiefly with the early Christian exegesis of biblical texts, our first task is to explore the nature of the texts themselves and then to see how they were used in subsequent biblical and extrabiblical literature before the first Christians came onto the scene. Paul's use of Genesis 1–3 is so sure footed that it can give the impression of being built on long-accepted readings. Yet the Hebrew Bible is nearly silent on the six days of creation and on paradise. Did Paul's reading, then, come out of nowhere? This introduction charts the long and bumpy journey leading to the NT Epistles and beyond.

The Text and Its Journey

The primary text whose early Christian interpretation is examined here comes to us, in the chapters assigned it in the Middle Ages, as Genesis 1–3. The broader context—Genesis 1–11, all of Genesis, the whole Pentateuch—is important, but the first three chapters, narrating the Hexaemeron and the story of Adam and Eve in paradise, have their own integrity and will be our primary focus here. Although an exhaustive critical survey is naturally beyond the scope of this study, we will raise questions about the redaction of the narratives and their respective character, shape, and emphases, as well as the project of their translation in the LXX, the text used by nearly all the interpreters examined in the chapters to come.

Two Narratives

Genesis 1–3 is unmistakably divided into two parts: that describing the "generations" of the creation and situation of the heavens and the earth (1:1–2:4a) and that focusing on the creation of the human person (2:4b–3:24). Because of this clear division, regardless of their respective provenance or how we may see them as interrelated and complementary, I speak of the creation *narratives* in the plural.

The presentation of creation from perspectives that narrate two different sequences, each invoking God's making of earth and heaven (1:1 and 2:4b), has been a prime factor in modern hypotheses identifying multiple strands of authorship. The Hexaemeron narrative emerges as the work of the alleged "Priestly writer" (P) and the paradise narrative as that of a less distinct, probably earlier "Jahwist" (J).[1] The particulars of Wellhausen's Documentary Hypothesis have been debated and challenged,[2] yet the respective details and narrative styles leave no doubt that we are dealing with two related stories or an overarching event described from two perspectives. There is equally no reason to doubt that an author/redactor saw fit to bring these accounts together, probably adding material to give them coherence (e.g., 2:4a), and to conceive of them as together forming the beginning of the book whose Hebrew title, *bereshit*, means "In the beginning." The evidence presented below will support the theory that this redaction took place quite late or, at any rate, that its entry into Israelite consciousness as a normative creation account did not take place until the first and second centuries BCE.

The Narratives' Logic

Let us look at some of the clearest overarching characteristics of what I will here call the Hexaemeron narrative[3] (or Gen. 1) and the paradise narrative (or Gen. 2–3). Genesis 1 is a primarily cosmocentric account, whereas Genesis 2–3 is anthropocentric—although it would be truer to say that both culminate in

---

1. The regnant theory that P is postexilic has been seriously challenged by some scholars who propose an earlier date, possibly even in the eighth century BCE. See Milgrom, *Leviticus 1–16*, 3–34. Regarding the difficulty in dating or even identifying a distinct J, see Carr, *Reading the Fractures of Genesis*.

2. For a summary of recent thinking on the Documentary Hypothesis and its particular strands, see Nicholson, *Pentateuch in the Twentieth Century*. For other significant challenges, see Whybray, *Making of the Pentateuch*, 75; and Niditch, *Oral World and Written Word*, 110–17.

3. One might also have called it the Heptaemeron, given the significance of the seventh day (which comes in Gen. 2). But the "six-day creation" has established itself in the popular and scholarly lexicon from early on.

a focus on the human person, though in different ways. The creation of the human person—here not simply by the fiat of the divine word "Let there be" but with the conscious deliberation of "Let us make"—is presented as the culmination or crowning point of creation, and the divine image—whatever this is taken precisely to mean—is at the very least an indication of the unique role of the human person within creation.[4] The movement in Genesis 1 is from chaos to cosmos: from the *tohu wa bohu* of formless void to an ordered creation, crowned by the human person, male and female. Aside from this movement toward the creation of humanity, Genesis 1 reflects the priestly interest in (cultic) order, in placement, and in distinction; the separation into "days" arguably speaks out of this concern rather than functioning as a historical or scientific chronicle.

Genesis 2–3 is not concerned with a first-to-last order; it begins already speaking as from the future, of a "time" when there were yet no plants, and is unconcerned with the heavens, or even very much with the earth except to specify the geographic location of Eden. Its chief subject matter is the human person. In a manner of speaking, we move from a void (no plants and no rain/mist) to cosmos (beautiful and tasty vegetation and finally human personhood, which is complete or "good" only when there is a complementary pair of persons) and back to chaos (the curse and expulsion from paradise).

Far from a redundant retelling, then, the two accounts fulfill different functions and are, for the purposes of subsequent thinking, both indispensable. Many observers have come up with ways of describing the complementary features and functions of the two narratives. Genesis 1 is about "showing": God's words are immediately transformed into action. Genesis 2–3 is about "telling": "In the day that the Lord God made the earth and the heavens . . ."[5] Genesis 1 is an objective account, culminating in the creation of humanity but defining it from the outside; Genesis 2–3 is a subjective account, beginning with the creation of humanity and defining it from the inside.

This kind of analysis, though utterly foreign to the writers considered in this study, remains useful in underlining for us both the distinction and the complementarity of the Hexaemeron and paradise accounts. The main question—whether the juxtaposition of two evidently distinct narratives is the work of a single author or a single redactor—does not have theological consequences that fit within the scope of this book. The fact is that they are enshrined next to one another in the scriptural canon and were read as such by the Christian interpreters here considered.

4. The idea that the image rests in gender differentiation (given the parallel place the two are given in Gen. 1:27) is unlikely, since the rest of animal creation is also thus differentiated. See Wevers, *Notes on the Greek Text of Genesis*, 15–16.

5. Hasan-Rokem, "And God Created the Proverb," 109.

Points of Departure: The Content of the Narratives

Every journey has a point of departure. The journey toward the Christian interpretation of Genesis 1–3 begins (after their composition, compilation, and redaction) with what the narratives seem to be saying as distinct from what was made of them in later imagination. Although it is unrealistic to pretend to a definitive account of the narratives' meaning or to aspire to unlocking authorial intent, we can at least try to return to a reading that ignores some of the later questions posed to the narratives and the interpretations foisted on them: much of the significance and many of the features we take for granted in the paradise narrative are absent from the text itself. The biblical text nowhere says that the serpent is the devil or that Eden is a heavenly garden where the righteous will live eternally; it does not even present itself as describing the fall of humanity. All of this comes from later interpretation, some of which is so powerful—and indeed so ancient—that it is difficult to extricate it from the scriptural narrative.[6]

In this chapter we will try to read the text on its own as a first step in plotting a trajectory of how the later exegesis developed. We will focus on just a few key features within the stages of the story: humanity before the distinction of "Adam" and "Eve," the result of their transgression vis-à-vis mortality, and their story in its wider context.[7] The emphasis will be on the human person as described in the paradise narrative (though with reference also to Gen. 1:26–27) because this is what chiefly engaged later interpreters.

The Hexaemeron also generated significant commentaries in the early church, but these neither vary greatly nor are they theologically complex. An observation at the outset, however: the Hexaemeron was not concerned primarily with establishing God as Creator of the world. True, it was significantly distinct from other ancient Near Eastern cosmogonies in that it presented creation as the work of one God, not the outcome of a battle of gods or the work of a series of demiurges. But "Israel had no need expressly to *believe* that the world was created by God because that was a presupposition of their thinking."[8] This disinterest also meant that the Hexaemeron did not set out to answer in a fixed way the question of *how* God created the world, because Israel was not terribly interested in this question—which is probably why the Hexaemeron account is unapologetically followed by a paradise narrative that recounts creation in a different sequence and why allusions to creation in the Psalms, Job, and Isaiah vary from it and from each other.

6. See Kugel, *Bible as It Was*, 53–82, which is indispensable reading about the layers of interpretation that accrued from early on.

7. I am particularly indebted to Barr, *Garden of Eden*, esp. 4–20, and the first two chapters of Ricoeur and LaCocque, *Thinking Biblically*.

8. Westermann, *Creation*, 5, emphasis original.

HUMANITY BEFORE ADAM AND EVE

The translation problem posed by the Hebrew *'adam* will be a recurrent theme in this introduction.[9] This word may refer to human beings generally ("man," ἄνθρωπος), to any particular person ("*a* man"), or to a particular person or character named Adam; the author or redactor of Genesis 1–3 exploits this ambiguity. The word first occurs in Genesis 1:26–27:

> Then God said, "Let us make *'adam* in our image, according to our likeness. ... So God created *'adam* in his image, in the image of God he created them; male and female he created them.

In 1:26 and 1:27a, it would be impossible to call *'adam* a particular person, and certainly not a male person. This is why the LXX has here ἄνθρωπος and the NRSV says "humankind." In Genesis 2, where the provenance of female (*išša*) from male (*iš*) is explicit and where the story tells of a particular man (and his mate), the Hebrew again refers to him as *'adam*. Here too the LXX and all English translations—with the notable exceptions of the King James Version and New King James Version—use generic terms. They do not speak of a male (ἀνήρ). It is clear therefore that before there are male and female, *'adam* does not refer to a particular male human being. Two preliminary observations: humanity is not really humanity—is not properly *'adam*—without sex distinction. Genesis 1:27 is classically understood in this way, although we will see below that, largely under the influence of the LXX translation, some interpreters saw a male, or possibly even an androgynous but particular "Adam," as preceding multiple, sex-differentiated humanity. The name *'adam* is only bestowed, however, on sex-differentiated humanity, as is all the more evident in Genesis 5:2. The other observation is that little is said about humanity before the description of the transgression. It is as if the transgression is more definitive of the existential human person than is a putative pre-fallen state. Other than the vocation of stewardship, the unashamed nakedness, and the proscriptive command, we have no data about humanity outside the transgression.

THE TRANSGRESSION AND MORTALITY

It follows from the above that the Genesis creation accounts do not suggest that first-created humanity was by nature immortal. The first couple do not die (in the sense of ceasing to exist) upon their transgression, nor is mortality as such a part of the resulting curse. Both omissions are significant. In 2:17, the Lord God says to Adam that he would die the very day that he partook of the tree; Eve displays her cognizance of the threat in 3:3. But they eat and

---

9. The table in the appendix will be useful in charting the different translations of *'adam*.

do not die.[10] Adam goes on to live to the ripe old age of 930.[11] Interpreting the effect of the eating as a "spiritual death" comes far later in the history of exegesis; such a reading is made more difficult in the LXX, which unequivocally says Adam will "die by death" (θανάτῳ ἀποθανεῖσθε); that is, he will die utterly upon eating of the tree. The disconnect between the divine threat and the resulting punishment struck several ancient authors. One common interpretation rests on the saying that "with the Lord one day is like a thousand years" (2 Pet. 3:8; cf. Ps. 90:4), concluding that Adam, living just short of a thousand years, did in fact die on "the day" he ate the fruit.[12]

The curse leveled on the serpent, the woman, and the man does not entail death as such. Rather, for each, the curse is mortal toil, anxiety, and frustration. Reading the paradise narrative on its own, one may conclude that "death is not the punishment, but is only the *mode* in which the final stage of the punishment works out."[13] Humankind does not begin as immortal and then become mortal as a result of the transgression. Their expulsion from paradise explicitly prevents Adam and Eve from becoming immortal by partaking of the tree of life (Gen. 3:22); to become immortal in their new mode of existence would have meant only eternal torture, or at any rate eternal unfulfillment.

But even if "there is no suggestion in the narratives of the creation and fall, nor indeed in the Old Testament as a whole, that man was created immortal and lost his immortality as a result of his disobedience,"[14] neither do the narratives say that human beings were created for death. However one analyzes the threat, the transgression, and the curse, they show that humanity was created *for life* and therefore *for immortality*.

Even before the transgression humanity was not perfect. The first couple did not enjoy an idealized existence. True, once they had been created, God pronounces all of creation "very good" (1:31a), yet prima facie this denotes neither immortality nor fully realized human perfection. Naked and unashamed (2:25) they may have been, but fully actualized human persons they were not. In effect, the scriptural account does not portray two sharply contrasted states of the human person, one (perfected, immortal, sinless, united with God) before the transgression and the other (fallen, mortal, sinful, separated from God) after. It describes, rather, a process, whose starting point is not perfection but *nascence*. The separation has begun already with the prohibitive

10. As Barr points out still more clearly in "Is God a Liar?" this is not a "lie" on God's part but an unfulfilled threat.

11. Barr suggests that the eight-hundred- to nine-hundred-year life spans attributed to the forefathers of Noah (Gen. 5:4–31) may be meant to indicate the near attainment of immortality. If a thousand years signified immortality, these forefathers nearly reached this mark, but all fell short of it; after their era, life spans (and physical size) decreased dramatically. See *Garden of Eden*, 81–82.

12. See *Jub.* 4:29; Justin Martyr, *Dial.* 81; and Irenaeus, *AH* 5.23.2.

13. Barr, *Garden of Eden*, 9, emphasis added.

14. Knibb, "Life and Death," 402, cited in Barr, *Garden of Eden*, 18.

commandment of God, which not only shows an intimacy between God and humanity unique to the whole of creation, but also indicates a distancing. The separation process continues with the temptation. What is in Eve, and Adam, that is already inclined to listen to the alien voice? Is theirs the behavior of fully realized and sinless human persons? The temptation, to which they accede with little hesitation, proceeds to the transgression, then the trial (and the denial and transmission of culpability), then the curse and expulsion.

PARADISE IN LIGHT OF SUBSEQUENT DECLINE NARRATIVES

The above observations lead to another: the transgression of Adam and Eve is not portrayed as an anomalous infraction that uniquely and permanently sullies a theretofore perfect humanity. Not only is there a prehistory to the transgression in Eden; there is a long sequel. Beyond Genesis 3 it becomes increasingly apparent that the paradise story—though justly singled out for concerning the first-formed persons—is just one in a series of decline narratives that find a particular, though not final, culmination in Genesis 6. Indeed, people's sins after the expulsion from paradise make Adam and Eve's partaking of the tree seem a petty offense, even if their gross disobedience is indeed terrifying. Cain's cold-blooded murder of his brother captures the attention of more early Jewish and Christian authors. The very first scriptural occurrence of the word "sin" (Gen. 4:7) regards Cain, not Adam or Eve. A far more convincing portrayal of the "fall of humanity" comes in Genesis 6:1–7, which describes the blasphemous irruption of the Nephilim into the world and God's dismay over their exclusively wicked acts, evil thoughts, and *violence* of people.[15] The transgressions of the generation of Noah, unlike Adam and Eve's, do bring on the punishment of near-universal physical death.[16]

Although Genesis 1–3 is an utterly remarkable and indelible capsule of Scripture, it needs to be read in context. As Stanley Stowers points out, Genesis 1–11 narrates a whole series of cycles or ages of human decline, ending with the age in which the reader lives. Adam and Eve, Cain, the Nephilim, and Babel all represent humans' wrongheaded attempts to transcend their natural earthly existence, and all these rebellions stand in contrast to the repentant descendants of Abraham.[17] Richard Clifford likewise notes that Genesis 2:4–11:26 presents "a single cosmogony." It not only forms a remarkable parallel to the Akkadian Atrahasis story (which shows that the contours of the story were part of the broader culture) but also shifts the focus away from the paradise narrative. It allows the broader story to function as an introduction to "the nations," with obvious implications for humanity in general. Genesis 1:1–2:3, then, functions

15. Much more is made of the Nephilim's blasphemy in *Enoch* and *Jubilees*.

16. Barr, *Garden of Eden*, 74, notes that in the Gilgamesh epic the tree (or plant) of life appears with the flood. Thus there seems to have been an ancient Near East tradition of a flood as a turning point similar to the one in the biblical paradise story.

17. Stowers, *Rereading of Romans*, 88–89.

as the redactor's preamble or overture, foreshadowing the themes developed in 2:4–11:26, if not in the entire Pentateuch.[18]

To obtain a larger sense of what the redactor was doing, we must look beyond the paradise narrative. Doing so will prevent us from reading the Pentateuch (or even the whole Bible) as a linear account of "creation-fall-redemption," a reading difficult to trace before the eighteenth-century notion of *Heilsgeschichte* but one that captured much modern theological and popular reflection. The Pentateuch was intended to show—and this is vital if by no means novel—creation and redemption as one contiguous act.[19] As Israel continued to see it, creation shows that God has the power to save, that creation *is* salvation:

> Yet God my King is from of old,
>   working salvation in the earth.
> You divided the sea by your might;
>   you broke the heads of the dragons in the waters.
> You crushed the heads of Leviathan;
>   you gave him as food for the creatures of the wilderness.
>   (Ps. 74:12–14)

Salvation is embedded by God in God's act of creation, and the redemption of a particular people is universalized to encompass humankind (Gen. 12:3).[20]

The transgression, too, is an ongoing reality or activity; Scripture does not present the fall as an event but as humanity gone awry, though this sense is not properly (for Israel, at any rate) identified with the tree in Eden. Scripture points beyond paradise, beyond Genesis 1–11, to existential life. "It is the *ongoing* sin of the human that returns the earth to chaos."[21] As we might deduce from Jeremiah 4:22–25 and Hosea 4:1b–3, it is not because Adam sinned that everything is askew; it is because everyone *is sinning*.

A completely detached summary of the paradise narrative, ingrained as it is in our minds, is impossible. But the attempt to do so will be a useful baseline in helping us see what aspect our early Christian authors take up—often in distinction from later widespread readings. The few details sketched above may suggest that some of the eventual readings of it were quite creative—if this is the appropriate word for the often great liberties taken with the evident sense and subsequent OT use of the text.

We must also examine the text that the majority of our authors had before them. The journey that began with the writing and redaction of Genesis and

18. Clifford, "Hebrew Scriptures and the Theology of Creation," esp. 521–23.

19. See also Ricoeur and LaCocque, *Thinking Biblically*, 3–29.

20. This idea is treated extensively in, e.g., Rad, "Theological Problem of the Old Testament Doctrine of Creation."

21. Ricoeur and LaCocque, *Thinking Biblically*, 7, emphasis added.

the Pentateuch and that would continue later with their Christian interpretation took a remarkable turn when the text was translated for a hellenized Jewish audience.

The Septuagint

Nearly all of the authors under discussion in the present study worked primarily in Greek, and their text was the LXX or Septuagint. A few words about the character and history of the LXX may help bring out its significance for our texts and our writers. The word "Septuagint" referred to different collections of texts in different eras, so that it is possible to speak of several "Septuagints." When the earliest Jewish sources refer to the Greek translation of Scripture, their scope is generally the Pentateuch.[22] It was only in later (Christian) reckoning—certainly by the time of Justin Martyr in the mid-second century—that the LXX was taken to include all of the books in Greek accepted by that time. By the fourth and fifth centuries CE, there were several comprehensive LXX manuscripts encompassing the books of the Hebrew canon, each with a varied listing of what came to be called in the medieval West "apocryphal" and "pseudepigraphical" books. Furthermore, the standardized text in use today is a collation of several manuscripts, and we do not always know precisely which recension was being used by an ancient author.[23] The creation narratives are not seriously complicated by these considerations, since the book of Genesis—probably the first to have been translated—was a part of the LXX from its beginnings in the third century BCE.[24]

What interests us more is the process of translation itself, its effect on interpretation, and therefore its possible repercussions for our Greek-speaking Christian authors. The translators of Genesis were working from a text that closely resembled the (far later) Masoretic Text, although it was not the vocalized Hebrew. One may observe both the attempt at fidelity to the original—complete with occasional awkward Greek phrasings that mirror Hebrew syntax—and periodic departures to accommodate Greek idiomatic usage.[25] But to translate is to interpret. There are points where the LXX translators made subtle changes to the sense of the Hebrew original, particularly where it referred to ideas that were rising in prominence during the Hellenistic period (angels, the resurrection of the dead).[26] William Loader suggests, for example, that the LXX translation of Genesis 2:3–4 deliberately smoothes out some of the discontinuities between

22. Tov, "Septuagint," 163.

23. On the manuscript tradition, see Jellicoe, *Septuagint and Modern Study*.

24. Dines, *Septuagint*, 14. It is owing to the LXX that we call the Bible's first book Genesis—its Greek name—rather than Bereshit, "in the beginning."

25. See ibid., 57, for an illustration that uses the text of Gen. 1:2. But consult also Wevers, *Notes on the Greek Text of Genesis*, an encyclopedic work.

26. See Longenecker, *Biblical Exegesis*, 7–8.

the Hexaemeron and paradise accounts of creation.[27] There are several varia-
tions between the Masoretic Text and the LXX in Genesis 1–3, many of them
at the syntactic level but carrying significant implications.[28]

For our purposes, the most important aspect of the process of translation
into Greek is how the word 'adam was translated in its various contexts. The
Hebrew word derives from 'adamah ("the ground," leading some to translate
'adam as "earthling"). As mentioned earlier, it can denote the human person
or humankind (in Greek ἄνθρωπος), or a particular person with the proper
name Adam, or (later on in the Pentateuch and possibly elsewhere) the land of
Adamah. 'Adam represents a brilliant play on words whose ambiguity speaks
volumes in the original language. Adam as humanity (ἄνθρωπος), Adam as a
character in a story, Adam as forefather of Noah and of the patriarchs—all
of these are held together in a kind of flux in the mind of the Hebrew reader.
Rendering the text in languages where the pun is lost forces the translators to
interpret the sense of 'adam in each instance.[29] It is of interest and significance
to note the approaches taken by the LXX and, for that matter, the various
English-language translators, whose respective solutions are sometimes at
considerable variance with each other.[30]

The Hebrew uses 'adam (אָדָם or הָאָדָם) and its cognates from Genesis 1:26
through 5:5 to speak of humanity in general or Adam as a particular person.
The LXX uses ὁ ἄνθρωπος for 1:26–27 and for the account of the creation of
the human person in 2:7. The first time the LXX uses the personal name Αδαμ
in 2:16, it is in a sense quite out of the blue. From this point onward through
5:5 (with the exception of 2:18 and 5:1a), every occurrence of 'adam is rendered
by the Greek (ὁ) Αδαμ, so that an individual person is named.[31]

The LXX's logic is in this sense consistent: when the Hebrew seems to be
speaking generically about humanity, it uses ἄνθρωπος; where the narrative
appears to concern a particular person, it uses Αδαμ. (The Greek text is also
fairly consistent in retaining the articular form of the Hebrew [הָאָדָם], rendering it with its respective article.) At Genesis 2:16, the LXX makes the decisive
move from ἄνθρωπος to Αδαμ probably because this is the first instance where

27. Loader, Septuagint, Sexuality, 30–32. He also indicates possible Platonic influences in
some of the LXX wording.
28. These are helpfully documented (though with a particular interest in gender/sexuality
issues) in ibid., 27–69.
29. Another Hebrew wordplay, between iš ("man") and iššah ("woman"), is also effectively
lost on the LXX, with results that reverberate. Even the English "woman/man" works better
than the Greek, where there is no etymological relation between γυνή and ἀνήρ.
30. The table in the appendix may be of use in charting the various translations of 'adam. See
also the useful chart in Loader, Septuagint, Sexuality, 33. For other English-language versions,
consult Weigle, Genesis Octapla.
31. The NETS follows the LXX and calls him Adam from this point onward, whereas the
NRSV refrains from using the name Adam at any point until 4:25. The RSV calls him Adam
beginning in 3:17. See table in the appendix.

God is not forming a generic humanity but speaking to a particular (male) character, one who will soon be joined by another particular (female) character. The story has shifted to individual persons—even if some subsequent exegetes interpret these characters as representative of wider humanity.

But the original text maintains the multivalence of 'adam. And so the LXX translators are forced to revert, in 2:18, to ἄνθρωπος, recognizing that the "not good" status of being alone pertains to *unsexed* (or one-sexed) *humanity*, not to a lonely Adam. More importantly ἄνθρωπος is used at 5:2, which stipulates that God gave humanity the name Adam *when he had created it male and female*. The Hebrew text never allows the reader to understand "Adam" as only the man in the garden, even as it refers to him by that name. The effect of the LXX translation is that even when "Adam" is an individual person, the *descriptive* character of that name ("human being," or "earthling") is lost. Eve fares somewhat better, as the LXX takes an entirely different approach with her. The Hebrew original is ignored where she first is named (3:20), and the translation gives her the Greek name Ζωή (life), as she is the mother of all ζώντων ("living things"). Once this wordplay has been established, from 4:1 onward she becomes Ευα, a transliteration of the Hebrew. Had the LXX taken the same approach for Adam, it might have originally called him ἄνθρωπος.

A more significant repercussion of the 'adam ambiguity rests with how 2:7–24, with its account of sex differentiation, relates to 1:26–27. In the LXX the "Adam" of Genesis 2—the male person out of whose rib Eve is formed—is too easily conflated with the 'adam/ἄνθρωπος of 1:26–27. The problem already exists in Hebrew but is exacerbated by the Greek translation, which uses ἄνθρωπος for both 1:26–27 and 2:7 but Αδαμ from 2:16 onward, as if they were the same "person." Read in such a way, the 'adam that God creates in his image in 1:26 *is* the male Adam, and the female is created in the image of the male. The identification of the male "Adam" with ἄνθρωπος is further suggested where the LXX uses ἄνθρωπος rather than ἀνήρ to translate the gender-specific Hebrew *iš* in 2:24. If, as the LXX has it, ὁ ἄνθρωπος leaves his father and mother and is joined to his wife, then it is all the clearer that ὁ ἄνθρωπος is somehow essentially male.

Finally, the LXX translation subtly reemphasizes woman's derivation from man in 3:16–19, which describes its reversal through the curse and punishment. In 3:16, where the Hebrew says that the woman's "desire" shall be for her husband, the LXX uses ἀποστροφή, "return." The cumulative effect of the curse is that Eve (woman) will "return," explicitly in a relationship of subjection, to Adam (man), from whom she derives, and that Adam will return, also in a relationship of servitude, to the earth, from which he derives.[32]

At the same time, the interpretation that the ἄνθρωπος of Genesis 1 is the Αδαμ of Genesis 2–3 is negated not only by 1:27 itself but by 5:1–2, specifically

---

32. Loader, *Septuagint, Sexuality*, 46–49.

in its LXX translation. In 5:1, where the Hebrew speaks of "the list of the descendants of Adam" (anticipating the narrative genealogy leading to Noah in 5:3–32), the LXX changes it to "the book of the origin of human beings," using the generic ἄνθρωπος in its plural form. In the same verse, the LXX then uses Αδαμ as a kind of fulcrum, identifying it/him both with the generic plural that immediately precedes and proceeds as well as with the person who would be the forefather of Noah. Then in 5:2 Αδαμ serves as the generic (or possibly even personal) term for a male/female humanity.[33] Here is the Greek text, with its NETS and NRSV translations (the latter evidently working from the Hebrew text):

Αὕτη ἡ βίβλος γενέσεως ἀνθρώπων, ᾗ ἡμέρᾳ ἐποίησεν ὁ θεὸς τὸν Αδαμ, κατ᾽ εἰκόνα θεοῦ ἐποίησεν αὐτόν, ἄρσεν καὶ θῆλυ ἐποίησεν αὐτοὺς καὶ εὐλόγησεν αὐτους. καὶ ἐπωνόμασεν τὸ ὄνομα αὐτῶν Αδαμ, ᾗ ἡμέρᾳ ἐποίησεν αὐτούς. (LXX)	This is the book of the origin of human beings. On the day that God made Adam, he made him according to divine image; male and female he made them, and he blessed them. And he named their name "Adam" on the day that he made them. (NETS)	This is the list of the descendants of Adam. When God created humankind, he made them in the likeness of God. Male and female he created them, and he blessed them and named them "Humankind" when they were created. (NRSV)

Given that the LXX constituted the Scriptures for Philo, Paul, and the Greek fathers, the influence of its interpretive choices, whether deliberate or not, was far-ranging indeed.

Silence and Irruption: First References to Genesis 1–3

The LXX translation was clearly a vital part of a vast journey that the Genesis narratives and their interpretation underwent on the way to Christian exegesis. Our study now examines where and when the Genesis narratives appeared within Jewish experience.

Silentium

To the extent that the authority of Genesis 1–3 for theology—or at least its influence in the history of ideas—is accepted unthinkingly, it seems puzzling that neither the primordial Genesis accounts nor most of the theological questions that they addressed (such as the origin of sin and death) play any role of consequence in the rest of the Hebrew Bible.

After the expulsion from paradise, Adam's function is purely genealogical, and he appears only twice. He is an actor in Genesis 4, leading to the narrative

33. Ibid., 50–51, alludes to ancient interpretations of the original male Adam as an androgynous figure and indicates a few Greek and Jewish reference points.

genealogy of Genesis 5, which establishes and fills in the generations leading to Noah. He turns up one last time in 1 Chronicles as the first in the genealogy of the patriarchs, claiming for them a primordial lineage by tracing the Abrahamic line to Noah, one of the line of the πρῶτος ἄνθρωπος ("first human being") himself, 'adam. (Luke 3:23–38 does the same to show Jesus Christ as being of primordial human lineage.)

When Scripture elsewhere refers to creation, to human disobedience, to agriculture, or to death, we do not find the vivid particularities of Genesis 1–3: the six-day creation, its culmination in the creation of the human person in the image and likeness of God, the disobedience of the primordial couple (under threat of death), and the curse and expulsion from paradise. In other words, Genesis 1–3 does not emerge as the obvious referent, though there may be allusions to it.

The Hexaemeron Narrative

Several OT passages mention the creation of the world. The only direct references to the six days of creation appear in the Pentateuch—Exodus 20:11; 31:17—to explain the Sabbath. In Scripture outside the Pentateuch, Psalm 104; Isaiah 42:5; 44:24; 45:12, 18; and Job 38–39 refer in general terms to creation in order to establish the absolute sovereignty of the Lord. While Psalm 103:29 LXX (104:29) seems to hearken to Genesis 2:7 when it speaks of God taking away the human's πνεῦμα ("breath"/"spirit") and of death as return to dust, the likelihood of this reference is lessened because it describes the death not only of human persons but also of all creatures. But the days of the Genesis account are never mentioned, although the Prophets and the Writings explicitly cite other aspects of pentateuchal narrative, for example, the details of the deliverance of the Israelites out of Egypt.

Themes recur, however, such as the chaotic waters brought to order by God in Genesis 1. In the OT, the waters are a powerful instrument of God's bidding in Noah's flood, at the crossing of the Red Sea, and in countless passages in the Psalms, Job, and elsewhere;[34] their taming is a sign of divine might and authority. When Jeremiah 5:22 speaks of God establishing the sand as bounds of the sea, this too is in the context of the assertion of fearsome divine might. And the theme continues in the Gospel accounts of Jesus subduing the waters (understood as a clear sign of his divinity)[35] and may lie at the root of the Revelation images of the sea of glass—utterly subdued by the might of the Lord (Rev. 14:6; 15:2). Genesis 1 is less likely the source for the prevalent water imagery than a key example of it.

The closest we have to a Hexaemeron reference may be Psalm 148:4–6:

---

34. Psalm 77:17–21 contains a near conflation between the creation narratives and the parting of the waters to deliver Israel.
35. See Batto, *Slaying the Dragon*, 179.

> Praise him, you highest heavens,
> and you waters above the heavens!
> Let them praise the name of the LORD,
> for he commanded and they were created.
> And he established them forever and ever;
> he fixed their bounds, which cannot be passed.

It is important, however, to be cautious when seeking such allusions. For example, Psalm 82:6 (81:6 LXX), "I say, 'You are gods, children of the Most High, all of you'"—a favorite patristic citation in support of the doctrine of *theōsis* (deification) and thus ostensibly a reference to Genesis 1:26—actually refers to the pagan gods who have dashed the psalmist's expectations.[36]

In all, the theme of creation functions in the OT mainly as an ongoing (and apparently oft-needed) reminder of the Lord's absolute sovereignty. The OT authors drew on any of several oral and written sources to make this point. The Hexaemeron does not seem to have captured Israel's imagination the way the Passover did. The Passover story remains part of the historical and etiological vocabulary for the establishment of Israel and hence a part of OT intertextuality; it would be hard to say the same about the particular details of the P creation narrative.

THE PARADISE NARRATIVE

What about when the Hebrew Bible seeks a progenitor, or first father? Adam plays this role just once after Genesis 5 when he appears at the beginning of 1 Chronicles (at 1:1), and never again. An exception may reside in Ezekiel 28:12–13, where the Lord calls the king of Tyre the "signet of perfection" and says, "You were in Eden, the garden of God." This glorification of the king—before he fell into violence and pride—seems to be inspired by a vision of the (glorious) first-made man. This at any rate is what both the rabbinic texts and modern scholars have inferred.[37] Ezekiel 31 and 36 and Joel 2:3 also appear to refer to the primordial paradise. If so, they would be rare cases of explicit reference to the paradise story outside the Pentateuch and before the second century BCE.[38]

So once again, searching the Hebrew Bible through the lens of the Pauline concept of Adam as first father, or especially as progenitor of sin and death, would be an exercise in frustration. The Hebrew understanding of death

36. Mitchell Dahood translates the verse as follows: "I had said 'You are gods . . .' yet you shall die as men do" (*Psalms II*, 268–70).

37. See, e.g., Greenberg, *Ezekiel 21–37*, 590–93 (reference to the *midrashim*, p. 590). Of further interest is that the patristic exegesis of Ezek. 28 takes particular notice of its treatment of Lucifer, the pre-fallen Satan. See Anderson, "Ezekiel 28."

38. Ezekiel wrote during the exile; Walther Zimmerli has suggested additions to the book from a later "Ezekiel school" (Zimmerli, *Ezekiel*, 68–74) but this theory is far from universally accepted. The sole authorship of Ezekiel (and the explicit rejection of the "school" theory) is a basic premise for Greenberg; see Greenberg, *Ezekiel 21–37*, 396.

is not theologically consistent, and there was no unanimity in viewing sin (especially the purported original sin of Adam) as the entry of death into an otherwise immortal humanity. The one time the Hebrew Bible speaks of a "first ancestor [who] sinned" is Isaiah 43:27, and the referent is certainly not Adam: it may be Jacob (see Hos. 12:2–3), or possibly Aaron (who makes the golden calf for Israel in Exod. 32).[39]

As mentioned earlier, in Hosea 4:1b–3—a passage that might be taken as representative of prophetic sensibilities generally—the cause for the corruption even of the natural world and animal life is not some primordial sin event but the ongoing sin of the people. Hosea 6:7 clearly refers not to the person but to the *land* of Adam, as it is followed by the locative "there" and its adjacent verses refer to other lands.[40] Since the verse refers to transgressing the covenant, it is tempting to interpret (and translate) it as, "But *as Adam* they transgressed the covenant . . ." But here and throughout Hosea the author consistently and explicitly universalizes sin.

There are other appearances of the Hebrew *'adam*. In Deuteronomy 32:8, for example, it refers to humanity, and *bene 'adam* is translated as "sons of men," as in the RSV (or "humankind," in the NRSV), even if the LXX preserves the word/name ἀδάμ. Other appearances that may refer to the person of Adam include Psalm 82:7 (81:7 LXX). In his continued disenchantment with the pagan gods (see above), the psalmist says that they will die *ke'adam* in the Masoretic Text, interpreted in the LXX as ὡς ἄνθρωποι and as "like men" in the RSV.[41] It is not impossible, however, to imagine the psalmist saying that the gods "will die like Adam," who is the representative of all humanity.

Finally, Job 31:33 reads, "I have concealed my transgressions from men, by hiding my iniquity in my bosom" (RSV). The Hebrew text, however, is perhaps more closely rendered, "If I hid my transgressions like Adam, concealing my guilt."[42] But if the latter reading is indeed more faithful to the Hebrew (the LXX omits a reference either to "men" or to "Adam"),[43] certainly no theological point is being made about Adam, either as father of humanity or as first sinner or the one responsible for human sin and death. It would show a rare instance of a prophet's being aware of the Adam narrative. Pity, then, that the composition of the Job story is notoriously difficult to date, for it would be useful to suggest when the paradise story was becoming widely known.[44]

39. See McKenzie, *Second Isaiah*, 59; Blenkinsopp, *Isaiah 40–55*, 231–32.

40. See Andersen and Freedman, *Hosea*, 432–36.

41. Dahood, *Psalms II*, 270, explains why he does so as well.

42. See Pope, *Job*, 199, 208.

43. εἰ δὲ καὶ ἁμαρτὼν ἀκουσίως ἔκρυψα τὴν ἁμαρτίαν μου (NETS: "and if too, having sinned haplessly, I hid my sin"). The NRSV follows the LXX more than the Hebrew text: "if I have concealed my transgressions as others do, by hiding my iniquity in my bosom."

44. Informed readers of the past two millennia have proposed dates from the patriarchal period (twenty-first to fifteenth century BCE) to the exilic/postexilic period (sixth to fourth century BCE). See the summary in Pope, *Job*, xxx–xxxvii.

It is difficult to be conclusive about mentions of the person of Adam after Genesis 5 because of the ambiguity in the Hebrew; the more apparently straightforward and obvious characteristics and characters of Genesis 1–3 are also anything but prominent in the Hebrew Bible, and this is significant given other examples of its intertextuality. The creation narratives are not foundational, authoritative etiologies for the world or for Israel until centuries after the exile, nor do they serve to ground a teaching about humanity, sin, or death as they do in later Jewish and especially in Christian thought.

The question then becomes this: if the idea of the creation of the world by God underlies Hebrew Scripture, which creation account, if any, is normative? Many were circulating in the ancient Near East. It has long been shown that Babylonian and Canaanite creation myths had considerable influence on the resurgent interest in, and the content of, the biblical creation narratives, even if the latter broke in significant ways from the other circulating myths. One compelling theory states that the J (preexilic) paradise story was based on the Babylonian myth of Atrahasis—whose flood story was also at the root of the one in the Gilgamesh epic—and that the Priestly author, addressing a battered exilic community, rewrote the J story while probably borrowing from the *Enuma Elish*.[45] Aside from their direct influence on Genesis 1–3, these and other ancient Near Eastern creation stories circulating in Babylon may well have informed the exilic and postexilic author/redactors in forming the accounts that came to be seen as canonical in the two centuries before Christ.

(Re)appearance

Awareness of the paradise and Hexaemeron narratives rose, first gradually and then sharply, during the second and first centuries BCE. Both the silence and the reappearance may be puzzling, but they are not inexplicable. The earlier silence may owe to the fact that until after the exile Israel did not have a canonical Scripture (or even a sense of scriptural canon) to which to refer. It is the cultic materials, oral and written, that endured in Israel's consciousness. The paradise story—unlike, for example, the deliverance out of Egypt—simply did not figure largely in that material. We know the Hexaemeron and paradise accounts did exist in some form long before, because Ezekiel and perhaps the other texts as suggested above could allude to them. But by the second century BCE, we see an increased codification of writing, an increased sense of "Scripture," and an awareness of particular texts within it. The development of the LXX is vivid testimony to this process. The Second Temple Jewish authors now had something to draw on.

The next portion of our study covers some of the Second Temple Jewish texts, an important part of the journey of Genesis 1–3 on its way to Christian

---

45. Batto, *Slaying the Dragon*, summary, 2–3.

interpretation. Readers wishing to go directly to ancient Christian readings may want to skip ahead to the treatment below of Philo (almost an honorary church father) or proceed directly to the next chapter. Of the wealth of texts that exist from the second century BCE to the first century of our era, our discussion here will be necessarily selective and brief, focused on the texts' demonstrable usefulness to Christian commentators. The books of Sirach and Wisdom are part of the LXX; *Jubilees* is not but is referred to by many of the Christian authors and is canonical in some Oriental Orthodox churches. Second Esdras and 2 *Baruch* are authoritative for some of the fathers, as they are in some churches to this day.

EARLY LXX TEXTS

While the silence on the Hexaemeron and Eden is characteristic of the Hebrew Bible; several of the later texts, some preserved in Greek and some eventually becoming a part of the LXX (thus forming a part of the scriptural canon of the Greek fathers), refer explicitly to Genesis 1–3, especially to the paradise narrative. These texts, as well as the LXX itself, were produced during a period characterized in some regions by degrees of linguistic, cultural, and theological hellenization, with concomitant and sometimes violent reactions against it. New thrusts in the Jewish literature of this period include an increased interest in philosophy and theology. Hallmarks of this interest are anthropological dualism, most notably in the sense of a soul that survives the death of the body, and the sense of an awaited general resurrection.[46] It is within this climate that we witness the reappearance of the Genesis material.

The paradise story, and particularly the person of Adam, is especially important in this literature. Genesis 1 remains unmentioned until the early to mid–second century BCE, where it is prominent in *Jubilees*. Sirach 16:26–27, of the same time period, speaks of the "divisions" and the "order" of God's creation—possibly an oblique reference to the logic of the six days. Yet more significant is the appearance, in the same book, of an effective prohibition on the discussion of creation. Sirach opens with examples from the created world as testimonies of the mysteries of God, which are impenetrable (Sir. 1:1–5). Coupled with 3:21–24, which cautions against prying into matters beyond human understanding, these verses may anticipate the Jewish sensibility arising later in the talmudic writings, according to which the manner of God's work in creating the heavens and the earth (*ma'aseh bereshit*, "the work of the beginning") should not be discussed except with great care and among more than one person of understanding. This prohibition stems from, and especially pertains to, the pre-Kabbalistic

---

46. Along these same lines, 2 Macc. 7:28 features a passing but possibly significant mention of creation out of nothing.

esoteric teachings on the creation of the universe, which in turn are based on Genesis 1.[47] It may also help explain the paucity of exploration of the Hexaemeron narratives.

As for Adam and paradise, in the two centuries before Paul we find a varied picture that resists systematization. As John Levison notes, these texts are not only different from each other but are characterized by an internal diversity. He therefore warns not only against treating them systematically but also against reading them through the lens of Pauline theology.[48] Still, the Jewish literature of the period is indicative of a recently gained awareness of the scriptural creation narratives and constituted a body of texts alongside which Paul produced his own.

The first writings before us, LXX texts of the second and first centuries BCE, form a part of the wider biblical canon of the Orthodox churches. Tobit 8:6 cites Genesis 2:18 in the context of a prayer, naming Adam and Eve as those from whom the race of humankind has sprung. More significant mention is made of the paradise narratives in Sirach and Wisdom of Solomon. These texts also see Adam as the first of the human race, although they also use him to signify all humanity. Sirach 17:1–3 associates human origins out of the dust and in God's image with the person of Adam, who represents all humans (Sir. 33:10). Adam, though the protoplast and prototypical, is not responsible for sin and death. Ben Sira emphasizes human free will "from the beginning" (15:14 NETS); later in 40:1–11 he asserts that death and suffering are not catastrophes brought on by Adam or by sin but are an integral part of God's ordering of the created world.[49]

Sirach is also the source of a famous though somewhat anomalous verse that places Adam as primary among the glorious heroes of Israel. Though Sirach 49:16 has been subject to a multitude of interpretations, Levison cautions us to take the verse in its context: it is Israel that is being glorified, and through Israel, Adam, its first father.[50] All the heroes are glorified (cf. 44:1–2), yet Adam is honored above them all. One must recognize here a nascent tradition of seeing Adam as a being endowed with primordial and royal glory, a tradition with possible reference to Ezekiel 28:13 and continuing through later Jewish literature.[51]

---

47. Biram, "Ma'aseh Bereshit; Ma'aseh Merkabah," 8:235. This rabbinic caution against the study of the creation passages of Genesis, the beginning and end of Ezekiel, and the Song of Songs is cited by Origen in *In Cant.* prol.1.7, where he refers to these scriptural passages as *deuterōseis*, or matters to be treated secondarily. See Origen, *Song of Songs* (Lawson, 313n7); and Lange, *Origen and the Jews*, 34–35.

48. See Levison, *Portraits of Adam*, 14–28, 161.

49. On the significance of the phrasing "from the beginning" in reference to Gen. 1:1, see ibid., 34–35; and Skehan and DiLella, *Ben Sira*, 271–72.

50. See Levison, *Portraits of Adam*, 44–45.

51. E.g., *Life of Adam and Eve* 12–16.

Still, Ben Sira portrays Adam's function and stature inconsistently. Adam is both all of humanity and a specific person, the founding father of humanity. As an individual, he is either glorious (Sir. 49:16) or ignorant (24:28). His role in the beginnings of sin is neatly sidestepped in the context of the author's misogynistic descriptions of the evils of woman (25:13–26). It is Eve, unnamed but serving nicely to illustrate the author's dim view of women in general, from whom is the "beginning of sin," and "because of her we all die" (25:24 NETS).[52]

The portrait of Adam in Wisdom of Solomon is similarly erratic. It contains references to a (generally unnamed) πρωτόπλαστος ("first-formed," Wis. 7:1). Of greater interest is 10:1–4, where Wisdom delivers or extricates (ἐξείλατο) the first-formed from his transgression, and it is the unnamed Cain who shuns Wisdom and ultimately brings on the flood through his sin. It was common for the later Jewish and early Christian literature to place greater blame on Cain than on Adam.

Wisdom of Solomon 2:23–24 ties together two themes, the *imago Dei* and the entry of death: "But God created man [ἄνθρωπον] for immortality [ἀφθαρσίᾳ], and made him an image [εἰκόνα] of his own proper being; it was through the devil's envy that death entered into the cosmic order, and they who are his own experience him."[53] Levison's theory is that "the enemy" (for this is how he translates this instance of ὁ διάβολος) is actually Cain, as is more explicitly the case in 10:3–4.[54] Such a theory, if correct, supports the absence of any sense that sin entered the world through Adam and Eve's transgression. Likewise, 7:1 does not mention that sin is the cause of death, only that the narrator, as a descendant of the first-formed, is mortal and earthborn like everyone else.

This anthropology is effectively an adjusted version of Genesis 2:7. The paradise narrative is about primordial humanity, earthborn and mortal from the start, falling just short of attaining immortality. Wisdom speaks of the "earthborn" being into which a spirit/soul is breathed (Wis. 15:11), a soul that can be demanded back (15:8). The soul's immortality is potential, or *provisional*, rather than natural (in the Platonic sense).[55] Wisdom of Solomon 2:23–24, after all, speaks of an *intended* immortality but a clearly unrealized one. We cannot find a consistent, thoroughly worked-out doctrine of sin or death in Wisdom of Solomon. Yet the overarching sense throughout the book

52. Sirach 42:13–14 goes so far as to say, "For from garments comes the moth, and from a woman comes woman's wickedness. Better is the wickedness of a man than a woman who does good; it is woman who brings shame and disgrace." For more on the origins of evil and sin in Sirach, see Collins, *Jewish Wisdom*, 80–96.

53. Translations are from Winston, *Wisdom of Solomon*, unless otherwise noted.

54. Levison, *Portraits of Adam*, 51–52.

55. See Reese, *Hellenistic Influence*, 64–71.

is that, although mortality and sin are related, one cannot say that Adam's sin is responsible for human mortality.

Jubilees, though roughly of the same period as Sirach and Wisdom of Solomon, is not part of the LXX,[56] yet several early Christian writers—for example, Hippolytus, Origen, Epiphanius, Didymus, and Jerome—cite it by name.[57] The book is part of the wider scriptural canon in the Ethiopian and some other Oriental Orthodox churches.

The author of *Jubilees* recasts the main episodes of the book of Genesis (and parts of Exodus) in a way that reemphasizes the law and the patriarchy of Israel in the face of Hellenistic influence. Thus what began as a trickle of interest and awareness in the Genesis creation accounts in Sirach and in Wisdom becomes a flood in *Jubilees*. From this point on, there is no doubt that the accounts in Genesis 1–3 as we know them are fixed in Jewish consciousness; indeed so is the rest of the book of Genesis. *Jubilees* 2 and 3 retell the Hexaemeron and paradise narratives. This respun account—with some details omitted and many added—traces both the law (*Jub.* 3:8–14) and the line of the patriarchs of Israel (3:27–32) back to the first-formed man, thus universalizing them and their authority. All of creation is shown to have taken place in obedience to the law (15:27). The two biblical narratives (Gen. 1 and 2–3) seem to be taken as a seamless whole: the land created on the third day includes the garden of Eden (*Jub.* 2:7), and the human person ("a man and a woman") created on the sixth day (2:14) is the very one who turns up exactly one week later, a male, apparently, who names the animals and has a woman fashioned from his rib.[58] To emphasize this continuity, the Genesis 2:7 account of human creation is omitted in the retelling.

Jubilees, which presents Adam in as flattering a light as possible, omits Genesis 3:8–13 (God's search for Adam and Adam and Eve's transference of culpability). For the *Jubilees* author, Adam is a patriarch, a glorified and priestly figure who makes a priestly offering after his transgressions. Conversely the wrath of God is against Eve and against the serpent, and Cain is considered more cursed than Adam.

The Hexaemeron and paradise accounts were evidently now so firmly ensconced in Jewish canonical Scripture that the author of *Jubilees* was able to draw on them as resonant foundational narratives. The nature of their

56. See Testuz, *Idées religieuses*, 34–39, and VanderKam, *Textual and Historical Studies*, 214–85. On the possible relationship between *Jubilees* and the Essene community, see Sanders, *Paul and Palestinian Judaism*, 383–87. Translations here are taken from Charles, *Book of Jubilees*.

57. See Charles, *Book of Jubilees*, lxxvii–lxxxiii.

58. Testuz, *Idées religieuses*, 45, argues that the original text of *Jub.* 2:14 (the MS tradition is huge) mentions only Adam, not the "male and female," which was an interpolation of later redactors seeking to harmonize it with Gen. 1:27. See also Levison, *Portraits of Adam*, 90.

authority apparently did not prevent him from playing fast and loose with the details: he reordered, augmented, and subtracted from the original texts. When he was done, their etiological function was enhanced and enlarged to incorporate his agenda of reinvigorating the Jewish sense of heritage and the centrality therein of the law. Adam as responsible for human sin and death would have damaged his case.

LATER APOCALYPTIC TEXTS

Two apocalyptic texts are worth examining, both composed just after Paul's own time in the aftermath of the destruction of the temple. As Jewish works, they had (and in some cases continue to have) currency in the Christian world. The first is 2 Esdras. Known in the Latin Vulgate as 4 Ezra, this book is probably of Palestinian Jewish authorship.[59] Although the author describes the historical line from Adam through Noah and the patriarchs, his depiction of the garden of Eden is parahistorical, planted by God's right hand *before the earth appeared* (2 Esd. 3:6). God names the first-created human Adam, not only before Eve exists, but even before he is infused with divine breath (*nefeš*) and is still a lifeless creature from dust.

The author's portrayal of Adam is anything but royal or priestly. Nor is Adam's blame exonerated or transferred to Cain. Adam is a transgressor and begins the cycle of sin and of death (3:7). Several passages show us Adam before his transgression and its effect. Adam's fall is clearly not one from an erstwhile immortal perfection. Nor did it *cause* sin and death for his descendants, even if it is the first sin and the first death. Adam, "burdened with an evil heart, transgressed and was overcome, as were also all who were descended from him" (3:21). The evil seed, Uriel says later on, was "sown in Adam's heart from the beginning" (4:30). We do not have here a perfect first-formed, and he does not cause universal sin. The evil heart is in Adam's descendants by God's deliberate and providential design, as 3:20 has it. As a result, all his descendants were burdened with an evil heart, transgressed, and were overcome.[60] The relationship of Adam's sin (and death) to that of his descendants is not one of causality.

In the third episode of the dialogue, however, the author presents Adam from a different angle: as the first-created human person. Drawing now on the Hexaemeron account of the creation of the world and of ἄνθρωπος, the focus in 6:38–59 is the dominion of Adam—not only over the plants and animals but also over the sun and the moon and the stars (6:45–46), indeed over all created things (6:54).[61] The author portrays Israel as the chosen descendant of Adam; it thus ought to be exercising the same rulership but instead is being overrun

---

59. See Myers, *I and II Esdras*, 119–21; and Sanders, *Paul and Palestinian Judaism*, 409–18.
60. Levison, *Portraits of Adam*, 118.
61. Perhaps also a reference to Ps. 8:4–9.

by nations that are like "a drop from a bucket" (6:56). And so his outraged grievance before God: "If the world has indeed been created for us, why do we not possess our world as an inheritance? How long will this be so?" (6:59).

In 2 Esdras 7, he continues to vascillate between the universality and the particularity of Israel. This lengthy chapter, concerned mainly with theodicy, seeks to explain that Adam's transgression forces people—especially Israel—to pass through pain to obtain glory. In the first part, Uriel presents Ezra with a vision of a city full of good things; its entry is narrow and bounded by fire and water. That Israel must pass through danger to obtain the prize is also Israel's portion. "For I made the world for their sake, and when Adam transgressed my statutes, what had been made was judged. And so the entrances of this world were made narrow and sorrowful and toilsome; they are few and evil, full of dangers and involved in great hardships" (7:11–12). The rest of the passage, however, pertains to all "the living." When Ezra cries, "O sovereign Lord, you have ordained in your law that the righteous shall inherit these things, but that the ungodly shall perish" (7:17), the conflation of Israel with universal humanity reflects the sense that Israel is the only nation that really matters. Israel *is* humanity, properly speaking.

As the chapter proceeds, Ezra's lament, and his fear of judgment and damnation, deepens. In a dramatic passage we see once again that Adam did not live as immortal before the transgression. Rather, the transgression prevents the attaining of that yet-unattained prize: "For what good is it to us, if an immortal time has been promised to us, but we have done deeds that bring death? And what good is it that an everlasting hope has been promised to us, but we have miserably failed?" (7:119–20). Given that people transgress, mortality mercifully severs the sin cycle. Yet all this is, for Ezra, a pitiful state of affairs: "It would have been better if the earth had not produced Adam, or else, when it had produced him, had restrained him from sinning" (7:116). Not daring to blame the Creator, he blames the earth. He censures Adam, although he, too, does not link Adam's sin and that of his posterity: "The fall was not yours alone, but ours also who are your descendants" (7:118). Ezra is of two minds, at once blaming Adam and locating the blame with each descendant. His lament knows no bounds.

Uriel's reply assures that the call to morality pertains to all, that Ezra's censure of Adam and the earth that produced him is misplaced, and that all will be judged according to how they live:

This is the significance of the contest that all who are born on earth shall wage: if they are defeated they shall suffer what you have said, but if they are victorious they shall receive what I have said. For this is the way of which Moses, while he was alive, spoke to the people, saying, "Choose life for yourself, so that you may live!" But they did not believe him or the prophets after him, or even myself who have spoken to them. Therefore there shall not be grief at their destruction, so much as joy over those to whom salvation is assured. (7:127–31)

Second Baruch is another apocalyptic text of the same general time period as 2 Esdras.[62] It was composed in Greek, but the most complete extant MS is the Syriac translation, which serves as the basis for the text as it comes to us, so that it is frequently referred to as the *Syriac Apocalypse* of Baruch. Its similarity to 2 Esdras may indicate that it was based on that book.[63] Like 2 Esdras, it features seven dialogues with an angel and reflects the shattered sensibilities of post–70 CE Judaism. That it was written when consolation was sorely needed strongly affects the function of Adam. Before his transgression, Adam is shown the heavenly Jerusalem as an encouragement not to sin;[64] this Jerusalem (unlike the one that had just fallen) is preexistent and eternal (*2 Bar.* 4:1–7).

In *2 Baruch*, Adam has a threefold function: genealogical, moral, and cosmological. As elsewhere, he is the "father of us all" in that he is the first-created human and all necessarily descend from him. But he is also the father of sin: in the present age of sin and death, everyone has a choice to follow this legacy or reject it. Finally, although he is not portrayed as "glorious," Adam—and all humanity—was created with the vocation of dominion and glory; those who choose to reject the "darkness of Adam" (18:2) and be subject to their Creator will again enjoy this dominion in the age to come. Adam's sin brought death, which spreads to "all that are born" (23:4). The dead are "guarded" in Sheol as long as this age lasts (23:4–5).

But the question again arises: does Adam's sin cause the sin of the descendants? Baruch has moments of exasperation—"O Adam, what have you done to all those who are born from you?" (48:42)—but he also says clearly that "Adam is therefore not the cause, save only of his own soul, but each of us has been the Adam of his own soul."[65] People *become* "descendants of Adam" only by sinning. The free will of each person is the crux of the matter.

What, precisely, has Adam's sin engendered? This text's answer in 56:6 is specific. When Adam transgressed, the first repercussion is "untimely death"[66]: not

---

62. The translations are taken from Charles, *Apocrypha and Pseudepigrapha*, 2:481–524. For an extensive discussion on the precise date of *2 Baruch*, see Bogaert, *Apocalypse de Baruch*, 1:270–95.

63. See Bogaert, *Apocalypse de Baruch*, 1:21–32, 401–5; also Sanders, *Paul and Palestinian Judaism*, 25n2, 409n2.

64. See the summary in Levison, *Portraits of Adam*, 130–31.

65. Some scholars have remarked on the similarity of this passage to the sense of Rom. 5:12. See Bogaert, *Apocalypse de Baruch*, 1:405–9. Bogaert points out that the earliest twentieth-century commentators, basing themselves on the erroneous Vulgate translation of Rom. 5:12 (where "all men sin [*in Adam*]"), describe the relationship between the two passages as one of *opposition*.

66. Cf. also *2 Bar.* 54:15.

mortality in itself but death by violence (cf. 73:3–4). The other consequences are anguish, pain, trouble, disease, Sheol's seeking of blood, the begetting of children, the passion of parents, the bringing down of humanity's greatness, and the languishing of goodness.[67] This rephrasing of the curse of Genesis 3:16–19 describes the existential situation of humanity.

Summary

Other texts from this period, including much of the Qumran material and those seminal to rabbinic Judaism, richly reflect on Genesis 1–3. The Enoch material would also fit well with the apocalypses above. The authorship and dating especially of *2 Enoch*—the book with the most relevant material for our study—are, however, mired in uncertainty.[68]

A wealth of other later Jewish material, notably the *Apocalypse of Moses* and the *Life of Adam and Eve* (with which it overlaps), has been the subject of important studies, although its fertilization of Christian literature is not easy to demonstrate.[69] The Qumran scrolls might be of greater interest in this regard; work on discerning the possible correspondence between these and the Pauline corpus continues.[70] The texts we have examined were chosen for their relevance to the formation both of the scriptural canon and of ancient Christian exegesis. Several points have already emerged out of the material we have cursorily reviewed.

First, the appearance and prevalence of texts that refer to or retell the paradise narrative (and, to a lesser extent, the Hexaemeron narrative) only emphasize the absence of such references up until the second century BCE, when they begin to trickle in, becoming far more prominent in the first century CE. Whatever allusions to Genesis 1–3 that may have been made in passing in the books of Ezekiel, Job, and Psalms do not approach the fascination that explodes onto the scene in the intertestamental period.

67. In alternative translations in the Greek, the list is "untimely death, mourning, affliction, illness, labor, pride, death's seeking blood, conception of children, passion of parents, loftiness humiliated, and vanishing of goodness."

68. The book is unrelated to *1 Enoch* (*Ethiopic Apocalypse*). The earliest surviving manuscript of *2 Enoch* (*Slavonic Apocalypse*) is a late Slavonic translation of a work that scholars date from the first to the tenth century CE.

69. See Stone, *History*; Anderson, *Genesis of Perfection*; Anderson, Stone, and Tromp, *Literature on Adam and Eve*. The manuscript tradition of these texts is not simple, and there are Christian additions to, as well as Christian versions of, several of them.

70. Several essays in Davila, *Dead Sea Scrolls* are indicative of the potential fruitfulness of exploring this connection. See esp. Bauckham, "Early Jerusalem Church"; T. Lim, "Studying the Qumran Scrolls"; and Golitzin, "Recovering 'The Glory of Adam.'" Longenecker, *Biblical Exegesis*, 113–16, discusses, without great assurance, the idea that Paul uses the *pesher*-style exegesis characteristic of the Qumran materials.

Second, the authors show themselves quite at liberty to take license with not only the purported "meaning" of Genesis 1–3 but also the detail of the text itself. We see especially in *Jubilees*, but also in other retellings of the narratives,[71] that details are freely omitted and others added to help support the authors' agendas. This may indicate that the gradually emerging concept of "Scripture" and "canonicity" was not one that fixed a particular reading. Indeed, the authors here reviewed tacitly acknowledged multiple possibilities of meaning in the scriptural texts and dealt with them not only on the level of what might be called their "plain sense" but also on that of implied or derived meaning.[72] This bivalence of Scripture, implicit for the books reviewed thus far, is made explicit in Philo, as we shall see below.

The variety of readings and interpretations is due in part to the different contexts out of which these texts came and to the authors' concomitant viewpoints. Some books (e.g., *Jubilees*) were written to reestablish the Torah and place it at the basis of creation itself. Other books (e.g., Wisdom of Solomon) show how the Torah may be made amenable to Hellenistic sensibilities. Genesis is plumbed for imagery, or retold and recast, in ways that serve these agendas. A further cause of diversity was the great divide between authors writing before and after the destruction of the temple in 70 CE. The books written within a generation of this cataclysm bear the marks of the tragedy, either in their apocalypticism or in rethinking the nature of Judaism and its worship and practice.

Third, during the centuries under review, and especially during the first century of our era, several of the key, enduring questions surrounding the creation and predicament of the human person as treated in Genesis 1–3 were already on the table, even if they were not yet receiving clear and consistent answers. In all the diversity of their portrayals of the first-created world and its first-created human beings, the texts we have discussed share an interest, implicit or explicit, in several issues that will continue to captivate Jewish and Christian imagination:

- Who was Adam, and how does the named character who figures in the story of paradise and who begins the genealogy leading to Noah relate to the ἄνθρωπος of Genesis 1:26? The texts so far seem to maintain a certain neutrality on this question, sometimes allowing "Adam" to stand for ἄνθρωπος and sometimes personalizing him, especially when he is seen to be the father of subsequent generations.
- Who was Eve? In the patriarchal culture from which these texts emanated, Eve tends to be invisible, since genealogies, with some notable exceptions in Chronicles 1 and Matthew 1, list only males. Yet she too

---

71. E.g., Josephus, *Jewish Antiquities*, composed probably around the time of 2 Esdras and 2 Baruch. Cf. Stone, *Jewish Writings*, 210–27.
72. Cf. Longenecker, *Biblical Exegesis*, 6–35.

plays a role, though rarely, both as first parent of the lineage of human beings (as in Tob. 8:6) and, at least in Sirach (and Philo), as the means of entry of sin into human life.

- What was the state of first-created humanity? The texts, taken as a whole, tend to preserve the ambiguity given in Scripture itself. They speak of Adam as a glorious figure, created in God's image—and in this period of increasing anthropological dualism, the image was often interpreted as denoting the immaterial soul. Adam has the vocation of dominion over most, if not all, creation. But they speak of Adam as a humble or even tragic figure, created from clay, ignorant of wisdom, and the first of all transgressors. Both of these tendencies became strong legacies as the centuries progressed. Although in contrast to the "new Adam," Adam lives on in much Christian thought as one whose example is emphatically not to be followed, a parallel "glory of Adam" tradition remained in both Jewish and Christian texts of the first four centuries of our era.[73]

- What is the effect of the first transgression on subsequent humanity? Many ancient authors comment on the legacy of the dominion Adam was given over all creation and how this may or may not be enacted by subsequent generations and nations—notably Israel. But the more general matter of the legacy of sin and death is taken up not in the Wisdom literature but in the apocalyptic texts, where one may find a near unanimity in *denying* the direct causal role of the transgression in paradise. Among the authors we have reviewed, some exonerate Adam and blame Cain. Others see Adam as the first of sinners and progenitor of humanity, much of which will succumb to sin. But especially the apocalyptic texts emphasize the free choice of subsequent human beings and even envisage the possibility of attaining "righteousness." In these texts, the "sons/children of Adam" are not his descendants because they proceeded from this first parent but because they choose the way of unrighteousness and disobedience.

There is a sense in which these texts, especially 2 Esdras and *2 Baruch*, agree with the Pauline "Death spread to all, because all have sinned"—a formulation that denies causality but acknowledges the existential fact of sin and death. But their apocalyptic sensibility, emerging from the fall of the temple, represents a context entirely different from Paul's.[74] Their interpretation of Adam, sin, and death—like Paul's—can already be found in earlier hellenized Jewish texts such as Philo's.

73. See Golitzin, "Recovering 'The Glory of Adam'"; Anderson, *Genesis of Perfection*.
74. See Stowers, *Rereading of Romans*, 88.

PHILO: A CODA

A study of early Christian exegesis cannot omit a discussion of Philo the Jew, owing to his vital place in the history of ideas, his own development of the same Platonic (and Stoic) legacy that would provide a backdrop for Christian patristic reflection, and his direct influence on Christian writers.[75] Since Philo was effectively ignored in the Jewish world, it is likely that his writings survived only because of their enduring fascination for Christians. Living from about 20 BCE until about 50 CE, Philo falls squarely within the time period under review in this chapter, but, as he makes no pretense at being either scriptural or historical in his approach, his work is treated separately. He was a prolific author about whom there is an immense corpus of secondary literature; we can touch only on the points most salient to our present study to identify them so they will be familiar when they arise again in our discussion of the early Christian writers.

With Philo we have the first sustained reflection about pentateuchal literature and how it should be read; hence a few words are in order about his hermeneutics. His thought follows on—and elaborates and "theologizes," if unsystematically—ideas of classical philosophers on the nature of interpretation. Yet Philo's reading of Scripture often follows (widely varying) Jewish exegetical principles already in place during his time.[76] In a more Hellenistic mode, he regularly discerns two broad levels of interpretation of Scripture—the literal and the allegorical—and although both have the potential for misuse, it is the latter that takes the higher place in his work.[77] The literal meaning is, as it were, a concession to people bound to history, and although Philo does not ignore allegory or dispense with it, he views it to be for those initiated in understanding. His objection to literalism is especially strong in the face of the possible anthropomorphization of God, and so this danger appears as one of his main motivations for favoring allegory.[78] But allegory of widely varying kinds is also invoked wherever the literal reading seems to cause logical or theological problems.[79] At any rate, his awareness of the senses of Scripture

75. All translations of Philo are taken from Colson and Whitaker, *Philo*, except those for *De opificio mundi*, which are from Runia, *Philo of Alexandria*. See the thorough catalog of patristic citations of Philo in Runia, "References to Philo," 111–21.

76. See Borgen, "Philo of Alexandria"; Longenecker, *Biblical Exegesis*, 6–35.

77. From among numerous studies, see esp. Borgen, *Philo of Alexandria*; Tobin, *Creation of Man*; and Dawson, *Allegorical Readers*, 73–126. A useful summary may be found in Borgen, "Philo of Alexandria," 259–64.

78. See Tobin, *Creation of Man*, 36–55.

79. See Levison, *Portraits of Adam*, 64: "The tree of life, for example, represents the earth, the seven celestial circles, the ruling part of the soul, etc. Conversely, a single allegorical concept attaches itself to many different biblical figures or features. For example, Adam, Cain, Pharaoh, the tree of life, the sun, etc., symbolize the 'mind.' Because Philo does not differentiate these levels of allegory, it is difficult to disentangle his ideas."

and his view of the allegorical as the elevated sense presages what we will find especially in Origen, not to mention his Cappadocian disciples.

Of crucial importance for Philo's view of Judaism is the fact that he shows so little interest in history. All emphasis is on structural elements, especially the place of the human person in creation and the relation of the human to the divine. He is also interested in the relationship between time and eternity, but he does not consider that an event of shattering importance could take place in the course of time as experienced here on earth; for example, he completely detemporalizes the six days of creation.[80] This separates him, to a quite marked degree, from other Jewish groups of his day and also from the incipient world of early Christian thought.[81]

The Pentateuch, in its LXX translation,[82] seems to be the only Scripture on which Philo feels the need to comment, and he devotes special attention to the exegesis of Genesis 1–3, particularly in *On the Creation of the World, Questions and Answers on Genesis,* and *On the Laws of Allegory* (also known as *Allegorical Interpretations of Genesis 2–3*). The first of these books forms part of a corpus—usually referred to as "Exposition of the Laws of Moses" since it follows the chronology of the Pentateuch—within the larger Philonic oeuvre. We have seen other retellings of Pentateuch narratives in *Jubilees,* and they can be found also in Josephus, *Jewish Antiquities,* and Pseudo-Philo, *Biblical Antiquities.* Other texts would follow over the centuries, such as *Genesis Rabbah* and the overlapping *Life of Adam and Eve* and *Apocalypse of Moses,*[83] a common feature of which is the casting of Genesis 1–3 as the primordial history of Israel rather than of all humanity. For his part, Philo does not add plot details so much as his own analysis regarding the existential situation of humanity with an explicit focus on Genesis 1–3's etiological function.

On the Creation of the World

In *On the Creation of the World,* the analyses are idiosyncratic. Philo's explanation of why the narrative has God speaking in the first person plural, "Let us," in making the human person (Gen. 1:26) is obviously not the trinitarian explanation that would become standard in the Christian patristic tradition. Rather, he writes that when human beings act badly, God is not implicated, since God evidently collaborated with subordinates who botched the job (*Opif.* 75). In his treatment of the Hexaemeron account, Philo does not use the name Adam, nor does he conceive of a particular person. He sees Genesis 1:26–27 as pertaining to the human race—the human being (ἄνθρωπος) as genus (γένος)

80. See Philo, *Leg.* 1.2; *Opif.* 13.
81. Runia, "Philo, Alexandrian and Jew," 12.
82. See Philo, *On the Life of Moses* 2.37, where he describes the translation of "the laws" and specifically the creation narratives.
83. See Nickelsburg, "Bible Rewritten and Expanded."

and male and female as species (εἴδη) (*Opif.* 76). When he treats the paradise narrative, he speaks of the "first human being" (ὅ πρῶτος ἄνθρωπος) as superior by far to all who would come later, or a noble person (*Opif.* 136). This first human was excellent in both body and soul (*Opif.* 137–39); God clearly took not just any clay to form his body but used the best material there was. He was in effect "the only real citizen of the cosmos" (*Opif.* 142).

Creation—and humanity within it—thus represents an idealized state, and the end-time will be a restoration of that state (*Opif.* 82). Philo focuses on the dominion of the human person over all created things—except the angelic (*Opif.* 84). The transgression is regarded neither as the greatest of sins nor as the cause of subsequent sin. Rather, subsequent sin becomes progressively worse, effecting an ever greater distancing from the noble protoplast (*Opif.* 145). The transgression itself is subject to several levels of interpretation even within the same passage. On one level, the transgression happens through the temptation of pleasure, which comes to the man through the woman. (Philo, perhaps in the tradition of Sir. 25:24, seems to suggest that man was doing fine until woman came on the scene [*Opif.* 151–52], although to him the reason has less to do with female depravity than with sexual expression and the sinful pleasure it engenders.) On another level, "man" comes to represent intellect whereas "woman" is sense perception (*Opif.* 165). In effect (in Runia's vivid translation), the senses act as "pimps" for the "prostitute" that is pleasure in that they seek opportunities for pleasure to ensnare and enslave the soul (*Opif.* 166). Again, Adam and Eve are neither the progenitors of sin nor the cause of subsequent sin or of death. Rather, they indicate the mechanism by which sin functions in the human soul generally.

Philo's dualistic anthropology leads to his conclusion (shared by some of the Christian fathers in their own dualistic modalities) that the image of God in the human person is the incorporeal soul (*Opif.* 69–71). This teaching brings us to one of the most commented-on ideas emerging from the *Opif.*: the teaching of the "two men," which is brought out in a short passage (*Opif.* 134–35) usually taken out of the context of the whole exposition of the creation, temptation, and transgression of human beings. It is an admittedly interesting passage, and the concept of "double creation" has both a noted past and a significant future in the history of thought. At first glance, Philo seems to be talking about the distinction between the first-created *anthrōpos,* the one created in God's image in Genesis 1:26, and the *anthrōpos* we learn about in Genesis 2:7, made through the breathing of divine spirit (πνεῦμα) into the clay from the earth.

The first *anthrōpos,* as Philo has already said in *Opif.* 76, is the idealized genus, immortal by nature and not yet differentiated between male and female. The second *anthrōpos* (of Gen. 2) is "sense-perceptible, . . . consists of body and soul, is either man or woman, and is by nature mortal" (*Opif.* 134). This is the prima facie interpretation—a clear distinction between the image-bearing generic immortal (ideal) *anthrōpos* and the particular, psychosomatic mortal *anthrōpos*. Such a reading squares with Philo's broadly Platonic anthropology, and it would not be the only case of distinguishing between the idealized and the sensible *anthrōpos*, linked with the two respective creation accounts.[84] But another interpretation holds that the "two men" themselves represent the rational and irrational components of the human person.[85] The passage concludes by envisioning the two united under one overall rubric and states that they reveal that the human being is on the threshold between mortality (in the material body) and immortality (in the immaterial soul). It is easy to see how these refer back to the "two men." Indeed, *Opif.* 139 also portrays Genesis 1:26 and 2:7 as being the same event.

Much as scholars like to side conclusively with one or another reading, Philo makes it unnecessary to choose definitively between the two interpretations. Levison likewise notes that it is Philo's nature to merge, rather than distinguish, different readings.[86] Philo could, in other words, be saying two different things at once. It would, at any rate, be impossible to discount the first interpretation, wherein the two men represent a kind of double creation, the one ideal and immaterial, the other fallen and material. This doctrine, whether through the mediation of Philo or that of other Platonists, would influence several of the Christian fathers.

Finally, this entire treatise, analyzing the Hexaemeron and the drama of paradise, comes down to five lessons that Philo hastily outlines in *Opif.* 170–71: (1) God exists, (2) God is one, (3) the cosmos exists, (4) the cosmos is one, and (5) God cares for the cosmos. We may be surprised to see how rudimentary these are, and perhaps more so since none has to do with sin or death (or even humanity as such), except perhaps the last, by implication. The nature of these summary points is evidently related to Philo's intended audience, since with each of these lessons he gives examples of people who believed otherwise and ought to have heeded what was written by Moses.

Allegorical Works

Philo thus contributed his own retelling and interpretation of Genesis 1–3, as did other Second Temple Jewish authors who came before and after him. And he revisits the Genesis texts in two somewhat overlapping treatises from among his "allegorical works," *Questions and Answers on Genesis* and *On*

---

84. A Qumran text (QG 2.56) espouses the same idea. See Levison, *Portraits of Adam*, 69, 85; Tobin, *Creation of Man*, 109–10.

85. See Levison, *Portraits of Adam*, 69, who attributes this interpretation chiefly to B. A. Stegmann. For a more detailed treatment, see Philo, *On the Creation of the Cosmos* (Runia, 321–29).

86. Levison, *Portraits of Adam*, 70.

the Laws of Allegory. Here (in *Leg.* 1.31–42 and *Quaest.* 1.4; 1.8; 2.56) we also find a "two men" idea with a potential for different interpretations, one reflecting a kind of "double creation," the other an anthropological dualism. These are far from mutually exclusive concepts; each can be traced to Platonic thought. We may also discern an ethical reading: the heavenly man represents any person who by his or her very nature lives a right life and the earthly man represents a person who has a capacity for either virtue or vice, and the two men represent "two ways of living: either according to the divine inbreathing or contrary to it."[87]

Philo's allegorical works are also of interest because of his explicitly figurative readings of the Hexaemeron. In *On the Laws of Allegory* 1.1–18, he states clearly that the Hexaemeron is not talking about six twenty-four-hour days. Rather, Philo explains the meaning of the six days partly through astronomy and partly through numerology. And Eden was not a garden that one could have walked through: "Far be it from man's reasoning to be the victim of so great impiety as to suppose that God tills the soil and plants pleasaunces" (*Leg.* 1.43). Likewise in *Quaest.* 1.8 he states that paradise was not a garden but, rather, symbolizes "wisdom."

Philo also shows an awareness of the problem in translating *'adam*, and of its implications for identity, when he cites Genesis 2:16–17 (the first instance where the LXX translates *'adam* with the proper name Αδαμ):

> We must raise the question *what* Adam He commands and who is this; for the writer has not mentioned him before, but has named him now for the first time. Perchance, then, he means to give us the name of the man that was molded. "Call him earth," he says, for that is the meaning of "Adam," so that when you hear the word "Adam" you must make up your mind; for the mind that was made after the image is not earthly but heavenly.[88]

Philo concludes that the scriptural redaction deliberately crafted and made canny use of this ambiguity concerning identity. Each reader must negotiate this through the use of the mind (νοῦς), a heavenly, God-like faculty. Philo's reasoning here reflects his interest in semiotics, manifest in several of his works. He was captivated by the relationship of things to their names (or signifiers) and thus was interested in the name Adam as well as in Adam's divinely ordained function of naming created things. This in turn plays into Philo's concept of scriptural language, inspiration, and exegesis.[89] These areas will also be explored by the Christian authors who are the focus of this book.

---

87. See ibid., 81–82.
88. *Leg.* 1.90, emphasis original in the translation.
89. Of the many accounts of Philo's interest in naming and language, see Dawson, *Allegorical Readers*, 83–113.

Already we have seen that Philo paved several paths that would be further explored by later Christian authors. Implicitly and explicitly he discussed the relationship between literal and allegorical exegesis in a way that would be taken up most clearly by Origen. His thinking—here, too, adapted from Platonism—about two dimensions, registers, or realms of creation would be taken in different directions by Origen, Basil of Caesarea, and Gregory of Nyssa. His thought on the divine image and its immaterial character would be denied by some Christian writers (such as Irenaeus) and embraced by others (such as Origen), as would also his ideas about the age to come as a restoration of ideal origins. As one of the earliest writers to take up the biblical creation narratives, he played a seminal role in their later appropriation.

2

At the Birth of Christian Reflection

Paul and the New Testament

The letters of St. Paul, together with the other letters traditionally associated with him, feature important material about creation. They portray God as the one who calls nonexisting things into being and identify Christ as the chief agent of creation. Although these fundamental tenets are not explicitly grounded in the Hexaemeron narrative, what Paul and the other NT authors did with the paradise narrative, and in particular with the person of Adam, was groundbreaking and seminal, based as it was on an inchoate portraiture emerging from Second Temple Jewish texts. Although we cannot attribute to Paul a fully formed "theology of creation," his importance for how Christians read Genesis is difficult to overestimate. It is because of Paul's theology that we see Adam as the forefather of humanity, the progenitor of sin, and a type for Christ. The patristic and liturgical tradition focusing on Adam as the "old man" that has to be put off so that the "new man," Christ, can be put on has its origins in Paul, even if his intentions in establishing this dichotomy rested primarily in his bid to establish a new relationship between Jew and Gentile.

Paul in Context

It is well known that Paul was a zealous Pharisee, but modern scholars have sought greater precision as to which Judaism or Judaisms influenced him. In Judaism during the Second Temple period, especially after the death of

Alexander the Great in the late fourth century BCE, Hellenic influence was a significant factor, especially in the Diaspora. Rabbinic Judaism, which is associated particularly with the period after the fall of the temple (70 CE), is most tangibly identified with the Mishnah, its central and definitive anthology of texts codified in the third century CE. Rabbinic Judaism was at least a nascent reality in Paul's time; it is generally this Judaism that modern scholars have seen as his reference point.[1] Yet scholars differ widely on the nature of the Jewish influence on him. For Samuel Sandmel and for his teacher E. R. Goodenough, Paul's Judaism reflected the hellenized Second Temple variety.[2] Sandmel believes that Paul and rabbinic Judaism have nothing in common except the fact that they both refer to the Bible, that they are even antithetical to one another.[3] For example, he notes that the rabbis see sin as an act that can be repented of but Paul sees it as a condition from which we are freed and redeemed in Christ. Several other writers, however, hesitate to partition Hellenistic and Palestinian Judaism too neatly, finding many of the seemingly Hellenistic ideas in Paul to be equally present in rabbinic texts.[4]

Much ink has been spilled over the questions not only of Paul's Judaism but of where he stood on the law, sin, and justification. The "New Perspective on Paul," spearheaded by E. P. Sanders, James Dunn, N. T. Wright, and several others, has been helpful in wresting Paul from (a) the stereotype of Judaism as an obsessively legalistic religion and (b) the confessionally colored (viz. Lutheran) perspective of a once-prevalent Pauline scholarship fixated on the purported centrality, in Paul, of a doctrine of justification by faith.[5] The discussion of Paul's Judaism has been helpful in arriving at a potentially less-biased representation of his thought.

For the purposes of our own inquiry, however, the concern is not so much to identify the precise pedigree of the Judaism that influenced Paul in general. It is sufficient to have reviewed some of the texts that may either have specifically contributed to his conclusions about the nature and function of Adam or, more generally, have been a part of the zeitgeist in which he functioned. Indeed, the previous chapter revealed several features that might serve as a context for Paul's use of the creation texts, especially the paradise narrative. But we must exercise caution at several points. First, in the texts from the second century BCE through the first century CE, we have neither a homogenous portraiture of Adam nor a consistent use of the Hexaemeron. Second, the texts that most clearly echo Paul's concept and use of Adam came from the other side of a

1. Sanders, *Paul and Palestinian Judaism*, 24–25.
2. Goodenough, with Kraabel, "Paul and the Hellenization of Christianity."
3. Sandmel, *Genius of Paul*, 55–60.
4. Sanders, *Paul and Palestinian Judaism*, 7, neatly summarizes these views.
5. For a masterful summary of this movement and for directions forward, see Westerholm, *Perspectives*.

historic dividing line, the destruction of the temple, and therefore cannot be seen as part of the context out of which Paul emanated.

Perhaps the most that may be said—although this is no small thing—is that these texts show that Paul did not pull Adam out of nowhere. The virtual silence on the Hexaemeron and Adam in the Law, the Prophets, and the Writings had been broken already in the Hellenistic wisdom literature, which was increasingly instrumental in establishing a protology for creation and humanity in general and (e.g., in *Jubilees*) for Israel in particular. The idea of Adam and Eve both as first-created and (albeit in an inchoate way) as first-sinning had been hatched, even if the mechanics of it all—the relationship between the first parents and their legacy—had not yet been sorted out or presented with any consistency.

The treatment of Paul below emphasizes the undisputedly Pauline letters (which, as it happens, are the richest in relevant material), but it does not hesitate to consider Ephesians, Colossians, and 2 Thessalonians as well under the "Pauline" rubric since the Pauline character and even the Pauline authorship of the latter Epistles no longer appear as far-fetched as during earlier decades.[6] The Pastoral Epistles, whose Pauline authorship is more seriously in doubt, are treated separately; I refer to their author as "the Pastor." The letter to the Hebrews, of unknown authorship, receives passing mention.

Paul and Scripture

For Paul and for the other authors and characters in the NT, "the scriptures" are the Hebrew Scriptures. Even if Paul's own writings are at one point named among the γραφαί (2 Pet. 3:16), "the scriptures" according to which Christ died and was raised (1 Cor. 15:3–4) are the OT Scriptures. Judging from comparisons between his citations of Scripture and the LXX, Paul's main text seems to have been the LXX. In the vast majority of cases, Paul's citations and the LXX coincide, and they are often at variance with the Hebrew.[7] The evangelists, too, relied on the LXX, as we know from the scriptural citations they attribute to Jesus, whether he may have spoken them in Aramaic, Mishnaic Hebrew, or Greek.[8]

Paul uses the Scriptures in a variety of ways, many of which evince his rabbinic training.[9] Besides making numerous allusions to passages and themes from Scripture, he also quotes it directly, especially in Romans, 1 and 2 Corinthians,

---

6. See Longenecker, *Biblical Exegesis*, 90–91. At any rate, particularly given the undisputedly Pauline associations of these letters, it will not be of great consequence to insist here one way or another.

7. Ellis, *Paul's Use of the Old Testament*, 10–20, 150–85.

8. See Longenecker, *Biblical Exegesis*, 45–50.

9. See ibid., 98–109.

and Galatians. These references, together with their introductory formulae, are rich material for study.[10]

Particularly since most of the passages that refer to Genesis 1–3 do so by allusion rather than by direct quotation, it is his use of indirect references that is of greater interest to us. Paul is willing (together with other Jews and later the Christian fathers) to recast OT passages without regard to what we today may call authorial intent. Many of his adaptations occur as part of his christological use of the Scriptures. In Romans 10:6–8, he uses the proverbial words of Deuteronomy 30:12–14 to speak of Christ's descent and rising from the dead.[11] In Galatians 3:16, Abraham's promised seed (Gen. 12:7; 22:17–18) becomes Christ. Romans 10:18 refers to the apostolic proclamation by drawing on Psalm 19:5, which in fact refers to the heavens and the firmament. And there are what Paul, referring to Hagar and Sarah in Galatians 4:21–31, calls allegories. Notably, 1 Corinthians 9:8–10 states explicitly that in Deuteronomy 25:4 Moses was speaking for *our* (Christians') sake. The precise way in which the Corinthians passage ought to be interpreted may be disputed, but it is one of several that help us conclude that for Paul, as for several other authors under review in this study, the literal sense is subordinated to an allusive or allegorical sense, even if the literal is not rejected.[12]

These broad observations identify the defining characteristic of Paul's use of the OT. To Paul—the first Christian interpreter of the OT—the Scriptures speak of, anticipate, typologize, *reveal* Christ and him crucified. In effect, Paul takes the spectrum of Jewish hermeneutical methods—literal, allegorical, midrashic—and uses these instruments in a completely new way. In so doing, he says things that are revolutionary to the Jews but in a language and framework very much their own. As H. St.-J. Thackeray said more than a century ago, "The arguments by which [Paul] tried to convince his opponents of the true meaning of the OT as pointing forward to Christ, are those by which they would themselves have employed for another purpose; and to some extent we need not doubt that they were selected for that very reason."[13]

This study of Paul's use of Genesis 1–3 focuses on three general areas. First it looks briefly at how Paul might have understood creation and how that understanding may be derived from aspects of the Hexaemeron account. Then it investigates the nature and legacy of the transgression. Finally it examines Paul's (and the Pastor's) use of isolated verses from Genesis to support arguments about gender, sex, and marriage, and the use of some of the same verses in the Gospels.

10. See ibid., 92–95. The Pentateuch citations—there are about thirty—are introduced with "Moses says," "the law says," or "it is written."

11. See also Eph. 4:8.

12. See Longenecker, *Biblical Exegesis*, 109–10.

13. Cited in ibid., 111.

Let us first look briefly at Paul's allusions to the Hexaemeron. Hebrews 4:4 makes a passing reference to the fact that "somewhere" it is written that "God rested on the seventh day from all his works." Paul does not cite the Hexaemeron narrative explicitly, nor do the rest of the NT authors, who show a strictly limited concern with the *process* of creation. Emphasizing the radical nature of God's act of creation, Romans 4:17b states in passing (in a manner echoing 2 Macc. 7:28) that God "calls into existence the things that do not exist" (καλοῦντος τὰ μὴ ὄντα ὡς ὄντα). Even if it would be hasty to read a clearly formed doctrine of ex nihilo creation, we see here that Paul's interest lies in establishing God as radically other than creation, rather than in the means or sequence by which creation takes place.

The greater breakthrough is the association of creation with the agency of Jesus Christ. Colossians 1:16–17 says of Jesus Christ, the Son of God, that "in him all things in heaven and on earth were created, things visible and invisible" (he is the means of God's creation and therefore of the coherence of the created world: "In him all things hold together").[14] Likewise 1 Corinthians 8:6 speaks of Christ as the one by/in whom all is created. The idea is not unique to Paul. Hebrews 1:2 contains a similar statement, as does John 1:3, and the doctrine was later enshrined in the Nicene Creed in the article on Jesus Christ, "through whom all things were made."[15]

Some of these authors, especially the Fourth Gospel's author, were likely adapting the older ideas of the personification of Wisdom and/or the Torah.[16] Hebrews 1:3, speaking of Christ as perfectly reflecting God, echoes Wisdom 7:26. And the Colossians and 1 Corinthians texts likewise refer to wisdom literature, something that Philo also appropriated.[17] (The prepositions [generally διά] that the NT authors employ to speak of the role of "the Word" or of "Jesus Christ" in creation serve to distance the NT concepts from the gnostic demiurges; the latter were described as assigned agents rather than as beings "through whom" creation came into existence.)[18] Now, even if Paul is in fact building on recent concepts and anticipating subsequent authors, why does he stress this point about creation through Christ? The one God is established among the Jews as the Creator of all. Paul did not have to establish to the Jews that God was the Creator of the world, nor did he need to discuss the means of creation. The Gentiles are another matter, and the Areopagus episode in Acts 17 shows Paul

14. On referring to Colossians as Pauline, see n. 6 above.

15. All of these examples, including the Creed, are hymnological and doxological in character, suggesting liturgical origins.

16. Philo, too, seeing the Logos as the world soul, understood the world as having been created through the Logos. See Chadwick, "St. Paul and Philo of Alexandria." On the connection between the Torah and Wisdom, see Sir. 24:23, where the Torah is shown, in effect, to be the subject of all the attributes given to Wisdom earlier in the chapter.

17. See J. Dunn, *Theology of Paul*, 267–81.

18. See Brown, *Gospel according to John*, 26.

adapting the "unknown god" of the Gentile pantheon. The main adjustment that Paul must instill in Jew and Gentile alike is the establishment of Jesus Christ as not only a prophet and not only a prophet to the Jews but also universal Savior and, still more, the one in whom is founded not just Israel but all of creation.

This is part and parcel of Paul's transformation of the scriptural message. Genesis becomes the story not just of the origins of Israel but of the beginning of universal humanity, and this in turn paves the way for stressing the universality of salvation in Christ for the Jew and for the Greek. Paul's universalization of the Scriptures and his understanding of the Scriptures as revealing Christ are thoroughly interrelated. Together they constitute the cornerstone of his work in the establishment of Christian thought.

Paul and the Paradise Narrative: Sin and Death

Romans 1

A long-standing exegetical tradition considers the first three chapters of Romans—in particular 1:18–32—as functionally a creation narrative (or more accurately an etiology) and, as such, implicitly dependent on Genesis 2–3 and on parallels in Wisdom of Solomon. James Dunn makes the point that Adam lurks behind the whole Pauline passage, especially 1:22.[19] Fitzmyer notes the relationship as well, citing several of its proponents, even as he cautions against reading too much of Genesis into the passage.[20]

It is Stowers who is the most bothered by reading Romans 1 in terms of Genesis 2–3 or, for that matter, in terms of any uniquely Jewish background.[21] In the first place, he views this passage in a broader context of the prevalent Hellenic and Roman topos of the "decline of civilization narrative." Genesis 1–3, Stowers emphasizes, is the first of a series of decline narratives that takes us through Genesis 11 and beyond. Subsequent Jewish readings of Genesis often de-emphasize Adam, or at any rate underplay his guilt for the first sin, blaming Cain instead. In any case, Jewish readings are more prone to see Genesis 1–11 in terms of the origin of Israel rather than of all humanity.

Second, Stowers asks, where exactly is Adam in Romans 1? Paul does not hesitate to mention Adam elsewhere in his corpus and makes deliberate use of him in Romans 5. Although we would not want to depend entirely on an argument from silence, Adam's absence here is telling. Most important, the epistle has a Gentile audience in mind, as is announced clearly (e.g., Rom. 1:13; 15:13–26). We cannot therefore see 1:18–32 as speaking first and foremost of a universal human fall.

19. J. Dunn, *Theology of Paul*, 91–93. Dunn lists several other scriptural referents.
20. Fitzmyer, *Romans*, 274.
21. Stowers, *Rereading of Romans*, 83–109.

These observations may rule out a reading of Romans 1 as an echo of Genesis 2–3, but I would aver that Stowers's argument from tradition is faulty. His reminder that the Jewish tradition up until Paul did not focus on Adam as the progenitor and cause of sin is correct. Yet particularly when considered alongside Romans 5, 1 Corinthians 15, and the entire Pauline project of universalizing the scriptural message, it is plain that Paul is in several key places deliberately *breaking* the tradition that came before him. Granted, like the pre-70 CE Jewish texts, Paul does not (despite later misreadings of him) attribute to Adam a specifically causal role in the sin of all humanity. But even if the "person" of Adam is in no way the subject of Romans 1:21–22, Paul does in fact envisage a fall and likely sees Genesis as being a protological description thereof.

Although this study has presented Jewish readings of the creation narratives in order to explore possible influences on (or, in the case of later texts, by) Paul, one must not straitjacket him with that tradition, as, for example, Dunn does. He asserts that Christ's status as "last Adam" for Paul is contingent on his becoming one with the first Adam, in his fallenness and death. He also maintains that this idea "would have gained a ready acceptance from many if not all of his fellow Jews—the idea of all men as somehow caught up in Adam's fall, of man as fallen Adam."[22] Levison rightly critiques Dunn's assumption that Jews would have agreed that a fallen humanity began in a fallen Adam.[23] But the fact that this notion was foreign to the Jewish tradition up until that point does not mean that this was not what Paul meant.[24]

To the extent we can identify a pre-Pauline Jewish tradition regarding Adam and human sinfulness/righteousness, it appears that Paul broke it. Making use of familiar language and methods, he forged something radically new.

Romans 5

In Romans 5, Paul explicitly focuses on the paradise narrative—specifically in the person of Adam. He is elsewhere cognizant of Eve as having been deceived (2 Cor. 11:3), but here, as in 1 Corinthians 15, he needs "one man" to act as counterpart to the "one man" Christ. Here it would also be fair to make a connection with Jewish tradition specifically in its patriarchal character, which, though not blind to Eve, had always focused on Adam as progenitor.

PAUL'S ADAM

Who is Adam for Paul, and what is his role in the existential situation of humanity? His answer—and that of the other Second Temple authors we have

---

22. J. Dunn, *Christology in the Making*, 106, cited in Levison, *Portraits of Adam*, 20.
23. Levison, *Portraits of Adam*, 20.
24. And would it be possible to suggest Pauline influence on the post-70 CE texts, notably 2 Esdras and 2 *Baruch*? They do take up something quite like what we find in Rom. 5.

studied, with the glaring exception of Philo—would be essentially the same. For the scriptural and deuterocanonical authors, Adam both represented humankind and also figured as a character in a scriptural narrative and, through this story, as the first ancestor in a genealogy that led to Noah and beyond. Paul was not averse to the sporadic use of allegory, but he did not allegorize Adam. Yet he is finally uninterested in the question of who Adam is, caring only about *what* Adam is and the role he plays in counterpoint to Christ.

Indeed, there is a sense in which Paul's use of Adam is simple and minimal. Putting Adam and Christ together in Romans 5 is merely a way of showing how the actions of one lone figure can have profound (though opposite) effects on many people. Romans 5:15–19 is all about showing how the effects of Adam and Christ are both broad and deep, the one leading to death and the other to grace and justification. However basic this may sound, one should not minimize the significance of the choice of Adam as exemplar in this context, since for Paul's Jewish predecessors Adam was not the most obvious example of the protosinner whose transgression brings mortal consequences. Paul might just as well have chosen Cain, Aaron, or Abraham; instead he ratchets up the importance of Adam as the first human *and* the first sinner. Asserting Adam's broad and earth-shattering significance for "the many," Paul establishes Adam as "a type of the one who was to come" (5:14).

So Paul's Adam is the first in a lineage of sin and, through sin, death. Linking Adam's function with his primordial setting makes him, in effect, chiefly a symbol: he is a stand-in for (fallen) humanity in general and subsequently a type for Christ, an icon of the "old self" that is to be put off in favor of the new. Yet given Adam's genealogical significance, he is at least implicitly a person before he is a symbol.

Adam is the first sinner, and he died; thus he stands as first in a universal lineage of sinners and mortals.[25] It is all the more interesting in retrospect to notice that the paradise narrative does not present itself as an account of the universal fall of humanity. The story describes God's creation of persons as works in progress, persons who overreached their proper place, thus failing to attain immortality and beginning a series of declines that led to the depravity of Genesis 6 and the flood. Making the first sinner and the first-made human being one and the same person has the effect of opening out the genealogy, the effects of sin, and therefore the scope of salvation, which now incorporates the Gentiles. The dividing line is no longer between Jew and Gentile but between the old dispensation (or old Adam) and the new dispensation in Christ.

This universalizing message in an epistle that has chiefly the Gentiles in view justifies the standard approach of deriving from Romans generalized statements about "sin" and "death." True, the situation for Gentiles remains

25. The universality for Paul may have differentiated between Jews and Gentiles if we follow Stowers's arguments outlined below, but the condition is universal nonetheless.

different from that for Jews, as Stowers shows through detailed argumentation.[26] Stowers analyzes the structure of the whole letter, especially through
Romans 11, showing Paul's double standard for the Jews and the Gentiles.
The Jews, for Paul, are righteous by default but are wont to turn from that
righteousness and need transformation and mercy in Christ. The Gentiles, on
the other hand, are unrighteous by default (Rom. 1:18–32) and need transformation and mercy in Christ.[27] Romans 1:1–14 (and 15:13–26) makes a Gentile
audience the probable main target of the letter. Romans 5–8, then, is likely
to be chiefly concerned with the particular transformation and reintegration
of the Gentiles.

Nonetheless it is evident that "sin" and "death" emphatically remain *generalized* categories. Jew and Gentile alike are "under the power of sin" (3:9),
and all who sin require God's mercy. Indeed, "God has imprisoned *all* in
disobedience so that he may be merciful to all" (11:32). Let us briefly explore
what Paul means by these categories, particularly as they relate to the paradise
narrative.

Sin

There are different theories about what Paul means by the sin that came
"through [the] one man," the sin that brings death. One is that "sin" is short-
hand for a demonic force that through Adam gains a grasp in the world (Rom.
5:12), ultimately reigning in it (5:21). This cannot be the only meaning, for
even if we look at the interim verses, the logic begins to fail. If sin is a demonic
power, how could it not be counted where there is no law (5:13)?[28] Rather,
"sin" for Paul in Romans 5 is evidently the collective term for the specific (and
aggregate) *sins* committed by people. But insofar as sin becomes systemic, it
can indeed be spoken of as a "reigning force." Thus both of these dimensions—
particular sins and sin's systemic nature—are integral to Paul's concept. Yet
Paul is frequently at pains to refute the idea that sin is embedded in human
nature in such a way that people should simply resign themselves to it. Sin as
natural to humanity would compromise free choice, so for Paul there is always
the choice either to put off sin or to "die to sin," as we shall see below.

The idea of Adam's transgression *causing* the sin of subsequent generations,
or the idea that guilt for Adam's sin was a bacillus that spread to all human
beings, such that (as the Vulgate translation has it) "all men sin in Adam,"
has been rectified in the RSV and NRSV renditions of 5:12: "death spread to
all because all have sinned." The idea of "original sin" as a causal factor lies
not with Paul but with Jerome and, on the basis of Jerome's translation, with

---

26. Stowers, *Rereading of Romans*, 251–55.

27. See Rom. 11:30–31: "Just as you [Gentiles] were once disobedient to God but have now
received mercy because of their [Jews'] disobedience, so they [Jews] have now been disobedient
in order that, by the mercy shown to you [Gentiles], they too may now receive mercy."

28. See Westerholm, *Perspectives*, 394.

Augustine. Neither in Paul nor in the rest of the Bible is there a doctrine of original guilt, wherein all are proleptically guilty in Adam.[29] John Chrysostom comments on Romans 5 (as if anticipating the distortions to come in later, primarily Western Christian history):

> There is nothing improbable about the idea that, when Adam sinned and became mortal, those who were descended from him should become mortal. But how should it follow that from his disobedience anyone else should become a sinner? For unless a person becomes a sinner on his own responsibility he will not be found to deserve punishment.[30]

Romans 5 also speaks of the "reign" of sin and death with reference to a particular era, from Adam (the beginning) to Moses (the law) (5:14). With the law, matters become different: sin "increases" (5:20) in the sense that deviations may be seen more clearly against the plumb line of the law. But obviously Jews and Gentiles alike remain under the grip of sin, and so they need to be reminded that their baptism means death to all of that. This leads us to Paul's concept of death.

Death

The last chapter noted that, although dying by death (Gen. 2:17 LXX) was the threatened outcome of partaking of the tree, neither Adam nor Eve died until centuries later. Death became the final (merciful, even perhaps honorable) end of the mode of toil and pain that now characterized their days. Their transgression did bring on something very specific, but not biological death, even if they did finally expire. The cause-and-effect relationship that Paul posits between sin and death leads us to ask what kind of death he was talking about.

If not from the Genesis texts themselves, then at least from Paul onward we must distinguish physical/biological death from spiritual death—even if there remains a definite link between the two. For Paul, it would seem that Adam and Eve *did* die, in a manner of speaking, as soon as they ate of the tree, since "death" comes to stand for the pointless and painful existence to which Adam and Eve were relegated after their transgression. This is how death, like sin, can act as a reigning force, though one that is overcome in Christ.

Death is a multivalent term for Paul. In order to overcome spiritual death and thus transform even biological death, one must "die" to sin (cf. Rom. 6). "Life" likewise means more than biological existence, and eternal life is not endless longevity of years. When in Romans 6 Paul speaks of baptism and of dying and rising with Christ, he is obviously not envisaging some macabre

---

29. In addition to the other sources already cited on this point, see Tobin, "Jewish Context of Rom 5:12–14."

30. John Chrysostom, *Tenth Homily on Romans* (PG 60:477). See *NPNF*[1] 11:403.

baptismal murder followed by a resuscitation into physical immortality; rather, the character and the mode of people's lives are transfigured when they "die to," or renounce, spiritual death. For Paul, sin leads to spiritual death, and spiritual death is finally linked with biological death. Life in Christ (ἐν Χριστῷ) is an overturning of (and death to) sin and spiritual death. Sin began with Adam and was sharpened and highlighted by the introduction of the law. Mercy and righteousness begin with Christ.

1 Corinthians 15

First Corinthians and Romans were written within a short period of time of each other, and even if 1 Corinthians preceded Romans, the function of Adam in the earlier letter does not raise as many theological difficulties and can thus be treated in a manner approaching a postscript.

In 1 Corinthians 15, which focuses on the nature of the resurrection (Christ's and ours), Adam enters the argumentation twice, each time with a different intention. In 15:21–22, his function is initially not unlike the fundamental role he fulfills in Romans 5, namely, to emphasize consequence: he and Christ are both pivotal figures whose deeds affect many. The relationship is again one of opposition: death and life, which refer both to origins (death δι' ἀνθρώπου [Adam] and life δι' ἀνθρώπου [Christ]) and to the present and eschatological future (death ἐν τῷ Ἀδάμ and life ἐν τῷ Χριστῷ). Here, too, as in Romans (though less explicitly), Adam is the first to sin and therefore the one by whom mortality spreads to all human beings.

In 1 Corinthians 15:45–50 Paul takes as his scriptural foundation Genesis 2:7, the creation of the human person from dust and the breathing in of animating spirit. Genesis 2:7 had already been brought into the discussion before Paul wrote, as evidenced by 2 Maccabees 7:23 and by the earliest exponents of rabbinic Judaism as well as by "gnostic" sects.[31] The idea against which Paul is arguing in 1 Corinthians 15 is a dualistic one: the resurrection will be asomatic, and this because *'adam* has been in-breathed with life-giving spirit. Paul's point is that all human beings indeed die, since all human beings are descended from Adam. What is breathed into Adam is life, not immortality. Adam and all human beings are living beings, but they are mortal, made of earth/dust. It is in Christ, in the age to come, that we *shall be* given the spiritual body and become as the man of heaven (cf. also Phil. 3:21).

Whereas in Romans the use of Adam had a moral character, focusing on sin and its relation to spiritual and physical death, in 1 Corinthians 15 it has more a physical or almost technical character. Here it is not about whom we choose to follow, the old man or the new, dying to sin, and so forth. Here it is a matter of showing, on the basis of Genesis 2:7, that Adam/humanity is εἰς ψυχὴν ζῶσαν,

---

31. On this and what follows, see Pearson, *Pneumatikos-psychikos Terminology*, 23–26.

a living natural being, in contrast to Christ, who is εἰς πνεῦμα ζωοποιοῦν, a life-making spirit (1 Cor. 15:45),[32] and that our resurrection in immortality is neither bodiless nor ours by right or by nature but is entirely ἐν Χριστῷ.

In this context, is it worth looking at the connection between Philo and Paul and between Philo and the entire NT?[33] Passages, such as this, that contrast the physical and the spiritual ἄνθρωπος raise the possibilities of corresponding theology or even possible influence. But whether Philo's "two men" meant the rational and irrational components of the human person or referred to a Platonic "double creation," the idea had nothing in common with Paul's point here in 1 Corinthians 15. Rather than suggest direct lines of influence between Paul and Philo, it is more accurate to see them each as drawing from some of the same elements in Jewish and, to a lesser extent, Greek philosophical tradition.[34]

Paul's Adaptation of Adam

Particularly with his Jewish background in mind, we must still ask how Paul arrives at Adam to lay on him the burden of being the agent of sin's/death's initiation into humanity. Several astute commentators in recent decades have deduced the observation that Paul did not start with and then enshrine a chronological scheme of creation, (Adamic) fall, and redemption. Rather, Paul's understanding of Christ and his saving work for humanity and for the world set him searching for ways to express more clearly what it was about the world that needed saving. As E. P. Sanders put it most succinctly, for Paul the solution preceded the problem: "The conclusion that all the world—both Jew and Greek—equally stands in need of a saviour springs from the prior conviction that God had provided such a saviour."[35] So likewise James Barr:

> To [Paul] the total and unqualified gift of salvation through Jesus Christ was the reversed image of the equally total and unqualified disaster brought about by Adam and through Adam transmitted to the entire human race. . . . It is easy to see how Paul, wishing to make clear the completeness and finality of Christ's victory over sin, looked to the story of Adam and found in it the typology that he needed.[36]

Or more succinctly, "Paul was not interpreting the story in and for itself; he was really *interpreting Christ* through the use of images from the story."[37] This way of putting it helps us understand how it could be that Paul has made of

32. The translation here is from Orr and Walther, *1 Corinthians*, 341.
33. Runia, *Philo in Early Christian Literature*, 64–86, helpfully refers to them.
34. Cf., e.g., Ellis, *Paul's Use of the Old Testament*, 64–80.
35. Sanders, *Paul and Palestinian Judaism*, 442–47, here 443.
36. Barr, *Garden of Eden*, 4.
37. Ibid., 89, emphasis original.

Adam and the paradise story something different from what it ever was before. He not only transformed thinking about sin; he was the first to make of the paradise story what it has remained for subsequent Christian generations—the primordial account of the fall of humanity. Paul's thinking on the fall admits differentiation at several levels: the fall would have different effects before the law and after the law; it would have different ramifications for Jew and Greek; it would mean different things before and after the coming of Christ. But its status as universal is established in the light of Christ.

But even this last point does not reflect the most profound level of Paul's thought. For his starting point and focus are not finally sin (which is old news) but rather that which is *new*: Jesus Christ, Lord and Savior. Paul does nothing less than define the direction and the sequence, as it were, of Christian reflection on Christ. This direction is not the one commonly associated with Christianity, namely, a kind of chronological sequence from a perfect pre-fallen state, to a one-event calamitous fall, and then to a salvation that comes in 33 CE. It is a sequence that begins with Christ himself: rather than Adam being a model or image for humanity or even the first real human being, it is Christ who is both. Christ is the first true human being, and Christ is the image of God and the model for Adam.[38]

Indeed, there is no mention in Paul of *the person of Adam* as created in God's image. Genesis 1:26 and 2:7 are distinct for him: Paul's Adam is not so much the first human being as he is the first human to sin. Although he sees that the human person is in God's image (1 Cor. 11:7), Paul does not write of Adam as glorious or image-bearing but, rather, as the "man of dust" (1 Cor. 15:47). For him (and for the author of Hebrews), it is *Christ* who is the image of God (Col. 1:15; Heb. 1:3) and to whose image humanity must conform (Rom. 8:29). As Karl Barth puts it memorably, "Adam's humanity is a *provisional copy* of the real humanity that is in Christ."[39]

Paul may reinterpret the paradise narrative in ways that stretch "authorial intent" and break with Jewish tradition up until his time. But he is, in fact, completely true to several crucial aspects of the original story: he does not posit a perfect pre-fallen state, nor does he attribute later human sin to the sin of Adam. Rather, he sees Adam as a kind of beginning—the beginning of a death-bound mode of life. But it is a beginning that does not need to be followed; it does not overcome human free choice. History, humanity—says Barth, again—

> constantly re-enacts the little scene in the Garden of Eden. There never was a golden age. There is no point looking back to one. The first man was immediately the first sinner. . . . [Adam] was in a trivial form what we all are, a man of sin. But he was so as the beginner, and therefore as *primus inter pares*. This

38. The last chapter will further explore this point.
39. Barth, *Christ and Adam*, 46–47, emphasis original.

does not mean that he has bequeathed to us as his heirs so that we have to be as he was. He has not poisoned us or passed on a disease. What we do after him is not done according to an example which irresistibly overthrows us, or an imitation of his act which is ordained for all his successors. No one has to be Adam. We are so freely and on our own responsibility.[40]

Certainly Paul came to focus on Adam as a result of his finding Christ. Although it would be difficult to say that Paul bears the sole responsibility for the movement toward typological readings of the OT, his reading of the OT as illuminated by and illuminating Christ was groundbreaking and became the guiding rubric under which the Christian fathers read Scripture. Saying that "the rock was Christ" or that Adam is a type of Christ stems from Paul's reading of the function of the entire (OT) Scripture. As he shows in 2 Corinthians 3:12–4:7, to read Scripture in sheerly chronological terms, as a history of the world or as the story of the nation of Israel, is to have a veil over one's eyes. One lifts the veil when one turns to the Lord (3:16). The Scriptures are about Christ, the treasure who lies within the clay jars (4:7).[41]

Written some decades later, the description of the meeting of the Lord on the road to Emmaus in Luke 24 ascribes the same function to the OT. There it is the risen Lord, unrecognized by the two disciples, who opens the Scriptures to them, showing how the Scriptures are about himself. Likewise in the other Gospels—John 5:46 and Matthew 12:39–40—parts or all of Scripture are shown to be referring to Christ. We will see how in the patristic and liturgical legacy Paul's Adam-Christ typology became elaborated to the point where few scriptural verses were left unexplored for their relationship to Christ, Mary, or the church.

Paul and the Paradise Narrative: Gender and Marriage

Paul's use of the paradise narrative in his concept of sin and redemption is separate from the NT treatment of marriage and gender/sex that refers to Genesis 2:24. The common element, we will see, is his interest in the narrative as a reference point and his shaping of it for his own particular use. As this study examines Paul's use of Genesis 1–3, it will naturally focus on his discussion of gender, sex, and marriage.

1 Corinthians 11:7–12

In 1 Corinthians 11:7–12 Paul explains the use or not of head covering for men and women during prayer. He does so in the context of a theme appearing

---

40. Barth, *Doctrine of Reconciliation*, part 1, pp. 508–9.

41. It is easy to see how Valentinians and even Marcionites might have seen themselves as faithful to Paul's suggestions of knowledge hidden under veils and within clay jars. See Young, *Biblical Exegesis*, 63.

again in Ephesians 5: the headship of the man over the woman. Here, insofar as he discusses the image of God, Paul brings into service Genesis 1:26, where man (Ἀνήρ) "is the image and reflection of God; but woman is the reflection of man." Further, Genesis 2:18–23 is the text behind Paul's statement that "man was not made from woman, but woman from man" (1 Cor. 11:7–8).

This use of Genesis appears to bring the Hexaemeron and paradise accounts together, making them functionally one. The creation in the image seems run together with the creation of woman from man as if the two events were a single account, perhaps as a consequence of the LXX translation of 'adam.[42] If, as stated earlier, the two narratives were treated as distinct in Romans 5, the passage examined here represents a different approach—far from impossible, given that Genesis 1–3 by no means had a fixed exegesis in Paul's day and Paul did not intend to establish one.

There are several theories about what Paul is saying about men and women in general and even about what he is addressing in the specific context of the Corinthian community. At first glance, he seems to be setting out a double standard for women and men but then—in a passage (1 Cor. 11:11–12) that in the RSV appears in parentheses, presumably because it seems out of place—appears to backtrack, mitigating the absolute subordination of women to men. A deeper reading is necessary.

Paul's argument here about the interdependence of women and men is nearly identical to what can be found in typical rabbinic exegesis of Genesis 1:26–27 and 2:21–23:

> In the past, Adam was created from the earth and Eve was created from Adam; from then on, "In our image, after our likeness," there can be not man without woman, there can be not woman without man, there can be not both of these without the shekinah.[43]

Paul, like the rabbis, takes the Genesis texts that speak only of Adam and Eve and generalizes them to undergird his point about man and woman. But his use of the text also differs from theirs. The rabbis, as Mary D'Angelo shows, distinguish between the creation of Adam and Eve and its aftermath—procreation. Eve's derivation from Adam was "in the past," and "from then on" the relationship is one of interdependence. For Paul, however, the distinction is much sharper: between creation and new creation.[44] As seen above, Adam (and Eve) functions for Paul as a symbol of the "old self" in contrast to the new. Here, too, the dynamic of derivation is part of the old dispensation,

---

42. As discussed in chap. 1, above.

43. This argument appears nearly verbatim in three rabbinic texts. See D'Angelo, "The Garden," 7–21; citation from p. 7. D'Angelo also points to another rabbinic exegesis of the passage that, like Paul, conflates Gen. 1:26 with 2:18–23.

44. D'Angelo, "The Garden," 23, and the remainder of the article.

one that is transfigured in Christ. This is the meaning of saying "In the Lord woman is not independent of man nor man independent of woman" (1 Cor. 11:11). "In the Lord," for Paul, represents the eschatological dispensation as being already realized now. And the phrase "All things are from God" in the next verse is echoed precisely in 2 Corinthians 5:17–18, which likewise speaks of the "new creation" that comes from being "in Christ."[45]

So, having advanced the argument of woman's derivation from man (both physically and in the sense of image-bearing) as a possible reason for the difference in headgear at prayer, he immediately *rejects* this argument, since the dynamic of derivation is part of the old dispensation, overcome "in the Lord." Rather, Paul recommends different deportment at prayer now not because of an exalted protology but because of contextual propriety: he tells the Corinthians, "Judge for yourselves" (1 Cor. 11:13). Commenting on the same verses, Fiorenza writes, "In the Christian community women and men are not different from each other. Differences which might exist on the basis of nature and creation are no longer present in the worship assembly of the Christians."[46]

The paradise narratives describe several situations that are of the old dispensation: sin, imprisonment to death, and the derivation of woman from man and her consequent subordination. According to Paul, these are transcended in Christ (Gal. 3:28). He echoes positive statements about human beings in Genesis 1–3: in the new Christian dispensation they are still made in God's image, they are still differentiated according to sex, and they still "cling" to each other to become one flesh (Gen. 2:24). We now turn to this last statement as it appears in Paul and the other NT authors.

1 Corinthians 6:16

The reference to Genesis 2:24b in 1 Corinthians 6:16 appears to have a simple function: to show that there is no such thing as casual sex, that sexual relations both presume and effect a profound unity between the partners. This portion of 1 Corinthians deals with immorality—specifically with morality that pertains to the body.

In 1 Corinthians 6:15–16 Paul conflates body (σῶμα) and flesh (σάρξ), terms that he is more likely to distinguish elsewhere. Here he takes the "one flesh" of Genesis 2 also to mean "one body," and becoming "one flesh" or "one body" to mean what happens through the sexual act. To visit prostitutes causes the sexually immoral to become one with them. Evidently, Paul interprets Genesis 2:24 not so much as marriage but as engaging in the sexual act (unless, that is, the Corinthians are making a practice of marrying prostitutes). Such behavior is an especially egregious offense because, for Paul, the body

45. Ibid., 24–25.
46. Schüssler Fiorenza, *In Memory of Her*, 229–30.

is a reflection of Christ's body—an interesting turn on 1 Corinthians 12, in which the church, in its corporate membership, constitutes Christ's body, the body in turn consisting of many interdependent members. In 1 Corinthians 6, the body is also seen as a temple of the Holy Spirit (1 Cor. 6:19) and as a member of Christ (6:15).

Ephesians 5:31

In Ephesians 5, Paul[47] takes the marriage theme of 1 Corinthians 6 even further, interweaving the ideas about intrahuman union into ideas about the union of humans with Christ. The language of Ephesians 5:22–33 constantly dances between phrasing about husbands and wives and phrasing about Christ and the church, all under the rubric of a profound and mysterious union, one with differentiation and mutual dependency. Paul here invokes Genesis amid a series of his favorite themes: practical advice on male-female relationships, the church as Christ's body, the union of male and female, and the union of Christ with the church. Genesis 2:24, now cited in its entirety (as is done elsewhere only in Matt. 19:5), serves the double function of indicating both the primordial blessing on the married state and the depth of the union, expressed in the organic term of "one flesh." Here the context suggests that the "one flesh" is not just about sex (as it was in 1 Cor. 6) but about the ongoing relationship and state of marriage.

Genesis 2:24 is in fact given a privileged place in this complex passage. It comes right before the climax, which speaks of "this profound mystery" (NIV). The referent in τὸ μυστήριον τοῦτο is not entirely clear, and the ambiguity may be intentional. *All* of what Paul has said above about men and women, Christ and the church, and union unto "one flesh" (again with the link between flesh and body) expresses a profound mystery, but it ultimately refers to Christ and the church. Another possible reading, however, views Ephesians 5:32 as referring to what immediately precedes in 5:31, namely, the citation of Genesis 2:24. The mystery of two becoming one flesh is profound, ultimately referring to Christ and the church and *by extension* to the union of men and women in marriage. It would not be impossible for Paul to interpret Genesis here once again in terms of Christ. Paul, after all, is the one for whom the rock that slaked Israel's thirst in the wilderness was Christ" (1 Cor. 10:4) and for whom Adam is a type of the one who was to come (Rom. 5:14).

Paul and the Evangelists

The Gospels twice—Mark 10:8 and its parallel in Matthew 19:5–6—cite Genesis 2:24 with reference to 1:27. The context is a question posed about divorce;

---

47. Authorship questions have been addressed above.

Jesus invokes Genesis 2:24 (possibly paraphrased in Mark) to emphasize both the depth of the union of the two (into the "one flesh") and the primordial character of this union, as it existed from "the beginning."

In Mark's account, Jesus first stresses sex differentiation, which leads "therefore" (in an apparently logical inexorability) to the joining of the man to the woman in union. In Matthew's account, the logical connection is not pushed so far. But Jesus's words in Matthew 19:4–5 remarkably conflate God and Moses: "Have you not read that the one who made them from the beginning [viz., God] 'made them male and female,' and said 'For this reason a man shall leave . . .'" If this conflation is deliberate, it has the effect of putting into God's own mouth the pronouncement that a man leaves his parents to become joined to his wife. This would serve to undergird even further Jesus's unbending response to the Pharisaic inquiry about divorce.

Jesus even says farther on, in 19:11, that not everyone can accept this teaching/saying (λόγος). It is not entirely clear what *logos* refers to; it may be the disciples' suggestion in 19:10 that it would be better not to marry. But given the context of the inquiry and the centrality and force of the Genesis verses, more likely the hard saying is that marriage is a union into one flesh and that divorce is not a right but a concession. The fact that the same Genesis verses elicited Paul's characterization of them as a "great mystery" in Ephesians 5 may be unrelated, but again it may indicate that Genesis 2:24, which in a sense we take for granted, was for first-century Jews and Gentiles a striking and challenging statement.

There appears to be another parallel as well. Like Paul in 1 Corinthians 11, Jesus uses Genesis here to contrast the original creation with the new creation. The subsequent verse in Matthew's text (Matt. 19:12), where Christ refers to the eunuchs for the kingdom, points to an eschatological orientation that entails a transfigured relationship to the Mosaic law that precipitated the Pharisees' inquiry. This same orientation is also the subject of the next episode in Matthew 19, which emphasizes a childlike detachment in anticipation of the "renewal of all things, when the Son of Man is seated on the throne of his glory" (19:28).

The Gospels take up certain key aspects of Paul's message. Like Paul, they use the paradise story as representing "the beginning" and, for Luke at least, Adam is the universal forebear. Yet it is perhaps more remarkable to note that the central Pauline tenets are conspicuously absent in the writing of the evangelists. Although Jesus does speak of saving people from their sins, he gives no sense of a universal fall, nor does he mention Adam as its instigator. Indeed, even the concept of "sin" (rather than "sins") in the Synoptics is found just once, in Matthew 13:41. Even in the later writings, which do speak of "sin" (John 1:29; 8:21, 34; 9:34; 16:8–9), if there is an origin to sin, it is associated with the devil, not Adam (1 John 3:8).

This significant disconnect between Paul and the evangelists will be of continued interest when we explore the patristic writings and their readings of Genesis 1–3. Still, there is a vital note of unity between the Pauline project and that of the evangelists, as seen in the role played by Adam.

Both Matthew and Mark recount Jesus as bringing Genesis 1:27 and 2:24 together into a virtually seamless whole. In both versions, Jesus cites these texts as indicating the state of things "from the beginning of creation" (ἀπὸ [δὲ] ἀρχῆς κτίσεως, Mark) or "from the beginning" (ἀπ' ἀρχῆς, Matthew). The Genesis texts are thus seen as universal creation stories, as they scarcely were before the post-70 CE texts. In addition, the first words of John and of Mark and also of 1 John are probably a canny reference to the opening words of Genesis; Christ's final words from the cross, "It is finished," (John 19:30) may likewise be seen in this light. For Luke, it is still more apparent that the creation accounts—or specifically the person of Adam—represent a universal beginning. This leads to a final observation concerning the Gospels' use of Genesis, Luke in particular.

Earlier we saw in Luke's account of the Emmaus Road how Christ puts himself at the center of the OT Scriptures; this is the culmination of a strong Lukan theme. In Matthew's Gospel the starting point of Christ's genealogy is Abraham, for he intends (Matt. 1:1) to show Jesus as descending from the Abrahamic and Davidic line in neat, symmetrical numbers of generations. In Luke's Gospel, however, the genealogy begins (or actually *ends*) with Adam, for its function is markedly different. Jesus is not only a child of Abraham and David; he is a child of humanity. There was no better way to express this than in the terms that the Pentateuch used to introduce Noah: a genealogy dating back to "the beginning," namely, Adam. Thanks to Paul, Christians had begun to view Adam as the forebear of all humanity. This was Luke's program: to further the revolution, begun by Paul, of universalizing the Jewish heritage. The Scriptures have not merely a new audience but a transformatively expanded message. The Savior is not just the Savior of the children of Abraham, Luke is saying. He is *ours*.

Let us review Paul's influence on exegesis.[48] He began the transformation of scriptural exegesis as a Jew steeped in Jewish Scripture and exegetical method. His message was bound up with the end of the old law, such that ethnic Judaism (and circumcision) was no longer a requirement for membership in the people of God. Paul only began to draw out the implications of a renewed approach to the Scriptures and to their enduring moral (and theological) authority in the face of their transformed message.

Gentile writers coming just after Paul, particularly Luke among the evangelists, took up his baton.

---

48. For a fuller account, see Young, *Biblical Exegesis*, esp. 286–88.

Can there be any doubt that Luke's outlook is that of a convert who has become convinced that this message of the kingdom of God is for the whole earth, that the universalizing community of the Church rightfully inherits the literature and history that once belonged to another community?[49]

Luke's message is framed in the language of Gentiles, addressed to Gentiles as well as to Jews, who were increasingly distanced from their roots. Adam, appearing in Luke 3:38, plays a momentary but fundamental role in Luke's schema.

Postscript: The Pastoral Epistles

Stylistic and linguistic features of the Pastoral Epistles have long caused scholars to doubt their Pauline authorship. Historical considerations (notably the advanced state of ecclesiastical ministry depicted) appear to indicate also a later date, perhaps even the end of the first century or the beginning of the second. Some serious scholars are nonetheless confident in attributing most or all of the pastoral material to Paul, even if he dictated it to a scribe or an associate.[50] Others, however, remain skeptical.[51]

The chief use of Genesis 1–3 in the Pastorals appears in 1 Timothy 2:11–15, whose prima facie meaning (about women's subdued role in the church and their salvation through childbearing and modesty) leads many readers today to cringe and perhaps even to feel grateful that Paul himself is probably not its author. A closer look at the nature of the epistle and its use of the paradise story is necessary. Two aspects of the paradise account are brought to the service of the Pastor's message: the difference between Eve's and Adam's origins and the difference between their roles in the transgression in the garden.

The Pastor's use of Genesis 2:21–23 is simple and practical. Adam was formed first, then Eve. This summation is shorter and less elaborate than that in 1 Corinthians 11, where Paul adapted an existing rabbinic exegesis and addressed the question of provenance. The Pastor does not speak of Eve's origin in Adam's rib but only of sequence: Adam was formed first, and that is that. The fact that this argument has all the moral force of a playground claim to the jungle gym is of no consequence. What is of interest is that there is no reference here to the *new* creation, where, as is well known from the Synoptics, the last and the first are reversed and the dynamic of primordial succession is superseded. As we have seen in Romans 5 and

49. Ibid., 288.
50. See Johnson, *First and Second Letters to Timothy*; Kelly, *Commentary on the Pastoral Epistles*.
51. Bassler, *1 Timothy, 2 Timothy, Titus*, among many.

1 Corinthians 11, this contrast is central to Paul's message and specifically to his use of Genesis. The paradise episode is part of the old dispensation that is *put off* in Christ and in the community of prayer (which is the concern of 1 Timothy 2).

The Pastor's use of Genesis 3:1–13 is likewise straightforward if one reads the Genesis text literally. The focus is on Eve, her personal dialogue with the serpent, and her deception, referred to again in 3:13. Adam is essentially a bystander, an accessory. He eats only because Eve gives him to eat, without entering into the moral conundrum. This, too, represents a departure from Paul's use of the story. Elsewhere Paul mentions Eve's deception, though very much in passing, in 2 Corinthians 11:3, but when it comes down to it, Adam is the chief actor and by no means the accessory. Admittedly, this is so primarily because the one man Adam makes a better τύπος for the one man Christ. But even so, 1 Timothy 2 is much more reminiscent of what we saw in Sirach 25:24, if not 42:13, than it is of Paul.[52]

Regarding the Pastor's message in 1 Timothy 2, one compelling theory suggests that he was concerned about the evident incursions of heretical teachings into the prayer communities, particularly among women.[53] Whatever his motivation, his use of the Genesis narrative is rather pedestrian and, as such, would be difficult to associate with Paul.

The link we do find with Paul (or perhaps even more with the Gentile Luke) is the overall mission of recasting the Scriptures in a way that shows that their authority and their law are not so much transcended as transformed and that salvation is opened up to all humanity (1 Tim. 2:4). The Pastor's and Paul's use of this narrative as a universal moral etiology was not necessarily a commonplace in the first century.

Indeed, the paradise narrative, as a story of universal origins, may be even more prominent in the Pastor's thinking than is indicated in 1 Timothy 2:13 alone. Bassler notices other aspects of 1 Timothy that implicitly react to the paradise narrative, whether in affirmation or in rejection.[54] For example, the Genesis curse on childbirth is reversed in 1 Timothy 2:15. In the Pastor's day, the idea of the tree of knowledge evidently inspired gnostic teachings, which may have prompted him to show that knowledge was the province of the church (4:3; 2 Tim. 2:25; 3:7; Titus 1:1). The cherubim who protect the garden against Adam's reentry and the attainment of eternal life may have been the inspiration for the Pastor's twice-repeated injunction to "guard what has been entrusted to you"—the παραθήκη ("deposit") of true knowledge that leads to eternal life (1 Tim. 6:20; 2 Tim. 1:14).

52. On the connection with Sirach, see Barr, "Authority of Scripture," 70–71; and Barr, *Garden of Eden*, 50–51.
53. For this idea and for much useful background material, see Bassler, "Adam, Eve, and the Pastor."
54. Ibid., 58–59.

Conclusions

From the first century BCE, Jewish writers had begun taking an interest in and citing the Genesis creation narratives enshrined in the LXX, mentioning the six days of creation and looking to Adam and Eve for insights into the origins of human life and genealogy. This portraiture of Adam was varied and scarcely detailed. Philo had a great deal more to say, however unsystematically. Paul, without reference to Philo but probably drawing on similar sources, does not describe Adam to any great degree, for Adam's characteristics outside the transgression are irrelevant to him, as are the characteristics of paradise generally. What matters to Paul is that Adam (through the influence of Eve) sins and comes to stand for the one through whom sin—and therefore death—came into the world. It was his transgression—not Cain's or Aaron's—that had a profound effect on subsequent generations. To see Adam as the original sinner was to establish him as the foil for Christ, the deliverer from sin and death. Christ could then be seen as the new Adam. We know this story well but must recognize Paul's genius in conceiving it. We also must know where to stop attributing theology to Paul: he did not say, for example, that all mortals sin "in Adam" or are born guilty of Adam's sin. Nor, in fact, did he say anything about "pre-fallen" Adam or his immortality or perfection, for Adam was but "the man of dust." Christ alone, for Paul, is the icon of God (Col. 1:15).

There is no great link between Paul's use of Genesis 1–3 and that of the Gospels. The exception (other than the texts about marriage) is Luke, who sees Adam as the first human, the one to whom the genealogy of Christ leads back—establishing Christ as being of the lineage of David and of the patriarchs and of everyone who existed. At the close of the first century, the early Christian writers could look to the book of Genesis and find authoritative narratives of the origins of the world, of humanity, and of sin. But even more than this, they could look to these narratives with unveiled eyes to see the person of Jesus Christ, through whom the world was made and in whose image and for whom Adam was made.

3

Recapitulation

The Second-Century Apologists

The second century produced a series of remarkable authors who, though just one or two generations away from the apostles, developed substantial theological principles that would endure for centuries. These authors were steeped in the Jewish Scriptures and were beginning also to see the Pauline and other NT writings as authoritative witnesses. To different extents, they took up Paul's pioneering approach to questions raised by Genesis 1–3 about the origins of the world and the human person and the nature and result of human transgression. Several of the key figures are treated here in roughly chronological order: Ignatius of Antioch, Justin Martyr, Melito of Sardis, Theophilus of Antioch, and Irenaeus of Lyons.[1] By way of introduction, let us first examine the context within which the second-century writers took up the Pauline and apostolic project.

The Scriptures of the People

As we have been seeing, already during the late first century the "Scriptures" (γραφάι) were beginning to be recast as universal texts thanks mainly to Paul. The Christian appropriation of Jewish Scripture soon went further. The

---

1. Some relevant material appears in other Christian writers, notably Tatian and Clement, but only the briefest mention of their contributions can be made here.

second-century authors took for granted that the scriptural message and its promise of salvation were universal, but they made it all the clearer that this universality lay within—and depended entirely on—the specifically Christian reading of the Scriptures. This perspective made the Scriptures into Christian texts, which meant in turn that Jews did not understand them in the right way. As Paul had already said, the Jews read (their own!) Scriptures with a veil over their eyes, and that veil was lifted only when the Scriptures were read in the light of Christ (2 Cor. 3:14).

This transformation took place through the creative thought of the earliest Christian writers. But second-century Christians were appropriating and universalizing the Jewish Scriptures in a material and practical sense as well. They were copying them from the sacred scrolls into papyrus codices—the equivalent of modern-day notebooks or even paperbacks. This was a bold move, shocking to second-century Jews. "The transference of the Law from its sacrosanct form to a format of no antiquity and little regard . . . must have seemed to the Jew an act of sacrilege."[2] But it put the Scriptures into the hands of anyone who could read.[3]

It would be difficult to overestimate the effect of this physical change in the transmission of the Scriptures. They were transforming from sacred texts (used in liturgical settings or debated among rabbis alone) into reference booklets, albeit of a particular kind. Even as reading them continued to be an oral exercise—they were usually read aloud rather than silently and privately—this could be done in more settings by more people. Read now together with the Christian writings that were also circulating in codex format, the Scriptures were truly becoming the property of Christians in a way that Jews naturally found alarming. Over time, even the LXX, though a pre-Christian, Jewish document, became largely disowned by Jews, identified as it was with this overall Christian appropriation of their Scripture.

Christian adaptation was therefore twofold. It concerned both production/dissemination and a thoroughly altered understanding of the meaning and place of the Scriptures. The law, already transformed in Pauline understanding, was now a code that, although not completely superseded, was transfigured in the light of the new covenant.[4] Its relevance by no means disappeared, but it was significantly altered. With the rest of Scripture, it was no longer a matter of study "according to the letter" but "according to the spirit." Scripture could now be read, discussed, and summarized in briefer segments and in florilegia; from the third and fourth centuries it could also be "read" visually on the walls of churches.[5] All of this took place—most explicitly by

2. Roberts, "Books in the Greco-Roman World," 61, cited in Young, *Biblical Exegesis*, 13.
3. For more on the significance of this shift, with reference to other modern authors, see Young, *Biblical Exegesis*, 9–16.
4. In Justin and Melito, however, we do find a clear sense of supersession; see below.
5. Young, *Biblical Exegesis*, 17.

Irenaeus—from the perspective of a "rule of faith," or "canon of truth," which spelled out Scripture's underlying sense and thus served as the lens through which it was read.

As early as Ignatius of Antioch (died ca. 108) we find the Scriptures being taught as books that took second place to the new criterion and reference point: Christ's passion and resurrection.

> Certain people declared in my hearing, "Unless I can find a thing in our ancient [scriptural] records [ἀρχεία], I refuse to believe it in the Gospel"; and when I assured them that it is indeed in the ancient scriptures [γέγραπται], they retorted, "That has got to be proved." But for my part, my records are Jesus Christ; for me the sacrosanct records are His cross and death and resurrection, and the faith that comes through Him. And it is by these, and by the help of your prayers, that I am hoping to be justified. (*To the Philadelphians* 8)[6]

It is not that the Scriptures are being relativized. Ignatius tells his (Jewish?) inquirers that the Christian teaching *is* in the Scriptures, properly understood. The cross, death, and resurrection as preached in the apostolic kerygma become the lens through which Scripture should be read and therefore themselves become the "sacrosanct records."[7]

The Jewish reading of the law, insofar as it was translated into the particularities of temple worship, circumcision, the Sabbath, and dietary laws, was early on subject to degrees of derision by Christian writers, as in the *Epistle to Diognetus* and, at greater length, in Justin Martyr's *Dialogue with Trypho*.

Justin Martyr

Justin is known chiefly for two documents whose vastly different audiences give them concomitantly different emphases and characters, based on different appeals to (OT) Scripture.[8]

Christ in the Scriptures

The *First Apology* and the *Second Apology*—more likely an apology and an appendix—were written for a Greek audience; in them he adapts Greek

---

6. Cited in Young, *Biblical Exegesis*, 16; and Louth, *Discerning the Mystery*, 102.

7. Ignatius refers to the paradise narrative twice, both times in the longer versions of *To the Trallians* (§10) and *To the Smyrnaeans* (§7)—meaning that these passages may be later additions. In each instance he refers to paradise as the primordial context of the entry of heresy and sin into the world at the hands of the devil, personified by the serpent. These references thus offer nothing that progresses from or differs from Paul.

8. For a summary of the manuscript issues in these texts (and others attributed to Justin), see Skarsaune, *Proof from Prophecy*, esp. 17–23.

Logos concepts to Christ.[9] This was neither a simple process of reception nor a straightforward personalization of a Stoic or Platonic Logos, as sometimes presented.[10] It entailed a way of discerning what it meant to call Jesus Christ the Logos or Word of God. The sense of the *Apologies* (and the *Dialogue with Trypho*) is that Jesus Christ, as Logos, reveals or expresses God. He does this by inspiring the words of Scripture, by being himself present in the theophanies recorded therein, and ultimately by becoming human.

In the *Apologies* the appeal to Scripture is based not on scriptural authority—which would have been irrelevant to his pagan audience—but on an oracular exegesis, that is, an argument from prophecy. The identity and the definitive events of Christ's life, Justin shows, were all foretold; they were fulfilled prophecies, thus they were neither novelties nor happenstance. They were events of profound and even ultimate significance:

> We will now offer proof, not trusting in mere assertions, but being emphatically persuaded by those who prophesied [these things] before they happened, for with our own eyes we see things that have happened and are happening just as they were predicted; and this will, we think, appear to you the strongest and surest evidence. (*Apol.* 1.30)[11]

The Jewish audience of the *Dialogue*, on the other hand, acknowledges the authority of Scripture but—says Justin—misreads it. He intends, therefore, to supply the correct referent to the scriptural words, events, and prophecies, namely, Jesus Christ.

> I have taken great care to prove at length that Christ is the Lord and God the Son, that in times gone by He appeared by His power as man and angel, and in the glory of fire as in the bush, and that He was present to execute the judgment against Sodom. (*Dial.* 128)

The same Christ who appears "by his power" in the OT theophanies is the one who comes "in the flesh" from the Virgin. This continuity of identity means, for Justin, that the only reading of the OT that really matters is that which leads to Christ. He takes his cue from Paul and the Hebrews author but also from Christ's words in the Gospels, perhaps especially his teaching as recorded at the end of Luke's Gospel:

9. Regarding the Scriptures, Justin frequently refers to the composition of the LXX. Occasionally his references to Scripture are from other recensions, perhaps from florilegia. For a thorough discussion of his scriptural sources, see Skarsaune, *Proof from Prophecy*, 17–92, 228–42. For a review of the question of whether one of the apologies is, rather, an appendix, see, Justin Martyr, *First and Second Apologies* (Barnard).

10. Edwards, "On the Platonic Schooling of Justin Martyr," and Edwards, "Justin's Logos and the Word of God," are instrumental in redressing such oversimplifications.

11. See also 1.53.

> When he had risen from the dead and appeared to [his friends], and had taught them to read the prophecies, in which all these things were predicted as coming to pass, and when they had seen him ascending into heaven, and had believed, and received power which he had sent from there, and when to every race of men and women, they taught these things and were called Apostles. (*Apol.* 1.50)[12]

The apostolic witness, then, declares that the texts are understood rightly when considered in light of Christ. This fact is not part of a secret gnosis imparted to a select few; it is the testimony of the apostles, there for anyone to understand and apply to their reading of Scripture. That reading will be thoroughly transformed, to the point where the original intention of the words is of no importance: when Trypho challenges Justin that Isaiah 8 refers to Hezekiah and not to Christ, Justin retorts that, although no one can prove that these events happened as written, "we Christians can show that it *did* happen to our Christ" (*Dial.* 77, emphasis added).[13] If Justin's reading of Scripture can well be classified as supersessionist,[14] he is not motivated by anti-Semitism; his Christian conviction simply permeates his entire understanding of the cosmos and its history.

Particularly in the *Dialogue*, Justin unfolds the OT as a series of events that not only predicts the life, passion, and resurrection of Christ but also foreshadows them as types. The one who fails to discern these types will misunderstand Scripture.

> The Holy Spirit sometimes caused something that was to be a type of the future to be done openly, and on other occasions He spoke of things of the future as though they were actually taking place, or had already taken place. Unless readers perceive this art, they will not be able to grasp the full meaning of the Prophet's words. (*Dial.* 114)

The types for Christ, the cross, the passion, the church, and the Eucharist that Justin discerns range across persons and events. He uses several terms to describe this character of OT Scripture: "mystery," "announcement," "signs," "parable," and "symbol," as well as "type." Willis Shotwell analyzes Justin's usage of each of these terms and provides a helpful antidote to a simplistic understanding of what we call typology.[15] Even if Shotwell concludes that, for Justin, these words are virtually synonymous, Justin's invocation of mystery, sign, parable, and symbol serves to expand an undifferentiated concept of type and antitype. We thus come to see clearly that in Justin typology is more than an exercise in hermeneutical manipulation; it entails an entire worldview or, more accurately, a thorough sense of divine providence.

12. See also *Dial.* 76.
13. *Dial.* 33–34 likewise shows that the "priest forever according to the order of Melchizedek" (Ps. 110) is not Hezekiah but Christ.
14. Rajak, "Talking at Trypho." See also Rokéah, *Justin Martyr and the Jews*.
15. Shotwell, *Biblical Exegesis of Justin Martyr*, 13–23.

Typology and Providence

Justin's idea of Scripture as prophetic prediction and as words and events that speak of and typify Christ is more than "a reflection of the deep connections between the Christian Gospel and the ancient past."[16] It emanates from a view of God's thoroughgoing foreknowledge and providential care for the world, wherein God's Spirit enters time and orders events that culminate in the coming of Jesus Christ. This presupposition engenders Justin's celebrated doctrine of the *spermatikos logos*, the Word of God sown as a seed. A vital passage of the *First Apology* deserves citing here at length, with some interpolated comments:

> For Moses is more ancient than all the Greek writers. And everything that both philosophers and poets have said concerning the immortality of the soul, or punishments after death, or contemplation of heavenly things, or doctrines like these, they have received such hints from the prophets as have enabled them to understand and expound these things. And hence there seem to be seeds of truth among all people; but they are proved not to have understood them accurately when they contradict each other. (*Apol.* 1.44)

Justin's *spermatikos logos* concept is popularly associated today with the inclusiveness of Christian theology, the idea that non-Christians alike may be attuned to the truth, even if not under the name of Christ. Several scholars limit the scope of Justin's "sown Word" to the Scriptures themselves,[17] and one can see why: Justin does say above that the sown Word is to be found *in the Scriptures*. This—together with "the argument from antiquity" (i.e., older is truer)—explains why he asserts that Moses predates the Greeks and that when the Greeks say something true it is because they picked it up from Scripture.[18] Yet even here Justin retains a parascriptural universality, particularly in his emphasis on the seeds of truth found among *all* (παρὰ πᾶσι). The "all" is not limited to the Greek writers but includes "all people," as properly translated by Barnard.[19] In the *Second Apology* the *spermatikos logos* is still more explicitly universal; hence Justin's famous statement "Whatever things were rightly said among all people [παρὰ πᾶσι] are the property of us Christians" (*Apol.* 2.13).[20] He is not referring to Scripture here but to the seeds (σπορᾶς) of the Logos

16. Torrance, *Divine Meaning*, 101.

17. See esp. Edwards, "Justin's Logos," e.g., 275.

18. Cf. also *Apol.* 1.59–60, where he considers Plato to have derived his doctrine of creation in the *Timaeus* from Moses. Justin and the other second-century apologists are examples of a wider dispute between Christians and pagans of their era as to who came first, Homer or Moses. See Droge, *Homer or Moses?*

19. Justin Martyr, *First and Second Apologies* (Barnard, 54).

20. Barnard points to a nearly identical phraseology in Seneca, who claimed that anything that is said well or true was "his own" (Justin Martyr, *First and Second Apologies* [Barnard, 200n73]).

implanted in the pagan writers. The providential care of God implanted the seeds of the Logos, however, in a particular way in Scripture:

> So that what we say about things yet to happen being predicted, we do not say as if they took place by inevitable destiny; but God foreknows all that will be done by all people, since it is one of our tenets that each person will receive from Him according to his deeds. He foretells by the prophetic Spirit that God's rewards will occur according to the merit of the deeds, always urging the human race to thought and recollection, showing that He cares for it and provides for men and women. (*Apol.* 1.44)

The sowing constitutes the inspiration of Moses's authorship of the scriptural words as well as the providential ordering of events. But neither inspiration nor events are ordained only for moral guidance: they exegete the one who would be incarnate and live among other humans.

> We have been taught that Christ is the First-born of God, . . . the logos of whom every race of men and women were partakers. And they who lived with the logos are Christians. . . . So that even they who lived before Christ, and lived without logos [i.e., without reason], were wicked and hostile to Christ, and slew those who lived with the logos [i.e., with Christ].[21] But for that reason He, through the power of the logos and according to the will of God the Father and Lord of all, was born of a virgin as a man, and was named Jesus, and was crucified, and died, and rose again, and ascended into heaven, an intelligent person will be able to comprehend from what has been already so largely said. (*Apol.* 1.46)

Justin's fundamental conviction of God's deliberate, all-knowing, and providential involvement in human events lies at the root of his insistence on seeing Christ as the key to reading the OT, and the OT as a key to reading Christ.

Justin's use of Scripture represents a marked development in the scriptural exegesis initially set out by Paul and the author of the Letter to the Hebrews. He has taken this material, together with the apostolic witness in the Gospels, and developed the most elaborate typological portraiture yet of the OT. He may have had help—Skarsaune has shown that the scriptural texts from which Justin was working came preloaded with christological exegeses[22]—but the synthesis is his own, as is the manner in which he grounds it in his understanding of God and creation.

Justin on Genesis

Both the Hexaemeron and the paradise narrative (especially in the person of Adam and in the serpent) figure significantly in Justin's writing. In the

---

21. Justin distinguishes between "logos" and "the logos," but they are not unrelated. See *Apol.* 1.5.
22. Skarsaune, *Proof from Prophecy*, 25–92.

Apologies, Genesis 1 indicates that God created all things of his goodness (rather than out of necessity), for the sake of human beings and "out of unformed matter" (ἐξ ἀμόρφου ὕλης, *Apol*. 1.10), and is of a piece with Justin's sense of providence. Although his suggested doctrine of *creatio ex nihilo*, "out of unformed matter," resembles a Platonic formulation of creation out of perhaps preexisting, though unformed, matter,[23] Justin derives his theory from Genesis 1 and not the *Timaeus*, which he evidently knew well.

Justin elaborates his sense of Plato's dependence on the Scriptures—specifically the *Timaeus*'s on Genesis 1—again in *Apol*. 1.59–60, which culminates in a demonstration of how Plato misread the Pentateuch (e.g., he saw the letter *chi* instead of the cross in Moses's snake raised on a pole), although he concedes that the Greek philosopher still came remarkably close to a right doctrine of God, Logos, and Spirit.

In the *Apologies* Justin refers to the paradise narrative only once, in a curious way. He writes that Moses's words "Behold before your face are good and evil, choose the good" were addressed to "the first-formed one" (τῷ πρώτῳ πλασθέντι, *Apol*. 1.44). One would have thought Moses was speaking to the Israelites. Either Justin unwittingly confuses Deuteronomy 30 with Genesis 2:16–17 or he is portraying Moses as addressing Adam as representative for universal humanity.[24]

He refers to Genesis 1:26–27 in the *Dialogue* just once, to note that the verses use the plural form for God. Here and in Genesis 3:22, God refers to himself as "us," a point that Justin also takes up in *Dial*. 62 and 129. Genesis 3:22 gives Justin evidence that "Scripture declares that the Son was begotten of the Father before all creatures, and . . . numerically distinct from the Father" (*Dial*. 129).[25] Otherwise he refers several times to the paradise narrative, and not the Hexaemeron, in the *Dialogue*.

Justin is interested in Genesis 2–3 mainly with regard to the person of Adam as the first-formed man and thus the universal human being (*Dial*. 100), and also as first sinner, the one who—by Eve's mediation—was deceived by the serpent (the devil) (*Dial*. 88, 103). Although Adam may be the protosinner, Justin makes plain that subsequent sin is a matter entirely of human free choice, not of destiny or the influence of some bacillus of original sin:

> Human beings, . . . were created like God, free from pain and death, provided they obeyed his precepts and were deemed worthy to be called his sons, and

23. Cf. *Apol*. 1.59, 67. Justin's contemporaries, including Theophilus of Antioch, were clearer in declaring creation out of nothing.

24. Barnard suggests the latter, as a residue of Middle Platonist thinking (Justin Martyr, *First and Second Apologies* [Barnard, 156]).

25. Contrast with Philo's explanation in *Opif*. 75. Once a clearer trinitarian doctrine was elaborated, it became standard for the fathers to interpret the first person plural of these passages as evidence of the Trinity.

yet, like Adam and Eve, brought death upon themselves. . . . They were considered worthy to become gods, and to have the capability of becoming Sons of the Most High, yet each is to be judged and convicted, as were Adam and Eve. (*Dial.* 124)

He uses the provenance of Eve from Adam as an *explanation* of how Christ comes to be born of a Virgin, "just as Eve was made from one of Adam's ribs, and as all living beings were created by the Logos of God in the beginning" (*Dial.* 84). Although Justin nowhere speaks of Adam as a type for Christ, he does make a typological association that would later become a liturgical commonplace in the church: that the tree of life in the garden is a σύμβολον for the cross (*Dial.* 86).

Justin, after all, saw the cross everywhere. He saw it not only in Scripture—in the tree of life, in the roasted Passover lamb (*Dial.* 40), in the serpent raised on a pole by Moses (*Dial.* 90, 94, 112), in the hovering of the Spirit over the waters (*Apol.* 1.60)—but also in the construction of the human body (arms outstretched), the human face (intersection of the nose and the eyes), a sailing ship, the farmer's plow, the mechanic's tools (*Apol.* 1.55), even the rhinoceros's horn.[26] Justin's references to Genesis 1–3, and especially to Adam, must be seen—like all of his OT references—in the context of Christ. For him, Adam's status derives from being the one from whom all humans descend and from being a "sinner," deceived by the devil and therefore saved by Christ, like everyone else who sins of his or her free will.

Much of Justin's methodology was accepted and elaborated by others, notably Clement of Alexandria, who would develop the theretofore implicit connection between the rule of faith and the Logos of God.[27] Justin's vast expansion of the typology of Paul and the author of Hebrews represents an approach that would become virtually universal in the patristic and liturgical formulations of the church.

Melito of Sardis

Like Justin, Melito, the second-century bishop of Sardis, best known for the remarkable poetic text *On Pascha*, opened the OT and saw Christ.[28] Melito wrote

26. According to Justin, the cross provides the *only possible* understanding of rhinoceros anatomy: "Now, no one can assert or prove that the horns of a rhinoceros represent any other matter or figure than that of a cross" (*Dial.* 91).

27. See Dawson, *Allegorical Readers*, 183–234.

28. Melito's authorship is reasonably assured in Melito, *On Pascha and Fragments* (Hall, xvii–xxii); and Stewart-Sykes, *Lamb's High Feast*, 6–8. Cohick, *The Peri pascha*, casts both authorship and text into more serious doubt; it is a pity that her text and the magisterial volume of Stewart-Sykes were produced within the same two-year period without reference to one another.

his text in the 160s,[29] not long after Justin, in the thick of the quartodeciman controversy over the correct date to celebrate the Lord's resurrection. Written in 105 stanzas, On Pascha betrays its author's high rhetorical training; the entire treatise follows a classical expository form even as it replicates Jewish exegetical patterns.[30]

As its title indicates, the work is founded on the concept that Christ's passion, or pascha, is the fulfillment of the Jewish Passover (or Pesach, Pascha). Melito puts into Christ's mouth the words "I am the Pascha of salvation / I am the lamb slain for you" (PP 103).[31] He then plays on the question of the meaning of the Passover service in Exodus 12:26:

> What is the Pascha?
> It gets its name from its characteristic:
> from *suffer* comes *suffering* [ἀπὸ τοῦ παθεῖν τὸ πάσχειν]
> Learn therefore who is the suffering one,
> and who shares the suffering of the suffering one
> and why the Lord is present on the earth
> to clothe himself with the suffering one
> and carry him off to the heights of heaven. (PP 46)

The Christian adaptation of the Jewish Pesach in the paschal liturgy was already an accepted reality in Melito's day; indeed he intended On Pascha as a liturgical homily or the text of a liturgical service.[32] An early example of a tradition of the Christian adaptation of Jewish (and pagan) rites and worship spaces, On Pascha adapts not only liturgical texts and rites but Jewish literary and exegetical forms, especially from the targum, midrash, and haggadah traditions.[33]

Melito's text is characterized throughout by the naming of types from the OT and their fulfillment in the NT. Stanzas 57–64 are emblematic of the whole: "The mystery of the Lord is new and old," for it is seen through *types*.[34] Just about any person or lamb who suffers in the OT prefigures Christ; he cites Deuteronomy, the Psalms, Jeremiah, and Isaiah. In short, "if you wish to see the mystery of the Lord," Melito writes, it is to these persons, events, and words that you should look.

His approach is not far from Justin's. But whereas Justin grounded his typology in the apostolic preaching of Christ and in his sense of divine providence,

---

29. Melito, *On Pascha and Fragments* (Hall, xii).

30. Stewart-Sykes (Melito, *On Pascha*, 14–17) lists the classical devices Melito employed. For further treatment, see Stewart-Sykes, *Lamb's High Feast*, 77–83. See also Bonner, *Homily On the Passion*, 20–27.

31. Translations are here taken from Melito, *On Pascha and Fragments* (Hall).

32. Melito, *On Pascha* (Stewart-Sykes, 20–23).

33. See Melito, *On Pascha* (Stewart-Sykes, 55–113).

34. In Hall (Melito, *On Pascha and Fragments*), τύπος is consistently translated as "model."

Melito's can be traced to other sources. Given his training in rhetoric, his interest in types lies in their potency as expository devices. Like Justin and the Johannine tradition, he works from an elementary supposition that Christ and Christian life supersede Judaism.[35] He berates Israel for misinterpreting the events and words of the OT and torturing and killing the Savior. Finally, he combines the text's liturgical character with an emphatically eschatological perspective, one naturally conducive to the ways typology confounds chronological time. As Thomas Torrance points out, after the NT the typological perspective grew quickly primarily through the liturgical rites of baptism and the Eucharist, which were seen to replace circumcision and Passover and "naturally became the focal points where the OT patterns and motifs were reinterpreted to bring them into line with the Christian rites."[36]

Typos *and* alētheia: *The Function of Typology*

At the same time, Melito gives systematic thought to the ontological implications of typology. In stanzas 34–43 he outlines carefully and precisely the logical rationale of type and antitype.[37] He suggests that the words and events of the OT are, in effect, a rough draft, a sketch, for something that would appear later in its realized form, "taller, stronger, beautiful." He echoes Ecclesiastes: "To each belongs its proper season: a proper time for the model [τύπος], a proper time for the material [ὕλη], a proper time for the reality [ἀλήθεια]" (PP 38). A significant recurring theme of this passage is that once the ἀλήθεια shines forth, the τύπος becomes obsolete, or in Melito's extreme terms:

> But when that of which it is the model arises, that which once bore the image of the future thing is itself destroyed as growing useless, having yielded to what is truly real the image of it; and what once was precious becomes worthless when what is truly precious has been revealed. (*PP* 37)

Later he adds:

> The people [ὁ λαός] was a model by way of preliminary sketch, and the law was the writing of a parable; the gospel is the recounting and fulfillment of the law, and the church is the repository of the reality.

> The model then was precious before the reality, and the parable was marvelous before the interpretation; that is, the people was precious before the church arose, and the law was marvelous before the gospel was elucidated.

35. See Melito, *On Pascha* (Stewart-Sykes, 25–27).
36. Torrance, *Divine Meaning*, 104.
37. This passage, pedagogical and philosophical in character, makes it difficult to accept that we are reading a homily or liturgical text, as is commonly supposed. The citations here do not reproduce the verse format followed by Hall and Stewart-Sykes.

But when the church arose and the gospel took precedence, the τύπος was made
void, conceding its power to the ἀλήθεια, and the law was fulfilled, conceding
its power to the gospel. . . .

The τύπος was abolished when the Lord was revealed, and today, things once
precious have become worthless, since the precious things have been revealed.
(PP 40–43)

The upshot for Melito is that the law is superseded by the gospel and that
the (Israelite) people are superseded by the church. We should now investi-
gate whether he draws out the implications in his treatment of the creation
narratives.

Melito on Genesis

Genesis 1–3 is Melito's foundation for the beginning of creation and of the
human person. Like Justin, he establishes the continuity of identity between
the one who created the world and the one who was born of the Virgin, an
identity that comes to the fore in the final verses:

> It is he that made heaven and earth
> and fashioned man in the beginning,
> who is proclaimed through the law and prophets,
> who was enfleshed upon a virgin,
> who was hung upon a tree,
> who was raised from the dead
>   and went up to the heights of heaven,
> who sits at the Father's right hand,
> who has power to save all [πάντα],
> through whom the Father did his works from
>   beginning to eternity. (PP 104)

He therefore understands Christ to be the Alpha and the Omega, the beginning and the end (PP 105; cf. Rev. 1:8; 21:6).

As for the connection with Genesis 1 and 2–3: in stanzas 81–86 Melito,
addressing the Jews, states that it was Christ who formed and named Israel
and that he, the firstborn of God, divided light from darkness, controlled the
deep, spread out the firmament, and lit up the luminaries. Melito also traces
the genealogy to Adam: "It was he [Christ] who chose you and guided you /
from Adam to Noah, from Noah to Abraham, from Abraham to Isaac and
Jacob and the twelve patriarchs" (PP 83).

Melito reads Genesis 1–3 as a harmonious whole: "When God in the beginning made the heaven and the earth and all things in them by his word [λόγος],
he fashioned from the earth man, and gave him a share of his own breath" (PP
47). He mentions that paradise was east of Eden and cites the divine command

concerning the tree. When Melito describes the transgression, he notes that the human person is "naturally receptive of good and evil, as a clod of earth is [receptive] of seed from either side" (PP 48). Adam (here simply called ὁ ἄνθρωπος) is a symbolic figure, then, marking the beginning of the genealogy and humanity; elsewhere Melito says that Christ's hands "formed *you* [the Jews] from the earth" (PP 79, emphasis added). Adam, then, is neither a holy, perfected figure nor pathetic. He is neutral, nonaligned.

But when Adam tasted of the tree, although he lived a long life, "he was dissolved and sank into the earth." His legacy is "not chastity but promiscuity, not imperishability but decay, not honor but dishonor, not freedom but slavery, not royalty but tyranny, not life but death, not salvation but destruction" (PP 59). These pairings identify chastity, imperishability, freedom, royalty, and immortality as characterizing the vocation of the human person. They do not imply that ὁ ἄνθρωπος ever embodied or actualized these attributes. And, much as Genesis 1–11 describes the matter, "the destruction of men upon earth became strange and terrible. . . . They were seized by tyrannical sin" (PP 50). Melito goes on to describe the generalities of human sin and some ghastly (and bizarre) particulars, such as mothers cannibalizing their children and incest (with an enumeration of seemingly every possible permutation of kinship).

The result of this rampant and systemic sin is that death divides body from soul. The body falls back to the earth from which it is taken; the soul is confined in Hades, so that "there was separation of what fitted beautifully"; and the human person "was being divided by death," so that "desolate lay the Father's image" (PP 55–56). This mode of death is what necessitates the coming of Christ and his own death in the flesh. Melito's list of "types" for Christ significantly omits Adam, even though the types do extend back to Adam's son: Abel (who was murdered), Isaac (bound), Joseph (sold), Moses (exposed as a babe), David (persecuted), and the prophets (who suffer) (PP 59).[38] Lovers of typology though they were, in their surviving texts neither Justin nor Melito identified Adam as τύπος τοῦ μέλλοντος (type of the coming one; cf. Rom. 5:14).

Additional relevant material appears in a short fragment found in a tenth-century Georgian manuscript whose attribution to Melito is likely but far from certain.[39] After quoting a mangled version of the postlapse curse on Eve, Adam, and the serpent, this homily says that "the same three [Eve, Adam, and the serpent] made sin." It goes on to link the tree through which sin came and the tree through which salvation came, closing with a series of lines glorifying the latter. But other than in this fragment, which may imply a human and satanic conspiracy in "making" sin, Melito does not suggest that

38. The list is repeated almost verbatim in PP 69.
39. This is *New Fragment III*, on which see Melito, *On Pascha and Fragments* (Hall, xxxix and 95–96).

Adam and Eve cursed humanity, which otherwise would have lived sinlessly. Nor does he follow Justin in emphasizing human free choice. But his work, which is either a homily or a ritual text, should not be expected to tease out all the implications.

As we have seen, the paradise narrative retained an etiological function for Melito. It represented the beginning of an ever-widening cycle of sin as well as the foundation of the patriarchs, kings, and prophets who all are τύποι for "the mystery of the Lord." As types, or models of the reality revealed in the church, they fade from significance in Melito's understanding of Scripture. Adam, however, in his genealogical role, does not.

Theophilus of Antioch

A contemporary of Melito, Theophilus, patriarch of Antioch, is known to have written several treatises, only one of which survives. The *Letter to Autolycus*, in three books of varying character, seeks to convince a pagan acquaintance about the authority of the Christian faith by using arguments that recall Justin's *Apologies* and others that are at considerable variance with them. The text gained immediate authority and was cited by Irenaeus, Tertullian, Novatian, Methodius, and Lactantius.[40]

Theophilus is not nearly so keen as Justin to show the wisdom or the good intuitions of pagan Greek literature. Although widely read in pagan classical literature, he has no taste for it; he despises its idolatry and polytheism. He once cites some of the Greek prophets, especially the Sibyl, at some length and in a positive light, as a tactic to reach out to his pagan audience (*Autol.* 2.36–38). In his view, however, the good bits do not commend the literature; rather, the bad ones corrupt it utterly.

> Even if something true seems to have been proclaimed by them, it is mixed with error. Just as some deadly poison when mixed with honey or wine or anything else makes the whole harmful and useless, so their loquacity is found to be pointless labor and causes harm to those who are persuaded by it. (*Autol.* 2.12)

He devotes a substantial portion of *Autol.* 3 to showing pagan literature's internal errors, contradictions, and immorality (including cannibalism) and concludes that the ideas of the Greek authors, including Plato, are "useless and godless" (*Autol.* 3.2–8; citation from 3.2). Like Justin, he is keen to show that Scripture predated the pagan philosophers, but he derives the primary importance of this point from the "argument from antiquity" rather than from the primacy of the christological reading.

40. See Theophilus, *Ad Autolycum* (Grant, xix).

Theophilus on Genesis

In *Autol.* 2, Theophilus seeks to establish as the true account of origins the biblical creation narrative in distinction from the pagan myths. This chapter begins with an attack on the emptiness of idolatry and mythology, which Theophilus believes go together (*Autol.* 2.2). Theophilus takes particular umbrage at Hesiod's account of the origins of the world. The fact that the ancient poet botches the question of the single divine Creator makes his entire corpus an abject failure, inconsistent with itself, and evil (*Autol.* 2.5–6).[41] More generally, Theophilus reviles the absence of a sense of divine providence in pagan mythology (*Autol.* 2.8). In contrast, he points to the God-inspired and truth-bearing account of origins found in Scripture, which is completely consistent with itself and features prophecies known to have been fulfilled.

In that light, Theophilus begins his discussion and analysis of the biblical account of creation with an explicit affirmation that God created out of nothing: ἐξ οὐκ ὄντων τὰ πάντα ἐποίησεν (*Autol.* 2.10).[42] There was no preexisting matter together with God. Rather, having brought forth his Logos—together with his Spirit, also referred to as his Wisdom and Beginning[43]—God creates everything by this Logos (*Autol.* 2.10). He cites Genesis 1 almost verbatim, with minimal paraphrasing, and only then begins his commentary on how each of the six days of creation makes sense (*Autol.* 2.13). He speaks of the light, that it was made good (i.e., good for the human person), and of the firmament as distinct from the invisible heaven.

Here the commentary suddenly becomes allegorical. Theophilus notes that "through [plants] the resurrection is signified, for a proof of the future resurrection of all [human beings]" (*Autol.* 2.14). As to the waters, the rivers and springs are like the Law and the Prophets flowing through the world, giving it nourishment. Islands—not mentioned in Genesis but implicit in the creation of the seas—are churches. Some islands are barren, and these are the places to which one is led by heresy (*Autol.* 2.14). Theophilus's interpretations continue to become further removed from the literal. The sun, always full and perfect, he says, is a type for God; the moon, which waxes and wanes, is a type for the human person. The three days before the creation of the luminaries are types of the triad (τριάς) that is God, his Logos, and his Sophia (*Autol.* 2.15).[44]

41. One thesis is that Theophilus's choice of passages from Genesis on which to comment is driven by Hesiod's account of origins. See Young, "Greek Apologists," 97–98; and Young, *Biblical Exegesis*, 55–57.

42. See also 1.4, where Theophilus cites 2 Macc. 7:28.

43. Origen will similarly say that the "In the beginning" of Gen. 1:1 refers to Christ, who is himself the Beginning. See chap. 4, below.

44. Given Theophilus's nascent understanding of how the three are related (he immediately adds ἄνθρωπος as a fourth), it would be anachronistic to attribute to him a "trinitarian theology" on the basis of this usage of τριάς.

This passage elicits two observations. Theophilus's argument for the factual/historical—as opposed to mythical—character of the biblical narratives is not compromised by his allegorical and typological interpretation, which is not intended to render the literal one obsolete. The allegorical is merely an added layer of interpretation; he considers it optional, if anything, inferior to the literal. This is also as far as Theophilus goes with typology. He has a very particular goal for his exegesis of Genesis, a goal that does not center on either the prophetic or the typological presence of Christ. Despite his strong sense of divine providence, Theophilus does not find Christ in Genesis as did his contemporaries and the NT authors.

The absence of Adam-Christ typology is an issue we have already observed and to which we will return below. The larger context in Theophilus is the absence of Jesus Christ in *any* element of this text. Indeed, Theophilus's exegesis and argumentation remain fundamentally Jewish; in several places he is remarkably close to Philo and to midrash on Genesis.[45] In the *Letter to Autolycus*, he is not only uninterested in the christological typology of Genesis, he does not even mention Jesus Christ by name despite numerous references to the NT. "Christ" is even excised from the appellation "Christian" by calling on the etymology of Χριστός: "We are called Christians because we are anointed with the oil of God" (*Autol.* 1.12). He speaks of the Logos in order to explain the immanence of God in OT passages and to show by whom the world was created; although he makes an oblique reference to John 1:3, he never explicitly connects this Logos with Jesus Christ. The churches may be island havens from the chaos of heresy, but the Christian faith itself is never presented. Robert M. Grant says that Theophilus, "like other apologists of his time, . . . never openly speaks of [Christ],"[46] but in fact Justin and Melito harbored no such reservations. Whether referring to Jesus Christ by name or obliquely, their writings are full of "the Lord," his birth from the Virgin, his cross, death, and resurrection—quite unlike Theophilus. Grant continues, "Apparently he viewed Jesus as second Adam, for of the first Adam he says that God intended him to progress, grow, and become mature, ascend into heaven, and become God." But the Adam-Christ connection is anything but apparent. Indeed, as Grant himself points out, Theophilus connects salvation with obedience to the divine commandments, so that *whoever* obeys them can be saved and inherit imperishability.[47] The particularity of Christ and his cross escapes all mention. We can only speculate that this reticence concerning Christ and the staples of Christian faith stems either from contextual realities (a perceived pastoral or

45. See Grant, *Greek Apologists*, 157–59, for other primary and secondary literature.

46. Theophilus, *Ad Autolycum* (Grant, xvii).

47. Ibid.; *Autol.* 2.27. Elsewhere Grant shows cognizance of Theophilus's "remarkable silence in regard to Jesus, Christ, the incarnation, and the atonement" (*Greek Apologists*, 165). But he maintains that Theophilus's descriptions of Adam's vocation—what he could have been—are tacit references to Christ (167).

political need to stifle explicit mention of Christ) or from a conversion from Judaism that was not fully realized in Theophilus's thought.[48]

Returning to the text and its treatment of Genesis, Theophilus now speaks in greater detail of the creation of the human person. God creates humanity together with "his own Logos and his own Sophia"—hence the plural of "let us make"—and Theophilus suggests that these are God's own hands (an image that will be taken up more famously by Irenaeus) (*Autol.* 2.18). This discussion leads directly to the paradise account, where Theophilus cites the text of Genesis 2–3 as the sacred history of the human person. Some passages elicit only brief commentary: God's "walking in paradise" does not describe the perambulations of the ubiquitous and uncircumscribable God; it is the Logos "assuming the role of the Father" (*Autol.* 2.22). We are not in an era of trinitarian theological precision, and Theophilus does not explain how the Logos circumvents the uncircumscribability essential to divinity; evidently he believes that the case for the Logos is simply different. God's calling to Adam, "Where are you?" is not a display of divine ignorance but divine patience and the hope of eliciting a confession (*Autol.* 2.26). Eve's provenance from Adam's side happens "so that his love for her would be greater" and so that no one could say that one god created man and another god created woman (*Autol.* 2.27). Other factors in the story, namely, sin and death, are the subject of more thorough investigation.

Regarding the tree of knowledge, Theophilus comments that knowledge in itself is not forbidden for human beings and there is nothing wrong with knowledge used properly and given at the proper time. Adam and Eve partook of it too early, in their infancy as it were. Furthermore, the real transgression lay in their eating it in disobedience to an explicit divine commandment. Theophilus likens the first couple's disobedience to that of children in the face of their parents. But however neutral the faculty of knowledge and however childlike Adam and Eve were, even in their sin, the consequence of their disobedience is profound: "It was not that the tree of knowledge contained anything evil, but that through disobedience [the human person] acquired pain, suffering, and sorrow, and finally fell victim to death" (*Autol.* 2.25). Yet this banishment from the life of paradise is a mercy, a "great benefit," in that it gives the opportunity for repentance and expiation (*Autol.* 2.26). In his understanding of the state of Adam and Eve in paradise and the nature of the tree and the transgression, Theophilus's ideas were seminal and influential; they were taken up and amplified in Irenaeus and later writers.

Regarding the curse/punishment, Theophilus notes that it bears out the truth of the paradise account, as shown by our own experience. Do we not see that women suffer in childbirth, that snakes creep on their bellies? This

---

48. "One cannot be sure that he reflects Christianity rather than Judaism or if, indeed, there was a clear line between the two in his mind" (Grant, *Greek Apologists*, 166).

"demonstrates to us the truth of what has been said" in the scriptural account
(*Autol.* 2.23). The fact that the punishment contained "death" does not mean
that Theophilus saw the human person as created immortal. Rather, he sees
humanity before the transgression as neutral, "neither mortal nor immortal
by nature" (*Autol.* 2.27). If the human person were created immortal, it would
be like creating another god. But to have created humanity mortal would
mean that God is the author of death. So the choice is left with the human
person himself or herself. Eve, the first deceived, is therefore the "pioneer of
sin" (*Autol.* 2.28). The consequence of Adam and Eve's transgression on the
rest of humanity is not spelled out. Earlier in the text, Theophilus did indicate that this human sin affected the animals, which were not created evil or
poisonous: "When [the human person] transgressed they transgressed with
him" (*Autol.* 2.17). Likewise they will return to tameness when humanity is
restored to its natural state.

Myth versus History

In sum, Theophilus's argument rests on interrelated antitheses that he sees
as fundamental and inexorable. On the negative side are myth and novelty,
which are linked with deceit. On the positive side are factual history and
antiquity, which constitute trustworthiness. It is this divide that dictates his
every thrust in the *Letter to Autolycus*. His presuppositions may have been
clear enough in the first two books, but they become still more explicit in
the third. There, his drive to establish the antiquity of the prophets and their
Scripture leads him painstakingly to calculate the chronology of events, based
primarily on the ages and dates mentioned in Scripture (*Autol.* 3.24–28).[49]
He summarizes his findings, giving the time in years between the key events:
from creation to the flood, 2,242 years; from the flood to Abraham, 1,036;
from Isaac to Moses, 660; and so on until the death of Marcus Aurelius
(*Autol.* 3.28). Historical chronology is of utmost importance to Theophilus,
but not for its own sake. He couples historicity with facticity, emphasizing
that the events described in the OT are not "mere myths" like those of the
Greeks. At the end of his chronology, he remarks, "From the compilation
of the periods of time and from all that has been said, the antiquity of the
prophetic writings and the divine nature of our message are obvious." He
follows this point immediately with its conclusion, which summarizes his
entire approach: "This message is not recent in origin, nor are our writings,
as some suppose, mythical and false. They are actually more ancient and
more trustworthy" (*Autol.* 3.29).

For Theophilus, the argument against polytheism (versus monotheism
and Christianity) goes hand in hand with the argument against myth (versus

---

49. For the precise scriptural (and Roman-historical) basis of his calculations at every point,
see Theophilus, *Ad Autolycum* (Grant, xxiii–xxv).

factual accounts). Facticity is part and parcel of the argument against poly-theistic mythology, for he considers that myths are by their very nature false. Although he admits the truth of allegory and a cautious typology, the concept of "true myth" is an oxymoron for him. Ancient, trustworthy, and factual stand in contrast to novel, deceitful, and mythical. The other apologists reviewed here so far would likely have seen the matter the same way if pressed, but their christological-typological reading dominated their argumentation, allowing them to identify and focus on types—which they also called parables, mysteries, symbols, and signs. They thus understood the creation narratives through the lens of Christ and the church. Absent the typological exegesis—in effect, absent *Christ*—Theophilus was left to defend the Genesis creation accounts entirely on the basis of their factual historicity.

The Greek writers make mention neither of creation before the flood nor of the things that had yet to come since they "lived long after [the prophets] and introduced a multitude of gods. For this reason it is plain that all the rest were in error and that only the Christians have held the truth—we who are instructed by the Holy Spirit who spoke in the holy prophets and foretold everything" (*Autol.* 2.33).

From here on, this study will be concerned with far more prolific authors than the ones so far treated and so will be more selective in its focus. Irenaeus, Tertullian, Origen, and the Cappadocians were the authors and the subjects, in turn, of a large body of texts, and the presentation here makes no pretense to comprehensiveness. Our sights are set on a limited spectrum of material from each author, even if general comments are made about the author's use of Scripture.

Irenaeus of Lyons

With Irenaeus and his main extant works—*Against the Heresies* and the *Demonstration of the Apostolic Preaching*—we witness a parabolic leap both in the exegesis of Scripture and in the identification of its canonical books. Since the heresies against which he was arguing had a great deal to do with both a misreading of Scripture and an addled reckoning of which books were to be understood as canonical, Irenaeus's aim is to show how the books of Jewish Scripture and the Christian Gospels and Epistles relate to each other and how they should be properly read and understood. In reading Irenaeus, we watch something like what we know as "the Bible" take shape before our eyes. The Jewish Scriptures (LXX) remain the chief referent for the word "Scriptures" (αἱ γραθαί), but the four Gospels, some of St. Paul's letters, the book of Acts, Revelation, 1 Peter, and 1 and 2 John are, in effect, a scriptural body for him as well.[50] Irenaeus was the first to call these compilations the Old and the New Testaments (*AH* 4.9.1).[51]

Irenaeus's attention to the proliferating theologies originating from an unchecked use of Scripture led him to identify its underlying sense, which would therefore act as its hermeneutical key. The NT's relationship to the OT was crucial, and here Irenaeus builds substantially on the groundwork of his predecessors and contemporaries. He is probably aware of Melito; he cites Theophilus anonymously in several places, sometimes taking up his ideas (such as the trope of the Son and the Spirit being God's "two hands") and sometimes correcting him.[52] He cites Justin twice: in writing that Jesus Christ recapitulates everything in himself (*AH* 4.6.2) and that the prophets spoke of Christ in parables and allegories (*AH* 5.26.2). Both ideas are very much in line with his own hermeneutical sense, though Irenaeus is more emphatic and more systematic than his predecessors about finding Christ in the (OT) Scriptures. Christ—the *crucified* Christ, as Irenaeus is keen to specify—is the one by whom we rightly read the Scriptures, and when we read the Scriptures through him, we understand both them and him correctly. Irenaeus describes a double dissemination: Christ is sown in the Scriptures, and the Scriptures in their turn announce, or "disseminate," the coming of the Son of God (*AH* 4.23.1).

Irenaeus's hermeneutic stems in part from his profound (anti-Marcionite) understanding of the unity of the Bible and of the one God who speaks through both Testaments. In a celebrated passage in *Against Heresies*, he speaks of this unity and of how Christ is present both in the sowing (OT) and the reaping (NT)—a presence that should guide our reading of Scripture:

> If any one therefore reads the Scriptures in this manner, he will find in them the Word concerning Christ, and a prefiguration of the new calling. For Christ is the treasure that was hidden in the field [Matt. 13:44], that is, in this world—for "the field is the world" [Matt. 13:38]. [Christ is] a treasure hidden in the scriptures, since he was signified by means of types and parables that, humanly speaking, could not be understood before the fulfillment of the things that were prophesied—in other words, before the coming of Christ. . . .

> For any prophecy, before it is fulfilled, is nothing but enigmas and ambiguities. But from the moment that the prediction is fulfilled, it finds its proper interpretation.

> And so it is that in our own day when the law is read by the Jews, it is [to them] like a fable [μῦθος], for they do not possess the exegesis of all things in order

---

50. The Gospels, e.g., were already being referred to as "Scripture" in other second-century texts; see *Barn.* 4.14; *2 Clement* 2.4; 14.1.

51. His chief point here is to affirm the unity of OT and NT in the face of the Marcionite tendency utterly to segregate them.

52. See Grant, *Greek Apologists*, 184–86.

to know the human coming of the Son of God. When read, on the other hand, by Christians, [the law] is indeed a treasure hidden in a field, revealed and interpreted by the cross of Christ.

Read in this way, he says, the law

enriches people's understanding and shows the wisdom of God, making known his dispensations with regard to the human person. It prefigures the kingdom of Christ, announcing beforehand the good news of the inheritance of the holy Jerusalem. It predicts that the person who loves God will grow into seeing God and hearing his word, and that he or she will be glorified in the hearing of this word to the point where others will not be able to look upon his or her glorious face. (*AH* 4.26.1; my translation)

As Irenaeus reminds us with an allusion to Luke 24, this is also how Christ after his resurrection instructed his disciples to read the Scriptures. Irenaeus interprets Christ's words during his earthly ministry, "Moses wrote of me" (John 5:46), to mean that Moses's words—and by extension, those of the other prophets—were Christ's own words (*AH* 4.2.3).

This christological reading of the Scriptures—the uncovering of types, parables, and prophecies that foretell, illuminate, and are illumined by the crucified Christ—is part and parcel of what Irenaeus comes to identify with a greater precision than writers before had: the rule of faith (κανών τῆς πίστεως), or rule of truth (κανών τῆς ἀλήθειας), by which one reads Scripture and the whole of creation.

Rule of Faith

The rule of faith or canon of truth as the principle of Scripture that Irenaeus identifies comes within his broader purview of the relationship between faith and truth. The opening to his *Demonstration of the Apostolic Preaching* centers on an exhortation to Marcianus and "to all who are concerned about their salvation" to hold to the faith, to make their way by faith. This introduction culminates in the charge to "keep the rule of faith unswervingly and perform the commandments of God, believing in God and fearing him (for he is Lord), and loving him (for he is Father)." The rule of faith is linked to people's love of God and their acting on God's commandments. But, Irenaeus concludes, faith is not an empty exercise; it is grounded in reality: "Truth brings about faith, for faith is established on things truly real, that we may believe what really is, as it is, and, [believing] what really is, as it is, we may always keep our conviction of it firm" (*Dem.* 3).

Irenaeus in this way gives firm grounding to his canon of faith, and the rest of the *Demonstration* elucidates this faith. It begins with an outline of the three articles of faith—God the Father and Creator; God's Word/Son,

Jesus Christ, by whom all things were made and who becomes incarnate to recapitulate all things; and the Holy Spirit, through whom the prophets spoke and who is poured out now on the human race in a new and renewing way (*Dem.* 6). These are the three articles through which we receive baptism; this is why we see here the kernels of existing and future trinitarian creedal statements.[53] He follows Genesis 1–3 to describe the creation of the angelic realm and the human person (together with the fall, or "apostasy" of humanity); he then races through the rest of Genesis, Deuteronomy, and the Prophets to arrive at the incarnation and death of Christ on the cross as the fulfillment of everything else that has been described.

The trinitarian core of Irenaeus's rule of faith is also reproduced twice in the first book of *Against the Heresies.* The context in both cases is the same, expressed first positively and then negatively. In *AH* 1.10.1 he uses the rule of faith to prove the unity of the church. To wit, although the church is disseminated throughout the world, the faith it receives from the apostles is one and therefore the church is one. In *AH* 1.22.1, essentially the same trinitarian faith definition is given as a means of identifying heresies, of showing who has strayed from the truth of the church and how. Irenaeus's goals—that the genuine truth be proclaimed and the genuine church retain its integrity—were threatened by the varied and unregulated readings of Scripture, primarily by the Valentinians. He illustrates the problem with one of his best-known images: Scripture is like a beautiful mosaic of a King (Christ), whose tesserae some people rearrange to portray something completely different, say a dog or a fox.[54] Worse, they then claim that this distortion is actually the beautiful image of the King. "Such is their system, which neither the prophets preached, nor the Lord taught, nor the apostles handed down" (*AH* 1.8.1).[55]

The apostles play a key role in the circularity of the rule of faith as it emanates out of Scripture and acts as the lens through which Scripture is properly read. If Scripture inexorably produced the rule of faith from itself, it would be impossible to emerge from reading it with the portrait of anything but the King. The *apostolic witness*—what the apostles preached based on how Christ taught them to understand the Scriptures—is what produces the rule, or canon, of faith. Apostolic witness thus functions as a criterion for right interpretation (κανών, or *regula*, refers to the plumb line or straightedge that craftsmen use as a standard). More than an interpretive key, it functions as a hermeneutical key because it first of all summarizes the entire underlying

53. Matt. 28:19; see also Justin, *Apol.* 1.61, although it would be anachronistic to equate the rule of faith with a formalized "creed." See Blowers, "*Regula fidei.*"

54. Later he uses an alternate image, that of people taking Homer's verses and rearranging them into a new order, thus forming an entirely new narrative (*AH* 1.9.4).

55. Irenaeus consistently holds to the ordered trajectory, the *traditio* that follows from the prophets to the Lord's teaching to the apostolic preaching (and to the succession of bishops), such that he considers its desecration by the heretics especially tragic. See *AH* 3.24.1.

sense and coherence principle, or ὑπόθεσις, of Scripture.[56] Holding to the rule of faith, then, naturally enables the Christian to reconstruct the mosaic of the King correctly (AH 1.9.4), even as it also serves to unite him or her to the true church. Irenaeus readily admits, however, that Scripture does not present explicit solutions to all questions or completely penetrate the mysteries (e.g., of theodicy, the angels, the incarnation, or the economy in general). It is our responsibility to take what Scripture presents "in parable" and explicate its meaning by accommodating it to the "hypothesis of truth" (AH 1.3.10).

Despite having concerns—most notably the right reading of Scripture—common to the other second-century apologists, Irenaeus distinguishes himself in several ways. He was not captivated by the argument from antiquity, probably because his opponents had no claim that their literature or its interpretation antedated the Scriptures nor do they attack the Christian position for its alleged novelty. What sets Irenaeus apart is his precision in defining the principle of Scripture. It was not just a matter of reading the words and events depicted in the OT as foreshadowing Christ. Irenaeus's typology and his signature concept of recapitulation may have been the most elaborated of any writer yet (and of most subsequent thinkers as well), but he also saw an explicit and precise trinitarian principle as constituting the inner logic and coherence of the whole of Scripture.

Recapitulation and History: Irenaeus on Genesis

Although he treats the creation narratives as a single whole, Irenaeus's chief focus is on the creation and salvation of the human person. Two emblematic elements of Irenaean thought derive from Genesis 1. His trinitarian consciousness, both nascent and utterly central to his thinking, leads him to make explicit the role of Father, Son, and Holy Spirit in the establishment of the world through the famous image of the Son and Spirit as God's two hands (AH 4.pref.4; 4.20.1; 5.1.3; 5.6.1; 5.28.4). Second, spurred by gnostic ideas about emanation, Irenaeus developed a meticulous teaching of creation ex nihilo. In his schema, Plato scores higher marks than the gnostics for his understanding of God and creation (AH 3.25.5). Justin, as we saw, equivocated in his thinking on creation: he gave no clear sense that he did not envisage a preexisting substrate. Theophilus, in a step forward, understood God as first creating amorphous matter and then giving it form (see Autol. 2.4; 2.13). For Irenaeus, the key was that God does not work from preexisting matter; God creates and shapes matter in a single act in a manner unexplained by Scripture and best left unexplored (AH 2.28.7).[57]

---

56. See Fantino, Théologie d'Irénée, 18–28; Behr, Way to Nicaea, 30–37; Blowers, "Regula fidei," 225–28.

57. On the difference between Justin, Theophilus, and Irenaeus in their doctrines of creatio ex nihilo, see Osborn, Irenaeus of Lyons, 65–73.

Irenaeus uses the Genesis creation narratives primarily to elaborate the concept of ἀνακεφαλαίωσις—"recapitulation," "summing up"—as it refers to the person and work of Christ. Although he was not the first to use the word in a Christian context,[58] recapitulation is the key to Irenaeus's understanding of the divine economy as expressed in Scripture. It is not simply another way of speaking of the typological interpretation of Scripture, even if it involves the same sense of divine providence and recasting of chronological time that we saw already in Justin. It is a complex concept. Eric Osborn sees in it a matrix of no fewer than eleven ideas: "Unification, repetition, redemption, perfection, inauguration and consummation, totality, the triumph of Christus Victor, ontology, epistemology and ethics . . . are combined in different permutations."[59] Osborn makes a unifying sense of the concept in part by noting that "everything that God does is part of his economy and every part of his economy is defined in relation to its recapitulation,"[60] but he maintains that it is impossible to do justice to Irenaeus's ἀνακεφαλαίωσις without covering all of the variables he names. Let us therefore examine his understanding of the relationship between the formation of the human person and the incarnation of Christ.

Recapitulation in Christ influences the precise nature of Irenaeus's Adam-Christ typology. But the larger matter is his view of history itself, outside which his perspective on the Adam-Christ relationship is scarcely new. Irenaeus's understanding of Christ and history resembles his understanding of Scripture: the NT is not simply more Scripture, new material added to the OT, but rather it describes Scripture's fulfillment and underlying sense. The incarnation of Jesus Christ is the fulfillment, the summing up (recapitulation) of the presence of the Word throughout history.

> For we have shown that the Son of God did not begin to exist when he became incarnate, and was made man, [for he was] eternally with the Father; rather [when he became incarnate] he recapitulated in himself the long narration [*expositionem*] of human beings, furnishing us, in résumé [*in compendio*], with salvation, so that what we lost in Adam—to be according to the image and likeness of God—we might recover in Christ Jesus. (*AH* 3.18.1)[61]

Justin, among others, had already identified Christ, the Logos, with the presence of God in the OT theophanies. But Irenaeus, writing at greater length and with more theological precision, emphasizes that we are not working with a linear chronology or a "biography" of the Logos that begins at creation,

58. Fantino, *Théologie d'Irénée*, 240–42. On Irenaean rhetorical use of this term and others, see Grant, *Irenaeus of Lyons*, 46–53.

59. Osborn, *Irenaeus of Lyons*, 97–98.

60. Ibid., 98.

61. These translations of *AH* are reworded from Behr, *Way to Nicaea*.

continues in the theophanies and the incarnation, and ends at the "second coming."[62] Instead, all history is summed up in the incarnation, as is testified by the apostles, a "résumé" that illumines everything coming chronologically before and after.

What does this mean for Irenaeus's understanding of Genesis 1–3, especially his understanding of the person of Adam? Adam is a key figure in Irenaeus's understanding of the human person, and especially the vocation of deification. Therefore a discussion of Adam in Irenaeus necessarily entails a treatment of wide-ranging issues that stem from the human person's creation, knowledge of good and evil, apostasy, and salvation.

Irenaeus's sustained argument in *AH* 4.37–39 provides a concentrated exposition of several recurring themes. The guiding question here is why the human person, though created for glory, was not created automatically good but neutral and free. The preliminary answer is that it is not God's nature to coerce (*AH* 4.37.1), and human beings, though flawed, inherently know what is best. The logic is as follows: if human beings are shown what God is like and are given the option either to follow God and go the way of life or to disobey God and go the way of death, they will naturally choose life. But virtue is pointless and meritless if coerced or achieved by mere programming. If people were created either bad or good by their nature, they would be neither praiseworthy for being good nor worthy of punishment for sinning as they would be simply behaving according to their nature. "Their being good would be of no consequence, because they were so by nature rather than by will" (*AH* 4.37.6).[63]

Irenaeus answers this question more deeply when he discusses the nature of the knowledge of good and evil. As Theophilus had already suggested (*Autol.* 2.25–26), God did not begrudge us this knowledge; the problem was that the first couple partook ahead of their time, while only innocent children.[64] Irenaeus goes further. Not only was this knowledge "not withheld" by God, but it is integral to genuine human personhood. A pragmatic dimension to Irenaeus's argument causes him to ask at several points in *AH* 4.37–38, "How, if he had no knowledge of the contrary, could he have had instruction in that which is good?" It is only when the human person

> knew both the good of obedience and the evil of disobedience that the eye of the mind, receiving experience of both, may with discernment choose the better things . . . and learning by experience that it is an evil thing which deprives him of life, . . . may never attempt it at all, but knowing what preserves his life, he may diligently keep it with all earnestness. (*AH* 4.39.1)

62. See Behr, *Way to Nicaea*, 128.
63. This is a common patristic argument, found also, e.g., in Gregory of Nyssa (*Antirrheticus adversus Apollinarem* 41; *In Cant.* 5).
64. This point is emphasized in *Dem.* 12, 14. See also *AH* 4.38.1.

The human person must act out of freedom and experience; for this to happen, the human person has to encounter evil and so become all the more grateful for what is good. In this way, too, the human being is delivered from pride, from having too high an opinion of him- or herself (see also *Dem.* 15). This argument is clearer in *AH* 5.3.1 and 3.20.2, with allusion to Paul's idea of humanity being consigned to sin (Gal. 3:22), or "in disobedience so that [God] may be merciful to all" (Rom. 11:32). God allows the apostasy because he knows it will foster in the human person both gratitude and humility. Irenaeus develops this theme in *AH* 3.20.1–2, where he indicates it is God's will that, like Jonah, all of humanity be swallowed up by the great whale, namely, the author of evil himself, knowing that God is thus "preparing the plan of salvation which was accomplished by the Word, through the sign of Jonah," that is, his deliverance from the leviathan (*AH* 3.20.1).[65]

Pastoral pragmatism also leads Irenaeus to the conviction that without the knowledge of good and evil, one cannot even be properly human: "If you were to divest yourself of the knowledge of both [good and evil], and the double faculty of perception, you would divest yourself of the character of a human being" (*AH* 4.39.1). In other words, God has very deliberately and benevolently adopted a particular course for human beings. He did not make them gods from the start but first merely humans. Irenaeus cites Psalm 82, "I say, you are gods . . . you shall die like mortals," and sums up the pedagogical nature—indeed, the necessity—of the apostasy thus:

> For it was necessary that, at first, this [created, weaker] nature should be manifest; and after this, that what was mortal should be conquered and swallowed up by immortality, and the corruptible by incorruptibility, and *that the human person should be made after the image and likeness of God, having received the knowledge of good and evil.* (*AH* 4.38.4, emphasis added)

Irenaeus—the first Christian writer to comment extensively on the divine image and likeness—sees our being made in God's image and likeness as a primordial gift as well as a calling to be realized. In one passage, he anticipates a later patristic trend by distinguishing between the image (as inalienable gift) and the likeness (as lost in the apostasy and restored in Christ). The likeness (ὁμοίωσις) is lost with Adam's transgression, and salvation in Christ is a συνεξομοίωσις ("assimilation") to the Father through the Word (*AH* 5.16.2). Humanity cannot attain to this divine likeness without the knowledge of good and evil; the reference is to Genesis 3:22, where God says, "See, the man has become like one of us, knowing good and evil." In God's deliberate plan, the only way to salvation, to deification, even to being conformed to his likeness, is by first being created, weak, corruptible, and knowing good and evil. Only

65. On the sign of Jonah, see below, p. 81.

thus will human persons be raised in Christ ("who came to us, . . . recapitulating everything . . . in a manner that we could behold him," *AH* 4.38.1), by having participated in their own deification through repentance and humility. The apostasy remains a tragedy brought on by human complicity with the provocation of the devil. But the knowledge given to humanity through this apostasy forms part of the realization of human personhood and of the divinely ordained process of salvation:

> God has displayed long-suffering in the case of human apostasy; while the human person has been instructed by means of it, as the prophet says, "Your own apostasy will instruct you" [Jer. 2:19 LXX]. God thus determined all things beforehand for the bringing of human beings to perfection, for their edification, and for the revelation of His dispensations, so that goodness may be made apparent, and righteousness perfected, and that the Church may be "conformed to the image of His Son" [Rom. 8:29], and that the human person may finally be brought to such maturity so as to see and comprehend [or "seize"—χωρεῖν] God. (*AH* 4.37.7)[66]

Irenaeus's understanding of the apostasy sheds light on (and is illumined by) his understanding of recapitulation in Christ, which in turn is the framework for his understanding of Genesis 1–3, for Christ is at the heart of the entire "Irenaean theodicy." As seen earlier, the "sign of Jonah" refers simultaneously to two realities: it is humanity/Adam, swallowed up by, and delivered from, the apostasy, and it is Christ (cf. Matt. 12:39–40), who is in the heart of the earth for three days, to be delivered from it. The primordial apostasy and its healing in Christ may seem to act as bookends to the divine economy, but to express it in this way would be utterly unfaithful to Irenaeus's concept of time and history, which is anything but chronological. For him, Adam is not the real beginning nor is Christ the end. Rather, the passion and resurrection of Christ are the recapitulating center and underlying sense of the trajectory of human personhood.

Beginning with Christ's becoming human as the recapitulation of Adam's own formation, Irenaeus sees typological or recapitulative significance in every detail: Adam born of virginal earth through the agency of the Word and the Spirit; Christ born of the virginal Mary (herself descended from Adam) through the action of the Word and by the agency of the Spirit (*AH* 3.21.10; 3.22.1–2; *Dem.* 32). Christ also recapitulates every stage of human life: infant, child, adult. To this end, Irenaeus takes exegetical pains to extend Christ's life to an older age, putting Jesus in his forties at his death (*AH* 2.22.4–6). He

---

66. Behr aptly notes that, despite appearances to the contrary, Irenaeus is not seeking to "privatize the relationship to God of each human person . . . emphasizing the need for each to gain personal experience" (*Asceticism and Anthropology*, 46). Hence his emphasis above that *the church*, as community, is conformed to the image.

also transfigures chronology when he exegetes the Lukan genealogy, stretching as it does to Adam. Irenaeus considers Luke 3:23–38 to exist expressly to show that Christ joined the end to the beginning, recapitulating all nations, languages, and generations in himself. Citing Romans 5:14, where Paul names Adam as "a type of the one who was to come," Irenaeus explains that "the Word, the maker of all things, had formed beforehand for Himself the future dispensation of the human race, connected with the Son of God." He further asserts that since God exists eternally as the Savior (προϋπάρχοντος γάρ τοῦ σῴζοντος), "it was necessary that one who would be saved [Adam] should also come into existence [ἔδει καὶ τὸ σῳζόμενον γενέσθαι], in order that the One who saves should not exist in vain" (AH 3.22.3). In other words, Adam exists because God saves, or insofar as Christ represents God's saving economy, Adam exists because of Christ's saving passion.

This is why, as Irenaeus goes on, there is also "interchange [ἀνακύκλησιν] between Mary and Eve," another example of chronological time being inverted in Christ:

> This is why the Lord said that the first should indeed be last, and the last first [Matt. 19:30]. And the prophet, too, says the same, saying, "Instead of your fathers shall be your sons" [Ps. 45:17]. For the Lord, having been born "the first-born of the dead" [Rev. 1:5] and receiving into his bosom the ancient fathers, has regenerated them into the life of God, having been made the beginning of the living, as Adam became the beginning of those who die. This is also why Luke, commencing the genealogy with the Lord, carried it back to Adam, indicating that it was He who regenerated them into the Gospel of life, and not they Him. (AH 3.22.4)[67]

In the divine scheme of things, Christ comes first, then Adam. This is not to be mistaken for another assertion that the "preexisting Logos" was the agent of the creation of the cosmos, including Adam. In effect, *the crucified and risen Lord* comes first, and Adam is made with reference to him. The nature of the recapitulation, which puts Christ at the center of the human trajectory from creation to salvation, is therefore such that Irenaeus can speak of Adam as being made in the image of the incarnate Christ (AH 4.33.4).

Irenaeus's understanding of the human person in the divine image runs contrary to a patristic tendency to locate the divine image with the immaterial soul or intellect (νοῦς); he understands the image of God to be reflected in the human body.[68] There is no disembodied human person and therefore no disembodied image of God. This is more than a holistic anthropology,

---

67. Elsewhere Irenaeus makes the more obvious link between Christ's obedience and Adam's disobedience; cf. AH 4.30.3.

68. This comes out especially clearly in Fantino, *L'homme image de Dieu*, 87–89, 103–6. But see, e.g., *Dem.* 11, which shows how God sketches his own form on his material handiwork.

for Irenaeus, in fact, takes little interest in the soul as such. Irenaeus understands that an image presupposes both *form* and *material substrate*.[69] Yet he well recognizes that an image has to resemble what it images. The problem then becomes, How can the corporeal human being be in the image of the incorporeal God? The answer: God also must become corporeal—hence the incarnation. It is only in the incarnation, the coming of the Son in the flesh, that we may properly say that the human person is made in the image of God. In a manner of speaking, the incarnation actualizes the image. "For this reason He appeared in the last times: *to render the image like himself*" (*Dem.* 22, emphasis added). The creation of the human person and the image-bearing character of the human person (both as gift and as eschatologically realized calling) are all founded on the recapitulating incarnation of Jesus Christ.

> When the Word of God was made human, He assimilated Himself to humanity and humanity to Himself, so that by means of the human person's resemblance to the Son, he might become precious to the Father. For in times past, it was well said that the human person was created after the image of God, but this was not [actually] shown. For the Word was as yet invisible—the Word after whose image the human person was created. . . . But when the Word of God became flesh, He confirmed both: for He both showed forth the image in all truth, becoming Himself what was His image; and He re-established the similitude in a stable manner, *rendering humanity completely like the invisible Father through means of the visible Word.* (AH 5.16.2, emphasis added)

Irenaeus's Adam

But who is Irenaeus's Adam, and what is his paradise? The answers are embedded in a matrix of interrelated issues. Irenaeus conflates the two accounts of the creation of humanity so that the Adam formed from the earth in Genesis 2:7 is the same one created in God's image in 1:26–27. The context of all of these passages is christological: they show that the incarnation recapitulates the formation of Adam, who himself was made in the image and likeness of God (*AH* 3.18.1; *Dem.* 32).[70] Yet chronologically understood, there is a sense in which Adam is not made in God's image. The corporeal manifestation of God's image—the incarnate Son—had yet to be revealed; Adam himself is also a work in progress. Irenaeus's Adam was neither a royal figure nor the scapegoat for human sin. He judges Adam quite gently; he interprets Adam's fig leaves and his transferal of blame onto Eve as indicative of his genuine *repentance* (*AH* 3.23.5). Cain's sin was far worse than Adam's. And what Adam did—partake of the tree of knowledge of good and evil—was something we all meant to do anyway. Adam did it ahead of his time, in

---

69. This idea forms part of an argument against the gnostic identification of image with the immaterial aeons. See *AH* 2.7.1–7; 2.19.6. See Fantino, *L'homme image de Dieu*, 103–6.

70. See also *Dem.* 11, outside the christological context.

his God-endowed freedom and in childlike innocence.[71] The pathos of human disobedience remains, but the primary blame rests with the devil (*AH* 4.40.3; 3.23.3; *Dem.* 16), and the outcome is very much part of the divine plan for the human person's union with God.

Like Paul and most of the other authors considered so far, Irenaeus has no romantic notions of an Edenic pre-fallen state of humanity. He never clearly or consistently articulates the question of the physical and historical reality of paradise, maybe because he presumes it, but in any case he considers it scarcely consequential. The six days of creation and the time in paradise are—at least in one context—not composed of twenty-four-hour periods but "delineated works" (*AH* 5.23.2).[72] Elsewhere he states that just as the world was created in exactly six days, so it will last exactly six thousand years (*AH* 5.28.3).[73] Yes, paradise itself was beautiful and good, "better than this earth," with the Word of God ever strolling through it. But that paradise prefigures the future, a type for the church (*Dem.* 12).[74] To the extent that Irenaeus even gives thought to the human condition "before" the apostasy, he sees it as one of unreadiness, of humanity in infancy. Adam and Eve are pure in their innocence, hugging and kissing like children (*Dem.* 14). The apostatizing Adam is neither a vilified scapegoat nor an example to aspire to. Adam's transgression, though not an infection transmitted to subsequent generations, does lead to death, which Irenaeus (like Theophilus) interprets as a mercy (*AH* 3.23.6).

Adam, the scriptural first-formed human being, has a primarily symbolic function for Irenaeus. Adam's creation and predicament represent those of the human person generally and reflect the logic of the divine economy. Adam's historic existence, seemingly taken for granted, is not a factor in the discussion (even of the Lukan genealogy, which is about Christ only) except in one instance. In *AH* 3.23 Irenaeus argues against Tatian, who (in a nonsurviving work) had said that Paul's trope "all die in Adam" means that Adam himself was not saved. That will not do: Irenaeus avers that the person of Adam was, in fact, saved with all of us. He sets out a clear and sustained argument featuring a vivid analogy: Imagine a group of people who had been imprisoned, who had children while in captivity. Would it not be unfair to free only the children and leave their parents in bondage (*AH* 3.23.1–8)?[75] Working backward, therefore, from salvation in Christ and provoked by Tatian's logic, Irenaeus must conclude that the scriptural person of Adam,

71. Regarding freedom: *AH* 4.37.1–7. Regarding innocence: *AH* 4.38.1; *Dem.* 12, 14.

72. This helps Irenaeus explain how God kept his promise and how Adam and Eve died "on the very day" that they partook of the forbidden tree. (Osborn finds no fewer than five different solutions to the problem of the "day" of their transgression; see Osborn, *Irenaeus of Lyons*, 71.)

73. This belief was not uncommon; see *Barn.* 15.

74. See Behr, *Asceticism and Anthropology*, 110.

75. The analogy is in 3.23.2.

as not only representative of protohumanity but also the first forebear, must himself be saved in Christ.

Until lately, Irenaeus's genius was like a treasure hidden in a field.[76] The modern critical edition of his work was completed relatively recently, and only a small proportion of his work has been translated into contemporary English. But the scholars who have commented on him within the last two decades agree in finding him to be thorough and broad-ranging, if unsystematic. The latter criticism is unfair, however, for he does sustain and develop particular trains of thought over the course of multiple chapters of *Against the Heresies*, and the *Demonstration* forms a coherent whole. The clarity of his exposition is such that much of the secondary literature does little more than trace his arguments as he presents them.

Indeed, the problem for our own study has been that Irenaeus's thought is so coherent that it is difficult to present his reading of Genesis 1–3 without reviewing his treatment of anthropology, theodicy, economy, and history. The all-consuming rubric of ἀνακεφαλαίωσις is itself a recapitulation of Irenaeus's thought. To paraphrase Osborn, cited above, this concept includes the unity of the Bible, christological typology, human image-bearing personhood, theodicy, divine providence, and the divine irruption into chronological time.[77] All of these find their meaning in the recapitulation, in Christ, of all of the generations and events of humanity that ever were and are to come.

Conclusions

This chapter has reviewed five thinkers who took the legacy of the first century and advanced it by leaps and bounds, partly because persecution and heresy left them no choice. The proliferation of widely divergent writings and movements with varied and overlapping theologies and understandings of Scripture and its exegesis compelled them to codify normative Scripture. They had to refine and argue the Christian faith before variously oppressive authorities, acquaintances, and preachers of false gnosis. They had to argue from logic, aesthetics, and antiquity. The second-century apologists took several approaches directly relevant to Genesis 1–3. Indeed, the biblical creation narratives, which had become standard authoritative reference points less than a century earlier, were foundational to their theological reflection. That reflection may be summarized along the following lines.

76. Particularly useful among modern scholarly treatments are Behr, *Asceticism and Anthropology*; Donovan, *One Right Reading?*; Fantino, *Théologie d'Irénée*; Grant, *Irenaeus of Lyons*; Osborn, *Irenaeus of Lyons*; Sesboüé, *Tout récapituler dans le Christ*.
77. Osborn, *Irenaeus of Lyons*, 97–98.

The Relationship of Old Testament Scripture to the Gospels and Epistles

The overwhelming conviction in the nascent Christian church held that the Scriptures, in both the law they dictated and the salvation they promised, were transfigured in Christ: the law took on an entirely new character subject to Christian faith, and salvation was available to Jew and gentile alike. The physical metamorphosis of Scripture—from sacred scrolls to popular codices—went hand in hand with the gospel message of the universalization of the Scriptures' audience and promise. The theological underpinning of the entire transformation was the interpretation of the Scriptures in the light of Christ. The broad directives in the Gospels[78] reflect the more specific indications in Paul and Hebrews about the fulfillment of OT words, characters, and events in the person of Christ; these blossom into a fully fledged typology in Justin, Melito, and especially Irenaeus, whose rule of faith was both explicitly trinitarian and, in a thoroughgoing and applied way, christological, nowhere more so than from the perspective of christological recapitulation.

The Relationship of the Divine Economy to Human History

These second-century writers were anything but mechanical in their elaboration of Christian typology. To them, seeing paradise as a type for the church, Adam for Christ, Eve for Mary, the tree for the cross was a clear sign of divine providence. For Irenaeus, it was this and more: it indicated a complete transformation of the meaning and character of history. History was not a linear trajectory from Adam—first created perfect, and then fallen—through sinful humanity to Christ and beyond. History began with the incarnate Christ, such that Adam was made in *his* image. In this, Irenaeus took up an idea latent in Paul, who himself did not reflect much on the meaning of the divine image but also never mentioned Adam as the image of God, for this status belonged properly to Christ, to whose image all are to be conformed.

Creation ex nihilo

These writers came to see the importance of declaring that creation was not an emanation from God or a shaping by God of preexisting matter. This, too, was clearest in Irenaeus, who faced the most obvious (gnostic) opposition to the ex nihilo view. The authors in this century also continued the Pauline and Johannine emphasis on the agency of the Logos/Son and, to a different extent, of the Spirit in the creation of the cosmos. The clarity with which they affirmed that creation was a *total* event, in the sense of denying any existing material substrate, effected the clearest delineation yet between created and

---

78. E.g., Luke 4:21; 24:26; 24:42; John 5:45.

uncreated—two categories that would prove of decisive importance throughout the formative period of Christian theology.

The Human Person and Sin

These authors each had much to say about the human person through the lens of the one whom Scripture recorded as the first-formed. None of the authors was interested in commenting on Adam's character, either as royal, pure, perfected, or ignorant. The tendency among them was, if anything, to moderate Adam's guilt by deflecting it onto the devil or accusing Cain of being much worse. The sense among Theophilus, Irenaeus, and also Clement of Alexandria—whose *Hypotyposeis*, a lost work, is supposed to have treated Genesis in some detail—was that Adam and Eve were like children, not yet fully developed, who partook of the intended fruit ahead of their time.[79] These authors also emphasized the complete human freedom in which Adam was created and that all human beings descended from Adam continue to enjoy. The concept of the divine image, which (like the rest of Gen. 1) is conspicuously absent in most of the NT,[80] began to be developed especially with Irenaeus, who took a holistic understanding and subsumed it under his framework of recapitulation in the incarnate Jesus Christ. The sin of the first couple is linked with death, but Theophilus and Irenaeus notably see death as a merciful dispensation in view of the reality of sin—a closure of what would have been an endless cycle of sin and the whole mortal mode of life.

These are the chief concerns that the second-century apologists addressed as they explained and defended the Christian faith in the face of theological challenge and political threat. Their articulations took place together with marked developments that distinguished their context from that of the first century: the increased consciousness of codified Old and New Testaments, the wider availability of these writings for reading and interpretation, and the development of principles for the exegesis of Scripture based on an explicit or implicit christocentric rule of faith. In all of this, the importance of Genesis 1–3 also grew exponentially in comparison to its role in first-century Christian reflection.

---

79. Regarding Clement, see *Protr.* 11.111.1; *Strom.* 3.17.103.1. The transgression, sexual in nature, lay in partaking too soon, not waiting for God's will. Adam had been perfect (and immortal) in the sense that nothing was lacking (*Strom.* 4.13.94.1), but this perfection was unrealized—an idea Clement conveys through the distinction between "image" and "likeness" (*Strom.* 6.12.96). See Floyd, *Clement of Alexandria*, 41–60.

80. Possible exceptions include Col. 3:10 and 1 Cor. 11:7.

4

Senses of Scripture

The World of Origen and the Origin of the World

The third century brought a new intricacy and depth to scriptural exegesis, and a new way of engaging and transforming the Greek philosophical climate. And if we can conclude that the third century ushered in a whole new world for theology, it was almost solely due to Origen. This is scarcely an overstatement. Origen's own thought, as well as the "Origenisms" that bore sometimes more and sometimes less relation to it, dominated his time and left an indelible mark on Greek Christian thought for centuries to come. This chapter is therefore devoted to the study of his thinking about Scripture, history, and allegory and how it bears on his reading of Genesis 1–3.

No formal material before Origen counts as Scripture scholarship; although Hippolytus might be considered Origen's counterpart in the West, we have but fragments of his exegetical work. Tertullian is the exception. He falls outside the geographical and linguistic purview of this study, but given his seminal role in the conception and interpretation of Scripture and of Genesis 1–3 in particular, his contribution deserves acknowledgment.

Tertullian and Origen, both of whom flourished in the first half of the third century, also share a vexed legacy. They are not among the saints canonized in the East or the West—Tertullian for his later affiliation with Montanism, and Origen for the complex reasons I refer to below. Yet both are indispensable reference points in the development of the church's enduring theology, not because of any dubious teachings, but by virtue of their pioneering insights.

This chapter deals primarily with the world of Origen, but because Tertullian shares his century, he shares his chapter too.

Tertullian

Tertullian was a prolific author who wrote on a broad range of theological topics between AD 196 and AD 212. His rich career produced ideas and formulations of acute insight. The challenges of docetism and modalism elicited from him groundbreaking reflections on the person of Christ and the unity in diversity of Father, Son, and Spirit, and many of his concepts and terms endured, mutatis mutandis, through the centuries that shaped Christian theology East and West. Because he shared several common opponents with Irenaeus—Marcion and several gnostic authors, including Valentinus—Tertullian took up many of Irenaeus's concerns from his own perspective, shaped by his North African background and his rhetorical training.[1]

Scholars debating the question of Tertullian's scriptural text come to a variety of conclusions.[2] It appears that where no existing Latin text was available to him, he translated ad hoc from the LXX. As to the NT, when he argued against Marcion he used his opponent's own bowdlerized text of Luke's Gospel. Perhaps his main goal as far as Scripture was concerned was to establish the unity of God and the unity and integrity of the Bible, OT and NT, subjects he developed in five substantial books against Marcion. Recalling the arguments of Justin and Theophilus, the third of these books rests on arguments from prophecy. Like Irenaeus, he was emphatic that the interpretation of the Scriptures rests within the church, and his argument in this regard was closely tied to his own understanding of the rule of faith. In *On the Prescriptions of Heretics*, he emphasized that the Scriptures are the property of the Christian church (*Prescr.* 15–17), of those who read and interpret them properly, that is, according to the *regula fidei* (*Prescr.* 19).

Tertullian codified his rule of faith as a succinct formula that, though resembling its precedents, anticipated more clearly the creedal formulas that would soon follow (*Prescr.* 13). The *regula* features in several of his works, figuring particularly in his arguments for the Christian interpretation of Scripture in *On the Prescriptions*. Scripture, writes Tertullian, is complex by design, containing material that God knew would be wrongly understood, because "there must be heresies" (*Prescr.* 39, citing 1 Cor. 11:19). Hence the *regula,* for the heretic can be defined as one who has fallen from the rule of faith (*Prescr.* 3). The rule of faith guarantees our continuity with the apostles and their preaching (*Prescr.* 19–21, 37). For Tertullian, as for Irenaeus, the rule constitutes Scripture's

---

1. For details on biography and context, see Barnes, *Tertullian.*
2. For a summary of contemporary views, see G. Dunn, *Tertullian*, 20–21.

underlying sense,[3] but by no means does it engender a single understanding of any passage of Scripture. As Paul Blowers observes, "It does not provide immediate and obvious answers to all prospective theological and exegetical questions. What it does provide is the fundamental makings . . . of a cosmic and evangelical narrative upon which basis the church must aspire to articulate its doctrine."[4] Hence Tertullian considered himself at liberty to exegete passages of Scripture in a variety of ways—isolated or in broader context—that suited his argument (or opponent) of the moment. Indeed, Scripture is designed by God in such a way that multiple methods would need to be used in order to read in terms of the *regula*. As T. P. O'Malley has shown, biblical language has a certain "otherness" or "strangeness" to it, wherein terms do not always mean what people think they do.[5] Thus much of Tertullian's exegetical work consists in making scriptural language comprehensible, to mean what it is supposed to.

When it comes to exegesis as such, Tertullian was suspicious of allegory, largely because of his distaste for its abuse at the hands of gnostics.[6] Yet he admitted that allegory may be useful if properly regulated. Elsewhere, however, he justified allegory as a method that Scripture itself requires so that the right meaning may be gleaned.[7] There are places also where his understanding of allegory is closer to what we call typology; he used *aenigma*, *allegoria*, and *parabola* as a matrix of terms that describe prophetic language generally.[8] He referred to prophecy that reports things that will occur in the future as if they had already taken place, such as "I gave my back to those who struck me" (Isa. 50:6) and the rock that sprang forth (1 Cor. 10:4). The teaching, derived from Genesis, that a man should leave his father and mother and be joined to his wife refers (as in Eph. 5:31) to Christ and the church (see *Adv. Marc.* 3.5). His use of the words *allegoria* and *aenigma*, whatever they in fact refer to, is reserved for a few occurrences.

Not so his use of the word *figura* and of the typological reasoning in general that appears throughout his works. Tertullian relied on it to establish the unity of OT and NT, particularly in arguing against Marcion. His treatise against the Jews also features several of the arguments of the second-century apologists—from prophecy, from typology—about the christological sense of Scripture. O'Malley makes the observation that Tertullian's use of *figura* often runs in

---

3. For a comparison of Tertullian, Irenaeus, and Clement on the rule of faith, see Osborn, "Reason and the Rule of Faith."

4. Blowers, "*Regula fidei*," 217.

5. O'Malley, *Tertullian and the Bible*. See esp. the concluding chapter, 173–78; also 26–37. Tertullian supplies alternate interpretations and glosses of words such as *Sophia, sermo, moechia, fornicatio, caro et sanguis, cor, adpretiatus, problemata*, and others (p. 173).

6. Ibid., 147.

7. Ibid., 156–58.

8. See ibid., 161.

tandem with *sacramentum*, with reference to Paul's concept of μυστήριον;[9] Tertullian thereby invokes sacrament as an overarching principle of unity.[10] Of still greater interest is that, unlike Melito, Tertullian suggests that in order for the type (*figura*) to be true, it has to have historical existence. If the bones in Ezekiel's vision (Ezek. 37:1–14) are allegorized to mean "the people of Israel," the vision cannot be a "true preaching of the resurrection."

> The metaphor could not have been formed from bones, if the same thing exactly were not to be realized in them also. Although there is a sketch of the true thing in its image, the image itself still possesses a truth of its own: something used figuratively to express some other thing must therefore have a prior existence for itself. (*De res.* 30)

In his treatise against Hermogenes, where he uses Genesis 1 to argue for creation out of nothing, Tertullian writes as follows about the prophecies of the return of creation into the nothing from which it came: "If in these passages there are allegories, they must necessarily arise from existing, not from non-existing things, because nothing can furnish anything of its own for a similitude, unless it itself be such that it lends itself to such a similitude" (*Herm.* 34). Tertullian's understanding here, and particularly its sharp contrast to Melitos's, is a significant factor in his understanding of the nature of history and narrative.[11]

Against Marcion contains a sustained discussion of creation and fall based on Genesis 1–3. Tertullian draws on the biblical creation narratives with the overall aim of showing that the God presented in the OT is not the monster of Marcion's conception. God is good in that he created someone to know him, someone who would recognize also the goodness of what was created before humanity (*Adv. Marc.* 2.3). Adam, the subject of both Genesis 1:26–27 and 2:7,[12] disobeyed God but owned up to his guilt and did not blame God for anything—nor should we (2.2; 2.4). Eve typifies Mary in a practical sense: God beneficently makes a helper for Adam, for "he knew that the femininity of Mary, and subsequently of the church, would be of advantage" (*Sciebat illi sexum Mariae et deinceps ecclesiae profuturum*, 2.4).[13] The giving of the commandment about the tree showed God's care of humanity over everything else (*Adv. Marc.* 2.4), particularly since the prohibition relied on and proved the gift of freedom, which (together with personal initiative [*potestas*]) is the hallmark of the divine image and likeness (2.5). God both bestowed

---

9. O'Malley, *Tertullian and the Bible*, 161–62.
10. See Bouteneff, "Mystery of Union."
11. See p. 180 below.
12. See also *Herm.* 26.
13. See also *De carne Christi* 17.

goodness on humanity and allowed the human person to be a participant in, and steward of, this goodness (2.5). In 2.8 Tertullian shows that the human person is made for life, not death: "That man was not made for death is proved by this, that God even now desires his restoration to life, preferring a man's conversion rather than his death" (cf. Ezek. 33:11). Death is the fault of the human person. Each of us in our own freedom may conquer the same devil when we are obedient to God. We are all therefore in the same condition as Adam.

At this point (*Adv. Marc.* 2.9) Tertullian embarks on an excursus regarding the human soul and its liability to sin. He points out that the Greek text of Genesis 2:7 speaks of breath (*afflatus*) and not spirit (*spiritus*).[14] The soul can therefore not be equated with God's Holy Spirit or God's very essence;[15] rather, it is "like a breeze in relation to the wind." It is "of God" but not divine or impervious to sin. It is now the *human* soul, and if by it the human being sins, God is not to be blamed. Even the creation of the devil is not cause for blaming God: the devil was, before anything else, an angel, the wisest of them, who of his own accord became corrupt (2.10).[16] In writing of the curse leveled on the serpent, Eve, and Adam, Tertullian—again at pains to maintain the goodness of God in the face of Marcion's objections—distinguishes between God's essential, eternal goodness and his providential strictness: "The goodness of God came first, as his nature is; his sternness came afterwards, as there was reason for it. The former was ingenerate, was God's own, was freely exercised; the latter was accidental, adapted to need, an expedient" (2.11). A lengthy argument on theodicy, based on human freedom and divine justice, ensues.

In this argument, explicit reference to Genesis 2–3 is rare. But at 2.25 it becomes clear that the paradise narrative has been in the background the entire time. Tertullian cites the remaining matters about which he would like to clear the air, the first being God's call to Adam "Where are you?" (Gen. 3:9). God is exonerated (at some length) of any ignorance as to either Adam's location or his motivation and of any other unawareness in other episodes of Genesis. We cannot be so literal as to envisage God strolling through a garden where Adam could escape the notice of the one who knows and sees all. And the question "Where are you?" is more like a parental rebuke eliciting repentance than a question based on ignorance.[17]

Tertullian's theology of creation, the human person, and the fall is based on the rough contours of the paradise narrative. His text here usually refers to the human person in general rather than to an individual Adam, and his goal in arguing against Marcion or elsewhere, as in his treatise *On the Spectacles*

14. Here is an instance of Tertullian providing his own Latin translations of the LXX text.
15. See also *De anima* 11.
16. Tertullian here relies on Ezek. 28:11–16, evoking as it does Eden.
17. See also Theophilus, *Autol.* 2.26.

(*De spect.* 2) was to demonstrate that God is good and that sin and the predicament of the human person is the responsibility of the creature and not the Creator. Finally, very much along the lines of Irenaeus, Tertullian could say that the human person was made in the image of Christ. Referring to the earth and clay from which the human person was created (Gen. 2:7), Tertullian writes:

> Whatever was the form and expression which was given to the clay [by the Creator] the thought was of Christ, who was to become human; . . . of the Word who was to become flesh. . . . For the Father had already spoken to the Son, saying "Let us make humanity in our own image, after our likeness" [Gen. 1:26]. And God made the human being, that is to say, the creature which he molded and fashioned; unto the image of God—in other words, of Christ—he made him. For the Word is also God, who being in the form of God, "thought it not robbery to be equal to God" [cf. Phil. 2:6]. (*De res.* 6)[18]

Genesis 1–3 was fundamental to Tertullian's understanding of God, the world, and the human person. His conclusions about the creation narratives, especially about humanity and its redemption in Christ, are basically Pauline, bearing also a close resemblance to Irenaeus. Although he did not take the paradise narrative literally, his reliance on typology and his understanding of its true sense and function were such that they would underscore the historical veracity of any scriptural narrative.

Origen

The last chapter noted the transformation of Scripture from sacred texts intended for the Jewish elite to codices that were no less sacred in their meaning but now widely available and preaching a message applicable to all. This universalization, taking place on the kerygmatic as well as the practical level, came now to the academy. Building on foundations laid by Clement and other Christian intellectual teachers, Origen was instrumental in placing biblical literature alongside classical literature in the academy even if, together with other Christian scholars, he frequently had to answer for the cruder language of much of the Bible. Christian literature, drawing on the exegetical practices of the Greco-Roman schools, became part of an alternative *paideia*.[19] Origen's life and career have by now been well documented.[20] Our concern will be to establish the role of biblical exegesis in his theology and to survey it for his understanding of Genesis 1–3.

18. The translation is reworded from Tertullian, *Tertullian's Treatise on the Resurrection* (Evans).
19. See Young, *Biblical Exegesis*, 76–96.
20. On Origen's life and work, see esp. Nautin, *Origène*; and Crouzel, *Origen*.

The Problem of Transmission

Origen's brilliance was almost matched by the degree of controversy that has dogged his reputation at every stage from late in his own lifetime to the various Origenisms constructed in late antiquity—including the ideas condemned from the fourth to the sixth centuries—and on through to the present day.[21] The difficulties that some early readers saw in his texts engendered a problematic manuscript transmission. Much of his output was destroyed and lost forever; other works survive only in transcriptions or translations by persons who sought either Origen's destruction or his rehabilitation and did not hesitate to manipulate his texts to suit their agendas. The resulting textual diversity has meant that assessments of Origen continue to fluctuate between condemnation and glorification.[22] Our understanding of Origen will therefore always be imperfect, and many of his texts—perhaps especially *On First Principles*—need to be read with an eye to the predispositions of those who translated or transcribed them.[23]

Indeed, any discussion related to *On First Principles* must begin with the problem of its transmission. The original Greek text is lost; what we have today is the Latin translation of Rufinus, who, during the turn of the fourth to fifth centuries, translated a substantial body of Origen's work. Rufinus, unlike his erstwhile friend Jerome, sided with Origen, and the extent to which he allowed his leanings to skew the translation is a matter of dispute.[24] What is clear is that Rufinus felt a responsibility to make doctrinal adjustments to the text from which he was working, especially since he had reason to believe that Origen's detractors had already manipulated it.[25] Thus the Latin version we have was subject to revisions by persons on both sides of the early Origenist controversy, even if the pro-Origen Rufinus had the last word. Greek portions of *On First Principles* have survived, notably in the *Philocalia*, the Origenist anthology attributed to Basil of Caesarea and Gregory of Nazianzus, but some of the Greek texts, too, were adjusted by later critics, including Justinian. Bearing all this in mind, Ronald Heine can conclude optimistically that "nevertheless, . . . on the whole, the substance can be regarded as representing Origen's thought."[26]

21. On multiple Origenisms, see Clark, *Origenist Controversy*, 6.
22. See Osborn, "Origen."
23. A useful summary of the transmission issues can be found in Torjesen, *Hermeneutical Procedure*, 14–18.
24. Ronald E. Heine provides helpful summaries of the situation in his translations of Origen's, *Homilies on Genesis and Exodus* (see pp. 27–39, where Heine summarizes the scholarly debate on the reliability of Rufinus) and of Origen's *Commentary on the Gospel according to John* (2:19–21). An important argument in favor of Rufinus's dependability as a translator may be found in Scott, *Origen and the Life of the Stars*, 168–72.
25. See Rufinus's preface to his own translation, reproduced in Butterworth's translation of *On First Principles*, lxii–lxiv.
26. Origen, *Homilies on Genesis and Exodus* (Heine, 38). Heine here notes that the theological statements on the Trinity and on the resurrection of the body are the exception, as it is likely that these teachings were the focus of the corrective translations of Origen's admirers.

Theology as Exegesis

Origen's scholarly interest in Scripture is nowhere more evident than in his compilation of the *Hexapla*, a six-column presentation of the OT in Hebrew (original and transliterated) and in four Greek translations, including the LXX. Origen often addressed the differences in the various translations in his scriptural commentaries. The commentaries thus relied on the text-critical work that produced the *Hexapla*, even as his basic reference text remained the LXX, to which he referred even as he noted divergences from the Hebrew. The project of the *Hexapla* and the fact that the bulk of his written work took the form of commentaries on Scripture[27] tell us that Origen was a Scripture scholar; they also indicate that, for him, theology *was* scriptural exegesis. Whatever may or may not be said about the hellenizing character of his reasoning must be subservient to this fundamental observation about his work. This, in turn, means that the kinds of questions we may pose regarding his "doctrine of creation" or his "teaching on Adam and the fall" may fall flat. As Caroline Bammel notes: "Origen's aim is to expound Scripture and to reflect the complexity of Scripture. He discusses the problems raised by the biblical text and searches for parallel passages that may provide illumination, airs rival views and arguments, but does not provide dogmatic answers."[28] Transmission difficulties notwithstanding, we have considerable data on how Origen read Scripture. For instance, he frequently describes his exegetical logic when he comments on scriptural passages. But he also sets out a systematic account of his method in *On First Principles* and his *Commentary on John*.

It is important to note that the separation of *On First Principles* into four books, each with chapters and sections, is late and therefore potentially misleading. Origen's systematic treatment of both the inspiration of Scripture and its exegesis in what we call book 4 of *On First Principles* does not simply constitute another item in a list of subjects; rather, it lays out the entire underlying sense of the work.[29] As said before, Origen's theology *is* exegesis.

Rule of Faith

Origen alludes to doctrinal fundamentals—a rule of faith—at several points in his works; with him as for several of his predecessors, these emanate from Scripture and constitute its underlying sense. In the *Commentary on John*, he suggests that if there were a hundred articles of faith to which one would

27. For a listing of works, based on Jerome's own cataloging, see Crouzel, *Origen*, 37–39.
28. Bammel, "Adam in Origen," 63.
29. "Scripture is not one question among others but is the primary reason for the existence of the *Peri Archon*, that Bk. IV.1–3 does not serve the function of legitimizing the philosophical doctrines derived from Scripture, but on the contrary that Bk. IV.1–3 serves the function of explaining what to do with the *Peri Archon*" (Torjesen, "Hermeneutics and Soteriology," 346).

adhere in order to "have all faith," then among them would be a few genuine essentials. He enumerates belief in the one God, in Jesus Christ, and in the Holy Spirit, but he also makes some refinements as to Christology that anticipate several of the heresies that would rock the church through the next century (*In Jo.* 32.187–93; see also *Sermons on Matthew* 33). But the most substantial exposition of his rule of faith can be found in the preface to *On First Principles*. Here he lists the sine qua non areas of doctrine on which he seeks to set out Christian first principles, the "necessary" teachings about which the apostolic proclamation is unequivocal as opposed to other, lesser teachings. His list is substantial; it begins with the Trinity. God comes first: the one God, Creator of all, the God of all the righteous, and here he lists Adam, Abel, Seth, and on down to the twelve patriarchs, Moses, and the prophets. Then comes Jesus Christ and his incarnation, and then the Holy Spirit. Origen next lists a range of anthropological teachings concerning the soul, its relation to the body, its free will, and its destiny in the age to come as well as teachings on the devil and the angels, the establishment and dissolution of the cosmos, and the Scriptures and their spiritual dimension, saying,

> The contents of Scripture are the outward forms of certain mysteries and the images of divine things. On this point the entire Church is unanimous, that while the whole law is spiritual, the inspired meaning is not recognized by all, but only by those who are gifted with the grace of the Holy Spirit and the word of wisdom and knowledge. (*DP* 1.pref.8)

Origen's prefatory catalog of "necessary" and "clear" doctrines is significant both for the broad range of what it enumerates and for its explicit acknowledgement of teachings that are "not yet known," such as whether the Spirit is begotten or unbegotten (*DP* 1.pref.4), and of teachings that are clear but whose underlying logic or full implications are not yet made plain. In such cases, he relegates the work of arriving at greater clarity to "diligent lovers of wisdom."[30]

The context for this rule and for the entire treatise is found in the first few lines of the preface:

> All who believe and are convinced that grace and truth came by Jesus Christ [John 1:17], and who know Christ to be the truth [John 14:6], derive the knowledge which calls persons to lead a good and blessed life from no other source but the very words and teaching of Christ. By the words of Christ we do not mean only those which formed his teaching when he was made man and dwelt in the flesh, since even before that Christ the Word of God was in Moses and the prophets. (*DP* 1.pref.1)

---

30. His idea that Scripture has not laid out everything clearly and therefore must be plumbed and explained is reminiscent of Irenaeus, e.g., in *AH* 1.10.3.

First, Origen locates the truth with Jesus Christ and his words. Second, these words are not limited to the sayings attributed to him in the Gospels, for he is embedded in the whole of Scripture and spoke through Moses, the prophets, and the apostles. These two points remind us of how the rule of faith and "necessary knowledge" are based in Scripture. Third, embedded in this little passage is the sense that these scriptural words exist to call us "to lead a good and blessed life." Although we will focus on several dimensions of Origen's exegesis, we ought never to lose sight that his entire exegetical project, however "spiritualizing," is finally a *paraenetic* exercise: what we glean from the Scriptures is intended for the living of a morally upright life. Karen Jo Torjesen has argued that *On First Principles,* often distinguished from the rest of Origen's work as either a systematic or a philosophical treatise, shares many characteristics of the exegetical corpus and is grounded in a primarily soteriological concern.[31] Similarly, Crouzel insists that the "unsystematic" scriptural homilies "are not aimed at producing history. It is for us Christians, as Paul says in 1 Corinthians 10:11, that Scripture has been composed."[32] For Origen, Scripture's usefulness and importance are not primarily historical but moral, pastoral, and, finally, soteriological.

In Origen's reading of Scripture, the rule of faith is also a proof of the necessity of spiritual (allegorical) exegesis. He states that the belief that Scripture ought to be interpreted according to the bare letter is tantamount to saying that it was composed by human beings alone, without inspiration. To those who believe in the inspiration of the Holy Spirit, Origen writes, "We must explain . . . what seems to us the right way of understanding Scripture for those who keep to the rule of the heavenly Church of Jesus Christ through the succession of the apostles" (*DP* 4.2.2).[33]

The "rule of the heavenly church" is not some disembodied ideal, by nature prone to vague spiritualization. Origen echoes Irenaeus in viewing it as the *apostolic rule,* founded by Christ and conveyed through the apostles. Moreover, the rule is best served through allegorical and spiritual exegesis, which in turn sanctions it. Spiritual exegesis is liable to bring out the (sometimes latent) rule of faith within the passages of Scripture that are hard to understand. Indeed, as Tertullian had suggested and as Origen would make plain in *On First Principles,* the difficulties have been placed in Scripture by divine design (*DP* 4.2.9).[34] The purpose of allegory, then, is to uncover Scripture's latent sense, the

31. See Torjesen, "Hermeneutics and Soteriology."

32. Crouzel, *Origen,* 63.

33. This translation, which is reworded from Butterworth's translation of *On First Principles,* is from the Greek text, but the sense is preserved also in the Latin.

34. For Origen, the σκάνδαλα inserted in Scripture are meant to lead us to loftier ways of reading. Tertullian's point in *Prescr.* 39 is that in God's wider plan "there must be heresies" (1 Cor. 11:19) and God therefore peppered the Scriptures with material for heretics.

embedded rule of faith. As we will see again farther on, this rule, Scripture's inner sense, is ultimately distilled in the person of Christ himself.[35]

Finally, Origen's perspective on the rule of faith evinces an observation that concerns *all* the fathers who spoke of it, and even those who did not do so explicitly: what finally matters in the reading of Scripture is the elucidation of the rule or "gospel" inset therein. Whatever manner of interpretation (historical/literal, spiritual/allegorical, typological) one uses, it is at the service of uncovering this *hypothesis* of Scripture. As Eric Osborn notes about Origen's predecessors, "The success of the second century was the affirmation that there was a true gospel; this was more important than any particular account of that gospel."[36] This sensibility is common to the fathers despite their incrementally differing articulations of the rule and its exact meaning. As Blowers writes:

> In the overall landscape of antenicene Christianity, the variations in accent among those renditions of the Rule of Faith that laid claim to catholic authority give the impression of a viable harmony, not a cacophony. The Rule appears in retrospect to be larger than any one of its individual renditions. The mounting pressure of heterodoxy—expressing itself ecclesially and institutionally as well as hermeneutically and doctrinally—may have induced some second-century writers to exaggerate the pure traditioning and uninterrupted history of a catholic Rule, but a maturing solidarity in Christian identity and self-understanding is discernible in this period, commensurate with a hard-earned balance of fixity and flexibility, conformity and freedom, unity and diversity.[37]

The rule was not only expressed variously, with different accents, but it also takes precedence over any particular method of exegesis, for the various approaches are finally only at its service.

On First Exegetical Principles

Scholars have devoted considerable attention to Origen's exegesis (with particular focus on DP 4.1–3).[38] Much of the debate concerns the distinction between allegory and typology, with some authors (notably Daniélou) seeing them as distinct categories and others (notably de Lubac and Hanson) showing

35. Clement reasoned similarly, connecting the rule with the Logos. The relationship between Clement and Origen is under question: Was Origen Clement's pupil, as Eusebius has it? If so, why is he utterly silent on his alleged teacher? See Dawson, *Allegorical Readers*, 220–21.

36. Osborn, "Reason and the Rule of Faith," 58. The rule of faith is not perfectly contiguous with the gospel, but Osborn's point regards the priority of the core message of Scripture.

37. Blowers, "*Regula fidei*," 226–27.

38. Several of their approaches are summarized by Torjesen, *Hermeneutical Procedure*, 5–12. See also Daley, "Origen's 'De principiis.'"

that the two are far from mutually exclusive in Origen's thinking. "Typology," although a twentieth century neologism, describes a long-established practice discussed extensively in the previous chapter. It is indeed treated—by Origen, Tertullian, and others—in a way that overlaps to various degrees with allegory. Nomenclature aside, what happens to the literal or historical sense of the scriptural type or of the event or person that is allegorized? We have seen that patristic typology focuses on the realization and fulfillment rather than on the substance of the type, although different ancient authors could reason differently on whether the OT type needed to have a concrete or historical basis. (For Melito, it explicitly did not; for Tertullian, it did.) These are some of the questions that will underlie our examination of Origen's reading of Scripture.

On First Principles 4.1 covers a broad range of topics, primarily the inspiration of Scripture. Its proof rests on the argument from prophecy, which itself is founded on an underlying sense of divine providence. Yet Scripture is a "treasure in clay jars" (2 Cor. 4:7), not only because its language and imagery are often unsophisticated but because it is veiled (2 Cor. 3:15–16). *On First Principles* 4.2 follows this reasoning, describing the pitfalls of a bare, literal reading of Scripture, for example, in the prophecies found in both Moses and the Prophets. (He calls such a reading Jewish because it fails to find Christ.) The further hazard of an overly literal reading (or one unguided by good teachers) is that it will be insensitive to the awesome mystery behind the words and thus produce an anthropomorphic portraiture of God.[39]

In 4.2.4 Origen begins to describe his celebrated threefold exegesis of Scripture, which he bases on scriptural texts as well as on passages from the Shepherd of Hermas, suggesting that different levels of the message are appropriate to different kinds of people. Scripture, says Origen, may be understood along an anthropological analogy according to three senses: the bodily, by which simple people may be edified; the psychic or soul-sense, which is open to those who have made some spiritual progress; and the spiritual, which is for "those who are perfect." Origen cites 1 Corinthians 2:6–7 as well as Romans 7:14 and Hebrews 10:1 (the spiritual law is but a shadow of the good things to come).

Some passages in Scripture, Origen goes on to say (4.2.5), have no "bodily" sense at all in that there is no possible literal interpretation. His example is unexpected: he refers neither to a fantastic and improbable vision nor to a piece of allusive scriptural poetry but to the six stone jars of water set before Jesus at the wedding in Cana. These, Origen says, can only refer to "those who are placed in this world to be purified"; he also connects the six jars to the six days of creation.[40] As to the first (bodily) level of interpretation, which

39. The "heretics" cited here are most likely Marcionites. See the commentary in Crouzel and Simonetti's translation, *Traité des principes*, 4:172.

40. Being the sum of its parts (1 + 2 + 3), six is a perfect number. See Philo, *Opif.* 13, *Leg.* 1.3. Origen's identification of the "obviously" historical and "plainly" nonhistorical portions

the Latin text calls historical (*historiali*, 4.2.6), it requires no supplementary argument; the meaning is evident to all. The second (soul) level can be seen where a text of the law (such as Deut. 25:4) is shown to have been written not about mere oxen but "for our sake" (1 Cor. 9:9–10). As for the third (supernatural) level, Origen conflates allegory and typology, for his examples are those of the τύποι (10:11)[41] and other "shadows of heavenly things," such as the rock that was Christ (10:4).[42]

Most discussions of Origen's exegesis treat only the bodily (literal) and the spiritual (allegorical) sense, without elaborating the intermediary (psychic) sense. This latter could be called a "figurative" reading, not straightforwardly literal or allegorical in pointing to another meaning altogether. It works simply to edify and morally encourage the reader through narratives that are not necessarily historical. Origen himself works with this intermediary sense only in a select few places of his written work.[43] But particularly as some—though not all—scriptural passages are open to multiple readings, we do well to be mindful of this intermediary figurative sense, for the examples that Origen brings forth in *DP* 4 from the paradise account—which he never identifies with any one kind of reading or meaning—may be well served by the figurative and paraenetic exegesis he identifies as that of "the soul."

Throughout 4.2 Origen carefully elaborates his idea that Scripture's divine inspiration took the form of an intricate pastoral placement of prosaic and poetic material. Origen's debt to Philo is clear in his acknowledgment of different modes of scriptural interpretation and, among them, the emphasis on the allegorical. But he is original in describing the divinely ordained braiding of different types of scriptural narrative. In 4.2 as well as in 4.3, Origen frequently uses the verb "interweave" (προσυφαίνειν) to describe how hidden meanings and ordinary history are intertwined in both the OT and the NT. Thus Scripture contains some narratives that would be benign, or perhaps edifying, at their face value but that the diligent should study in order to plumb their greater depths. The aim of the Holy Spirit is "to envelop [clothe] and hide secret mysteries in ordinary words under the pretext of a narrative . . . [i.e.] an account of visible things." Origen's example in 4.2, which he will elaborate further in 4.3, is the biblical account of the creation of the world and the first human being (4.2.8). Origen believes that the Holy Spirit even

---

of scriptural narrative is frequently baffling to our sensibilities. In *Homilies on Genesis* (2.2), he seems to defend the historicity of Noah's ark, explaining how it could contain all the species of animals, as "against those who endeavor to impugn the scriptures of the Old Testament as containing certain things which are impossible and irrational." Yet in the very same homily (2.6), he suggests that intrascriptural discrepancies about the ark's construction serve to remind us that there may not always be a literal sense to everything described in Scripture.

41. The NRSV translates this as "examples," the RSV as "warnings."

42. Given that all Origen's examples of the third level are taken from the corpus then assuredly thought to be Pauline, St. Paul is shown as one of "the perfect" who may reason at this level.

43. These are treated in Dively Lauro, *Soul and Spirit of Scripture*.

inserts what he calls (in 4.2.9) stumbling blocks (σκάνδαλα, *offendicula*)—things that could not possibly have occurred in history—in order to shake people out of an overly simplistic or literal reading.[44] The Spirit wants to lead us to the spiritual meaning of things. In some cases, this meaning coincides with a historical narrative, but in other cases, the Spirit had to "weave in" details or episodes that did not happen (συνύφηνεν ἡ γραφὴ τῇ ἱστορίᾳ τὸ μὴ γενόμενον), either because they could not have happened or because they could have but in fact did not. These "impossibilities" feature in some of the unrealistic commandments of the OT law as well as in the Gospels and Epistles.

What does the Holy Spirit want people to see behind the "garment" of the historical narratives? What have the inspired scriptural authors embedded in the stories? Origen answers in 4.2.7: "It is chiefly the doctrine of God, that is, the Father, Son, and Holy Spirit that is described by those persons filled with the divine Spirit. And then . . . they brought forth the mysteries of the Son of God, how the Word was made flesh and for what purpose he went so far as to take the form of a servant." Origen goes on to say that they also taught about earthly and heavenly creatures, the differences among souls, and so forth. In other words, we have in the preface to the entire treatise a recapitulation of the rule of faith, also called in 4.2.2 the "rule of the heavenly Church." It is this that the Spirit breathes into the narratives of Scripture.

In 4.3 Origen puts his exegetical principles into practice "so that [they] may be understood quite concretely," using as his test case the biblical creation accounts. His approach—stating that, in effect, these things did not happen in historical space and time—is consistent through other periods of his work, where he cautions against a literal interpretation of Genesis 1–3 that would anthropomorphize God or make of him something circumscribable, locatable, or capricious.[45] Earlier in *On First Principles* (3.5.1) he argued that there is no more dependable or enlightening (truthful) account of the creation of the world than that of Moses but that its power and clarity go far deeper than a recital of history. The Genesis account "enshrines certain deeper truths than the mere historical narrative, . . . and contains a spiritual meaning almost throughout, using 'the letter' as a kind of veil to hide profound and mystical doctrines" (*DP* 3.5.1, my translation). For Origen, "truthfulness" and "historical facticity" are distinct, not mutually dependent concepts. We have come a long way from Theophilus of Antioch.

On First Principles 4.3 gets right to the heart of the matter with some pointed rhetorical questions:

44. Tertullian, we will recall, had said that Scripture was complicated by design; see *Prescr.* 39. See also Pseudo-Dionysius, *Celestial Hierarchies* 2.3–5 (PG 3:141A–45A).

45. The *DP* probably dates from c. 230. But see also *De orat.* 23.3 (dating from 233) and *C. Cels.* 4.40; 6.60; 7.50 (dating from c. 249).

To what person of intelligence, I ask, will the account seem logically consistent that says there was a "first day" and a "second" and a "third," in which also "evening" and "morning" are named, without a sun, without a moon, and without stars, and even in the case of the first day without a heaven?[46] And who will be found simple enough to believe that like some farmer "God planted trees in the garden of Eden, in the east" and that he planted "the tree of life" in it, that is a visible tree that could be touched, so that someone could eat of this tree with corporeal teeth and gain life, and further, could eat of another[47] tree and receive the knowledge of "good and evil?" Moreover, we find that God is said to stroll in the garden in the afternoon and Adam to hide under a tree. Surely, I think no one doubts that these statements are made by Scripture in the form of a figure [*quod figurali tropo*] by which they point toward certain mysteries. (*DP* 4.3.1)[48]

The above is taken from Rufinus's Latin. In the Greek text, the concluding words outlining the approach of Scripture are still clearer: "I do not think anyone will doubt that these are figurative expressions which indicate certain mysteries through a semblance of history and not through actual events."[49] The spirit of this passage, like so much of Origen's exegetical theory, recalls Philo: "Far be it from man's reasoning to be the victim of so great impiety as to suppose that God tills the soil and plants pleasaunces" (*Leg.* 1.43).

ORIGEN AND THE HISTORICAL

Origen's rhetorical certainty—that no one could be so unintelligent as to doubt the ahistorical (yet truth-bearing) character of these narratives—was evidently a misjudgment. His treatment in *On First Principles* of passages that had become so dear, so foundational to Christians' belief about the cosmos and the nature and plight of the human person, was unacceptable to many (even intelligent) readers from the very outset precisely because it undermined that historicity, as Epiphanius would make abundantly clear the following century in his catalog of heresies[50] and as later reactions continued to attest.[51] But Origen himself is quite clear, as he continues in *DP* 4.3.1, that these (and other) things "are written as though they were really done, but cannot be believed

46. Origen treats these issues again in *C. Cels.* 6.50–62, alluding there also to passages in the (lost) *Commentary on Genesis.*
47. In the Greek text, the two trees are erroneously conflated. Rufinus's Latin corrects the error by adding "another" (*alia*).
48. The translation is from Greer's translation. I only substituted "figure" for his "type" in the last sentence.
49. Oὐκ οἶμαι διστάζειν τινὰ περὶ αὐτὰ τροπικῶς διὰ δοκούσης ἱστορίας, καὶ οὐ σωματικῶς γεγενημένης, μηνύειν τινὰ μυστήρια.
50. Epiphanius, *Ancoratus* 55.1; also 55.2; 58.6–8. See Dechow, "Heresy Charges," 115–17; Dechow, *Dogma and Mysticism*, 306–33. See also Bammel, "Adam in Origen," 65; Clark, *Origenist Controversy*, 86–104.
51. See the comments of Origen, *Traité des principes* (Crouzel and Simonetti, 4:194–95n2).

to have happened appropriately and reasonably according to the narrative meaning."[52] Citing examples from the Gospels, he concludes that careful readers will notice a great many passages where "among those narratives which appear to be recorded literally there are inserted and interwoven others which cannot be accepted as history" (4.3.1)[53]

One must always consider—and many have—the possibility that Origen means something quite different by "history" than we do. Frances Young is justly attuned to the anachronism inherent in applying modern conceptions of allegory, typology, and history to ancient sensibilities and writing.[54] Yet when we read Origen, it is difficult to see his understanding of history and the historical as much different from a modern one. Discussing the similarities of Origen's method with that of the Greco-Roman schools, Young's conclusions on his historical sense are contradictory. On the one hand, she says that despite their invocation of "the historical" and "history," the Greco-Roman critics meant something so different than we do by these terms that they cannot be said to have an interest in historicity. "Indeed," Young writes, "it is acknowledged that ancient literary criticism had no true historical sense." This is partly true. But can one really conclude that, in view of the obvious differences in the perception and weight of history and historicity between antiquity and now, the ancients were unconcerned with whether an event "happened" or with whether it was described accurately? Young concedes that Herodotus, for example, testifies to a sense of history that is "not totally dissimilar" to our own.[55] But the very fact that Herodotus, Thucydides, Polybius, and others were forthright about embellishing otherwise "historical" accounts shows that, although these historians may have adjusted the facts more than our own reputable historians do, their perceived need to periodically draw attention to these additions indicates that they took historicity—as we understand it—seriously.

D. A. Russel, on whom Young draws for her argument, notes in the classical writers an absence of a consciousness of clearly discernible periods or eras. Even so, the Greco-Roman literary critics "were undoubtedly concerned with two essential preliminaries to literary history: problems of authenticity, and biographical facts about authors."[56] They distinguished literary genres that were either more or less history-based, and were certainly, though inconsistently, interested in "fact" within historicity.

---

52. Verum ne nos opus, quod habemus in manibus, iusto amplius dilatemus, perfacile est omni uolenti congregare de scripturis sanctis quae scripta sunt quidem tamquam facta, non tamen secundum historiam conpetenter et rationabiliter fieri potuisse credenda sunt. Greek text: Καὶ τί δεῖ πλείω λέγειν, τῶν μὴ πάνυ ἀμβλέων μυρία ὅσα τοιαῦτα δυναμένων συναγαγεῖν, ἀναγεγραμμένα μὲν ὡς γεγονότα, οὐ γεγενημένα δὲ κατὰ τὴν λέξιν.
53. The translation is from Rufinus in Origen, On First Principles (Butterworth).
54. Young, Biblical Exegesis.
55. Ibid., 79.
56. Russell, Criticism in Antiquity, 159.

In the end, however, Young makes a compelling case for broadening our understanding of Origen's interest in history.[57] Allegorist though he was, Origen retained a keen faith in the historical—for example, providing explanations for Jesus's "brothers and sisters" in his *Commentary on Matthew*.[58] Young concedes that "the usual focus on his willingness to disregard 'history' in our sense fails to do justice to his exegetical practice."[59]

Crouzel, for his part, suggests that *DP* 4.1–3 is frequently misinterpreted to mean that the literal sense is superseded by the spiritual but that is because people misunderstand what Origen means by these terms.[60] But in general, Origen's notion of history is clear: he regularly calls attention to whether something happened or did not. He uses not only the potentially ambiguous word ἰστορία (and its derivatives) but also γίνομαι ("to happen," "to become," "to transpire"). Moreover, his sense of history is central to his study of Scripture: whether it is inconsequential that an event happened as written, he feels constrained to specify that some did occur and some did not. In *DP* 4.3.4 he addresses the slippery-slope question: if some events are fictitious, what is to stop us from saying that they all are, that even the commandments should not be taken at face value? His response—not particularly satisfying from a literary perspective—is that "in a great many cases" (later "more cases than not"), "the historical truth of the narrative meaning can and ought to be preserved. For who could doubt that Abraham was buried in the double cave in Hebron, as were Isaac and Jacob?" And "who would not affirm the commandment that orders 'Honor your father and your mother'?" In the end, each needs to "rely on great zeal and effort so that each reader may with all reverence understand that he is pondering words that are divine and not human and that have been sown into the holy books" (4.3.5).

Origen's suspicion—perhaps derived from the Stoics[61]—as to whether the events of "factual history" can be determined at all is nearly postmodernist. How do we know that something has happened or that it happened "as written?" In *Against Celsus* Origen finds himself countering claims that some biblical narratives—for example, the Holy Spirit alighting on Christ in the form of a dove at his baptism—could not have happened. Origen first asserts that "an attempt to substantiate almost any story as historical fact, even if it is true, and to produce complete certainty about it, is one of the most difficult tasks, and in some cases is impossible" (*C. Cels.* 6.42). Some doubt that the Trojan War happened, because of the improbable details that are bound

---

57. Young has in mind especially Hanson, *Allegory and Event*. Crouzel had already argued for a wider view of Origen, citing his spiritual interpretation but calling him also, "with Jerome, the greatest critical exegete and the greatest literal exegete of Christian antiquity" (*Origen*, 61).

58. Young, *Biblical Exegesis*, 86–87.

59. Ibid., 87.

60. Crouzel, *Origen*, 62–63.

61. See Watson, "Origen and the Literal Interpretation of Scripture," 75.

up with it, but the discerning reader, says Origen, "will decide what he will accept and what he will interpret allegorically, searching out the meaning of the authors who wrote such fictitious stories, and what he will disbelieve as having been written to gratify certain people" (6.42). After a lengthy excursus, Origen concludes that, although no one can substantiate that a dove landed on Jesus, neither can anybody doubt that, just as we sometimes dream in our sleep or see visions, certain prophets were shown visions that they then recorded. The prophets saw these visions in their mind, not in the objectively visible sky: "For I do not imagine that the visible heaven was opened, or its physical form divided, for Ezekiel to record such an experience" (6.48). And perhaps, Origen suggests, we can believe the same of the Savior's experience of the Holy Spirit in the form of the dove. Thus he asserts something quite profound: these things *happened*, but they happened *for Ezekiel* and *for Jesus* and, in their transmission, they happened ultimately *for us* and for our salvation. But they did not necessarily happen as events in physical space.

ORIGEN AND THE ALLEGORICAL

Origen's main task in *DP* 4 was to set out the different "senses" of Scripture: to explain the nature of its divine inspiration in terms of how the factual and the fictive are woven into a true account. Much of Scripture, then, is to be read in its spiritual (allegorical) sense and/or in its psychic (paraenetic) sense. The creation narratives, on which he wrote so controversially in his *Commentary on Genesis*, are his first case study. Although he constantly points to "hidden meanings," he does not indicate what he thinks these meanings are. We know from Methodius, Jerome, and Epiphanius (to name just a few) that some of the most damning accusations against him were precisely that he allegorized paradise to the extent that the biblical narrative was no longer recognizable.[62] The primary charge was that paradise and its trees were not physical realities on the earth.[63] The subsequent charges have to do with Origen's "spiritualization" of the waters above the heavens and under the earth. Although Origen did allegorize paradise in *On First Principles* and elsewhere, there is no evidence of his spiritualizing the waters in his surviving works, although it may have formed part of the lost Genesis commentary that had focused on Genesis 1–4. (From *C. Cels.* 6.49 we learn that Origen did specifically discuss the waters in that commentary, but we know little else.)[64] In the sixth century, Origen was criticized for allegorizing the sky and the stars; although Evagrius may have taken that direction, we have no evidence that Origen did.[65] Several

62. Dechow, "Heresy Charges," 116–17.
63. Origen's dehistoricizing paradise is no more radical than that in 2 Esdras, which asserts that the garden was planted before the earth came into being (3:6).
64. For a useful account of the commentary and the extant fragments, see Heine, "Testimonia and Fragments." See also Heine, "Origen's Alexandrian *Commentary on Genesis*."
65. See Dechow, *Dogma and Mysticism*, 344–45.

questions must be posed: How translational was Origen's allegory (i.e., did the allegorical interpretation always *supplant* the literal)? Were his critics always justified in charging that Origen wreaked havoc on biblical history? And were his critics indeed criticizing allegorical method as such, or Origen's alleged doctrinal conclusions?

To begin addressing these questions, let us look at Origen's spiritualization of the stars. As it happens, in the largest surviving segment of the lost Genesis commentary (preserved in the *Philocalia*), his discussion of God's creation of the stars is completely straightforward. His object was to argue against astrological determinism.[66] Although he believed the stars to be living beings, he considered them only as physical stars in the actual sky and not allegories for spiritual powers (*DP* 1.7.1–3).[67] We are not likely ever to know one way or the other whether he periodically allegorized geology and astronomy elsewhere; he remains rooted in the plain fact that God created water, earth, and all the heavenly bodies. In his Genesis homilies, he addresses the firmament and the waters above and below it; he never "spiritualizes" them to represent angelic powers.[68] He only gives them an added paraenetic dimension (to wit, each person should thus also become a "divider and discerner of that which is above and that which is below," *Hom. in Gen.* 1.2). His allegorical reading did not always supplant the literal or moral sense. Scholars justifiably question to what extent his immediate critics were trustworthy on the degree of his allegorization of the Hexaemeron and its supposed wanton arbitrariness.[69]

Let's look for a moment at the nature of his critics' accusations. Jon Dechow's work shows that Epiphanius made "uncharitable distortions of Origen's thinking," distortions that were used "to influence and purge the orthodox Christianity of his day."[70] Heine implies that Origen's alleged spiritualization of the waters did not come from him but instead was a reference in the lost Genesis commentary to Valentinian's readings of Genesis 1.[71] Frances Young has shown that even Eustathius of Antioch's critique, *On the Witch of Endor, against Origen*, was not, as is commonly held, an attack on his allegorical exegesis but a doctrinal conclusion based on Origen's *overly literal* reading of Scripture in this case.[72] The paradise narrative is another matter, and we must now account for what he says about it.

66. Fragment from *Comm. in Gen.* 3, in *Philocalia* 23.

67. The idea of stars as living beings has its own history, as documented in the appropriately titled book by Scott, *Origen and the Life of the Stars*.

68. Drawing on Rev. 12:9; 20:3; and Matt. 25:41, he only suggests that the "abyss" might be the place where the demonic forces would be cast.

69. See, e.g., Patterson, *Methodius of Olympus*, which discusses Methodius's simultaneous dependence on Origen and his criticism—the latter often as a result of misunderstanding.

70. Dechow, *Dogma and Mysticism*, esp. 346–47.

71. This is implied in Heine, "Origen's Alexandrian *Commentary on Genesis*," 68–73.

72. Young, "Rhetorical Schools," 193–95. Eustathius, in effect, was criticizing Origen's inconsistency: if he is going to allegorize the paradise narrative, then why treat 1 Sam. 28 literally?

ADAM, THE FALL, AND SIN

If Origen's paradise and its trees are ahistorical (or, in any case, not physical), then who, for him, was Adam? We are here again hindered by the loss of most of the *Commentary on Genesis*. All we have are the fragments preserved in some subsequent authors and what can be gleaned from Didymus the Blind's *Commentary on Genesis*, which at points explicitly depends on Origen. The exploration of these texts will take us still further into the inquiry of Origen's understanding of historicity and allegory and will also touch on Origen's wider thought on human personhood and its alleged preexistence. When it comes to creation, especially of human beings, in God's image, as body and soul, and as fallen, he makes different claims in different contexts. *On First Principles* and the Johannine commentary have led critics ancient and modern to believe that he distinguishes two human falls or two stages of fall: one of all the preexistent intellects or souls away from the heavenly realm into material bodies, and one primordial "Adamic" fall and its legacy. This is the contention of Caroline Bammel,[73] among others; however, Marguerite Harl shows that Origen speaks in different ways about the fall, depending on which *aspect* of the divine act of creation he is addressing. Her compelling claim is that Origen does not, in fact, teach the bona fide doctrine of preexistent souls that was later attributed to him.[74] Rather, in one mode of discourse about creation and the fall (where Origen seeks to explain the unity and diversity of creation), he makes no reference to the biblical paradise narrative; on the other hand, his discussion of the particularities of the human fall, as well as of biblical exegesis in general, hinges on it.

Indeed, Origen delineates two registers to reckon creation and the fall. In some passages, such as *DP* 1.6; 1.8; 2.3; and 3.5, Origen's main point is the unity and integrity of created things and the equality of rational beings.[75] Here he speaks of the "end times" in relation to ideal origins—a restoration (ἀποκατάστασις)—and his thoughts about the end and the beginning frequently inform each other:

> The end is always like the beginning; as there is one end of all things, so we must understand that there is one beginning of all things, and as there is one end of many things, so from one beginning arise many differences and varieties, which in their turn are restored, through God's goodness, through their

73. Bammel, "Adam in Origen," 68–69.
74. Harl, "Préexistence des âmes." The human intellects that were alleged to inhabit a preexisting (and coeternal) realm with God are better understood in terms of divine foreknowledge and providence—which is precisely how Origen refers to them later in his work, as Harl shows.
75. This concern may stem equally from a (Platonic) ideal of unity and simplicity as well as from a contention against the (gnostic) teaching that God created human beings in an arbitrarily unequal fashion.

subjection to Christ and their unity with the Holy Spirit, to one end, which is like the beginning. (1.6.2)[76]

This passage, which takes place within a discussion of the eschaton, when "all things will be made subject to Christ" and "the last enemy shall be destroyed" (1 Cor. 15:25–28), also calls attention, however, to "the beginning," as the end is a cyclic return to origins. The ideal characters of both origin and end are connected to unity, as opposed to plurality, diversity, and variety, which seek resolution and restoration. In this context Origen does not refer to paradise or to any aspect of the biblical creation narratives. His ultimate reference is to God, Christ, and the Holy Spirit, "for only in this Trinity, which is the source of all things, does goodness reside essentially," but he also has in mind all creatures, which have but one equal and simple beginning (*DP* 1.6.2).

Yet in his other mode or register of thinking about creation, Origen is squarely located within the paradise narrative. In some major texts, Origen distinguishes between the creation (ποίησις) in Genesis 1:26–27 (which is an immaterial creation in the image) and the fashioning (πλάσις) of Genesis 2:7 (where the body comes into existence).[77] The intelligences having fallen, Adam and Eve are fashioned; these "protoplasts" are the first "laborers" hired to work in the vineyard.[78] Yet Origen did not consistently teach that Genesis 1:26–27 referred to the creation and existence of bodiless human persons and that 2:7 referred to the addition of the body; his concept of the body itself (with reference to Gen. 2:7 as well as to 3:21) is complex and variegated—at any rate, not defined by materiality alone.[79]

There is a great deal of data in Origen's treatises and fragments thereof—about the formation of the human person (a microcosmic allegory of the universe), maleness and femaleness as referring respectively to spirit and soul, the divine image pertaining to soul only and not body, and the nature of sin and death (mortality being a result of sin but not something created by God).[80] But it is difficult to treat any of these ideas as definitive of Origen's thought.

Let us then pose a basic question to him: did Adam and Eve exist as historic human beings? This question is all the more pertinent as Origen discerned more clearly than his predecessors between things that happened or existed and things that did not. One important conclusion may be drawn regarding Origen's understanding of paradise: his concept of "restoration" to unified

<hr/>

76. The passage cited here is quite different in Jerome's translation. It is not clear whether Rufinus sanitized Origen or whether Jerome was working from (or propagated) a sullied version. Rufinus's rendition does fit more obviously with its wider context. See Origen, *On First Principles* (Butterworth, 53n3).

77. See *Hom. in Gen.* 1.13; *In Jer.* 1.10. See also Philo, *Opif.* 69–71, 134–35.

78. See Bammel, "Adam in Origen," 67.

79. See ibid., 70–74, 88n36.

80. Ibid., 71–74.

origins does not envisage a return to the paradise described in Genesis 2–3. Indeed, other than speaking in terms of unity, integrity, simplicity, and immateriality, Origen does not spell out the character of the eschatological restoration in any detail, certainly not in terms that are recognizable in relation to the book of Genesis.

We know that in *DP* 4 he considers paradise and its flora as being allegorical. Origen ridicules anyone who would take the trees as literal, the fruits as chewable; these point to unspecified other, deeper things. But he does not mention the persons of Adam and Eve in this context. Though he seems sure of what paradise *is not*, he never truly defines what it *is*.[81] Sometimes he sees it as a purely moral realm, the place where people choose the good, something that may be planted in our hearts. Sometimes he sees it as a divine "land" or "place" (χώρά), even if not a physical "space" (τόπος).

Adam and Eve, whether or not they were flesh-and-blood historical persons, operated within that divine space until their exile. But Origen's ambivalent treatment of paradise leaves ambiguous their status as historical persons. Within *On First Principles* Origen refers to biblical texts that could show Adam in a bodily or a spiritual sense. He cites texts that show Adam as having begotten Seth (1.2.6)—bodily—and as having prophesied (1.3.6)—bodily or spiritually. In 2.3.4 Origen speculates that if there is a parallel world anywhere or if one may come into existence, then "Adam and Eve will again do what they did before, there will be another flood, the same Moses will once more lead a people numbering six thousand out of Egypt . . . and . . . every deed which has been done in this life will be done again."[82] But for Origen, this theoretical cyclic repetition could just as easily occur on the historic plane, the allegorical plane, or both simultaneously; the repetition would presumably involve the same "interweaving" of events, images, and types presented in our Scripture. At many other locations in his text, Origen discusses the narrative about Adam and Eve in paradise, speculating about its details: if they had eaten from all the other trees, they would have remained immortal (*In Jo.* 13.223); Eve was susceptible even before her temptation, and this is why the serpent approached her (*De orat.* 29.18); and so on.

The primary evidence in *On First Principles* that might support Adam's historical existence is genealogical. Origen echoes Scripture in speaking of Adam in the same terms as the patriarchs and other persons considered historical; that is, he is one of "the righteous" alongside Abel, Seth, Noah, Abraham, and the patriarchs (1.pref.4). Further on in *DP* 4.3.7 (which we have in the Greek only), Origen blends historical genealogy and typology, saying that all the patriarchs "go back to Adam, who the apostle says is Christ." He continues,

---

81. See ibid., 73.

82. This translation in Origen, *On First Principles* (Butterworth), is from the Latin, which is the only surviving text of this passage. Butterworth (88n1) indicates the Stoic origin of the doctrine of identically recurring cycles.

For the origin of all families that are in touch with the God of the whole world began lower down with Christ, who comes next after God the Father of the whole world and is thus the father of every soul, as Adam is the father of all [people]. And if Eve is interpreted by Paul as referring to the Church, it is not surprising (seeing that Cain was born of Eve, and all that come after him carry back their descent to Eve) that these two should be [types] of the Church; for in the higher sense all [people] take their beginning from the Church. (4.3.7)[83]

In other treatises, Adam as a genealogical figure also collides in Origen's thought—much as it does in Scripture itself—with the fact that *'adam* means "humanity" (ἄνθρωπος). In *Against Celsus* Origen addresses the Pauline "all die in Adam" and the idea that we were condemned "in the likeness of Adam's transgression": "Here the divine Word says this not so much about an individual as of the whole race" (οὐχ οὗτος περὶ ἑνός τινος ὡς περὶ ὅλου τοῦ γένος), for "the story of Adam and his sin will be interpreted philosophically by those who know that Adam means *anthrōpos* in the Greek language, and that in what appears to be concerned with Adam, Moses is speaking of the nature of man" (*C. Cels.* 4.40). Similarly in the same treatise, Origen speaks of "the earthly region into which Adam, which means man, came after being cast out of paradise for his sin" (7.50). Origen follows Genesis 1–5 in deftly maintaining the ambiguity between Adam as historic person and Adam as the name of humanity: "What is expressed in the form of a story [can have] both something true in its literal meaning and also indicate some secret truth" (5.31).

But could Adam remain a mythical figure even if he stands at the beginning of a purportedly historical genealogy? In the Greco-Roman schools on which Origen is said to be dependent, the legendary and mythical regularly intruded on the historical. As Russell observes:

> The archaic Greek poets were to some extent persons of legend. Hesiod defeats Homer at the funeral games of Amphidamas. Sappho learns from the rock. Ibycus's murder is avenged by cranes. The eagle drops the tortoise on Aeschylus's head. Such legends may be based on poems, or they may be folk-tales given a new name and habitation.[84]

The Trojan War—whose historicity Origen knew was under suspicion (*C. Cels.* 6.42)—figures into ancient historical chronologies. Theseus was descended from Poseidon, Heracles from Zeus. "In the eyes of the [ancient] Greeks, Odysseus is as real, as historical, as Agamemnon."[85] It would have been unlikely for Origen to make the connection explicit between the scriptural Adam

---

83. Translation from Origen, *On First Principles* (Butterworth). Christ as Adam and Eve as the church are confirmed in Didymus, *Commentary on Genesis*, as well as in Socrates, *Church History*. See Bammel, "Adam in Origen," 74–75.

84. Russell, *Criticism in Antiquity*, 162.

85. Calame, *Myth and History*, 10.

and the figures of myth; Christians generally equated "myth" with "Greek myth," untrustworthy and superseded by Scripture. The term μῦθος had not yet undergone the transformation that would cast it in a potentially positive, truth-bearing light. Yet there may be an implicit connection with Greco-Roman sensibilities. Genealogies are preeminently functional in their character; their purpose for Origen and the scriptural authors is to establish a lineage that dates from universal beginnings. Arguably even if Origen had no particular reason to doubt Adam's historicity, it is of no consequence as such to his theological vision.

ADAM AS SINNER

Origen presents several different portraits of Adam as sinner. In the *Commentary on John*, he suggests in a speculative tone that, because God would not have created something imperfect or incomplete (ἀτελής) and certainly would not have entrusted the care of paradise to someone imperfect, Adam would probably have to have been perfect—at least until the transgression (*In Jo.* 13.237–41). In the same passage, Origen speaks of the "human fall" rather than "Adam's fall." Elsewhere he notes that Eve, for her part, was anything but perfect even before the transgression (*De orat.* 29.18). And elsewhere still, both Adam and Eve are said to have rightly shut the eyes of their senses and looked only with the eyes of the soul—until, that is, their transgression, when "the [sensory] eyes of both were opened" (*C. Cels.* 7.39, referring to Gen. 3:7).[86]

Like many of the Jewish and Christian authors mentioned earlier, Origen saw Adam's sin as a relatively petty offense, especially compared with Cain's (*In Jer.* 16.4). Irenaeus had stretched the scriptural evidence to say that Adam repented (*AH* 3.23.5); Origen does not go quite so far, but he still finds it better that Adam "hid himself" in humility whereas Cain "went away from the presence of the Lord" (Gen. 4:16). Like Irenaeus, Origen wanted to show that God's promise of death was "on the day" that the fruit was eaten. He was the first to conclude that the promised and actual death that occurred was spiritual in nature, "for the soul that has sinned is dead" (*Hom. in Gen.* 15.2). Origen can then say elsewhere that the devil murdered Adam not just as a particular individual but through him killed the whole human race, since "all die in Adam" (1 Cor. 15:22, *In Jo.* 20.225).

Origen frequently refers to 1 Corinthians 15:22, sometimes to call attention to the Hebrew pun on "Adam," which effectively departicularizes the man. The thrust of "all die in Adam" is thus not the identity of Adam or his responsibility in originating and propagating sin but the identification with sin itself (*C. Cels.* 4.40; 7.50). Adam, in this way, becomes an emblem for "sin."[87] "All die

86. See also *In Num.* 17.3.3.

87. Origen discusses why reference is made to Adam and not to Eve, who was technically the first to sin after the serpent. His argument rests on patriarchal genealogy (*In Rom.* 5.1.12–14).

in Adam," and sins "like the transgression of Adam" (Rom. 5:14) refer, again, to "the whole race." He interprets the elements of the story as universal: "The curse of Adam is shared by all people. There is also no woman to whom the curses pronounced against Eve do not apply" (*C. Cels.* 4.40). Yet he also sees them as particular to each individual, as each continues to bear the freedom to live in Adam or in Christ. Every person can, "in Adam, [be] cast out of paradise, and every person eats his bread by the sweat of his brow until he returns to the earth from which he was taken" (7.28). The beginning of *In Rom.* 5 sets out at length that "in Adam all die" does not mean that everybody dies. Instead, "many" will die, particularly those who sin in the likeness of Adam's sin (*In Rom.* 5.1.1–8), whereas "those who are dead to the world through Christ are strangers to death and sin" (5.1.16). Origen distinguishes "death," which is universal (as is some degree of sin), from "being under the dominion of death"—which helps explain Romans 5:14—but he leaves a certain openness as to how to interpret the spread of death to all people in Romans 5:12: this passage may be interpreted "either simply and straightforwardly, or it may be considered a mystery" (5.1.36). It depends on what exactly is meant by "sin" and "death" in this context.

Origen unapologetically espouses different views concerning Adam's sin and its transmission of death. On the one hand, he emphasizes Adam as progenitor of sin, and all human beings descended from him are therefore subject to what he began. But he also sets up Adam as a figurative emblem of sin, saying that any person who sins is, in effect, Adam; any person who is "earthly" and "bears the image of the earthly" (see 1 Cor. 15:47, 49) is one "through whom sin enters the world, and through sin, death" (*In Rom.* 5.1.15). Throughout his treatment of Romans 5:12–14, which he links with 1 Corinthians 15:45–49, Origen emphasizes both the precision of Paul's words and the unfathomable mystery to which they refer. Therefore he refrains from limiting the hermeneutical directions, drawing on the fruitfulness of the various possibilities, both genealogical and moral. As Bammel notes, "His aim was not to dogmatize or to force his biblical material into a straitjacket, but rather to do justice to the multiplicity, complexity, and variety of the biblical pronouncements concerning Adam, human nature, and the fall."[88]

ADAM AS TYPE

When Origen comes to comment on Romans 5:14b (*In Rom.* 5.1.38),[89] where Adam is said to be a τύπος τοῦ μέλλοντος (a type of the coming one), he calls this expression ambiguous. Is Adam a type of a future age yet unexperienced by Paul? Or is he a type of Christ? Technically, the verse could be translated

---

88. Bammel, "Adam in Origen," 83.
89. Rufinus heavily abbreviated Origen's treatment of Rom. 5:12–14. See Bammel, "Adam in Origen," 92n88.

either as "a type of the one who was to come" or "a type of that which is to come," but given its context—the Adam-Christ relationship—it is difficult to imagine the latter reading. Earlier, in 1.13.4, Origen had no problem speaking of the typological relationship between Christ and Adam, particularly where the relationship was not one of contrast: the first Adam was a type of "Christ the vine," and both vines have produced both fruitful and unfruitful branches. Origen takes a moment to reflect on the notion that it is a typology "on the basis of contraries" (*ex contrariis*). As he unfolds this revelation in *In Rom.* 5.2.2–15, he seems almost ashamed of the comparison between the one in whom the world was founded and the lowly creature whose only claim to fame, other than being "protoplast," is that he sinned and was evicted from paradise. Origen takes pains to make sure his readers understand that Adam is a type of Christ in a *contrasting* sense and that he led "many" to death but Christ led "even more" to life.

Elsewhere, too, Origen is quite comfortable typologizing Adam and paradise in a variety of ways, making links within OT Scripture as well as (most commonly) between the OT and the NT. Paul's own typological analysis resurfaces in *Hom. in Gen.* 9.2. There—the relationship of contrasts being explicit from the outset (drawing also on 1 Cor. 15:47–49)—the thrust returns to the moral: presented with the old Adam and the new Adam, all have the opportunity to participate in the one or the other. In the same passage Origen says that God's injunction to "be fruitful and multiply" (Gen. 1:28) prefigures what happens in the church when the gospel is preached to the ends of the earth.[90] Indeed, Origen's typological interpretation of Genesis 2–3 frequently encompasses also the church, with reference to Ephesians 5:32. In *In Matt.* 14.17 he cites Genesis 2:24 ("and the two will become one flesh" NETS) as the reference for Christ's fidelity to his former wife (the synagogue—it was she who revolted against him). The image is expanded: Christ fulfills Genesis 2:24 when he leaves his heavenly Father and his mother (the heavenly Jerusalem) to join to his wife, the church, and the two became one flesh (with reference to John 1:14).[91] Here and elsewhere Origen effectively links Ephesians 5:32—the mystery of Christ and the church—to Adam and Eve, in that Christ takes the church, even in an unworthy state, as his bride and gives himself up for her (see *In Cant.* 2.3). As already mentioned, in *DP* 4.3.7 Origen writes that "all go back to Adam, who the Apostle says is Christ." He then avers that just as Adam is the father of all human beings, so Christ is the father of all who are directed toward God. And since Paul equates Eve with the church, it seems reasonable to see Eve (and Adam) as figures of the church: "in the higher sense" all take their beginning from the church.

90. See also *In Cant.* 2.8.
91. Bammel, "Adam in Origen," 91n80, points us to Didymus, *In Gen.* 62.21–22, where likewise "every rational creature occupies the position of the female in relation to the Logos."

He also identifies other typological relationships that originate from paradise: Israel's descent to Egypt brings to mind two related *figurae*, the Lord's descent into the world to make the church, and Adam's descent out of paradise to struggle with the serpent (*Hom. in Gen.* 15.5); elsewhere he likens Adam's descent (expulsion) to the sending of John the Baptist (*In Jo.* 2.175–76). All of this testifies to Origen's unified sense of the Bible and to his understanding of time and chronology as centered on Christ.

The Centrality of Christ

Origen was yet another early Christian writer for whom Christ is the reference point of time, of creation, and of the divine image—concepts that are all tied together. Typology was but one of the mechanisms through which Origen indicated his thoroughgoing Christocentrism, which pervaded his entire exegetical project. Even the first words of the Bible, "In the beginning," to him signify not a temporal or chronological beginning but Christ, who *is* "the beginning."[92] He opens his Genesis homilies by quoting Genesis 1:1 and asking, "What is 'the beginning' of all things except our Lord and Savior of all, Jesus Christ, the first-born of every creature? In this beginning, therefore, that is, in his Word, God made heaven and earth, as the evangelist John also says in the beginning of his Gospel." He then spells it out: "Scripture is not speaking here of any temporal beginning, but it says that the heaven and the earth and all things which were made were made 'in the beginning,' that is, in the Savior" (*Hom. in Gen.* 1.1). In *On First Principles* as well, Origen takes note of the rooting of all rational beings in the archetype of the Logos (*DP* 1.2.2–3; 2.11.4). In his *Commentary on John*, he speculates more extensively on the various definitions of "beginning," observing finally that God is the beginning and the Word is in the Father (*In Jo.* 1.102). But he also notes that Christ himself is the beginning of those made in God's image and concludes that human beings are made in the image of Christ. Likewise in *Hom. in Gen.* 1: "What other image of God is there according to the likeness of whose image the human person is made, except our Savior who is the 'firstborn of every creature'?" (1.13). "For this reason," continues Origen,

> our Savior, who [himself] is the image of God, moved with compassion for the human person who had been made according to his likeness, seeing him, his own image having been lain aside, to have put on the image of the evil one, assumed the image of man and came to him. (1.13)

Everything, for Origen, comes back to Christ as its primary orientation point. Creation is rooted in this "beginning," Adam is the type of what was to come, and humanity is made in the image of Christ. As Origen elaborates in

---

92. See also Theophilus, *Autol.* 2.10.

In Jo. 1, Christ is the Word of God, by which is meant God's self-expression, the announcement of the divine "mind" (1.277), and yet he is a distinct being who can be said to be both "God" (i.e., truly divine) and also "with God," "with his own individuality" (ἰδίαν περιγραφήν, 1.289–91). Christ is God's spoken Word in and through the Scriptures. Thus it is in and through Christ that the entirety of the Scriptures are to be read and understood. The gospel, for Origen, is not limited to the good news as presented in the canonical Gospels. It is embedded throughout Scripture, even if we know this only retrospectively. The OT did not contain the gospel proclamation until Christ came in the flesh to explain it and "caused the Gospel to be embodied" in it (1.33). Elsewhere Origen exegetes the transfiguration, explaining that at first the disciples saw Jesus with Moses (representing the law/Pentateuch) and Elijah (representing the prophets), but when Jesus touched them, they opened their eyes to see only him, as Jesus, the law, and the prophets were no longer three but one in him (*In Matt.* 12.43).

Literal and Allegorical Exegesis Revisited

We are back, then, to the exegetical root of Origen's theology and to the christological root of Origen's exegesis. We also confront again the question of literal and allegorical approaches. The dynamic of "flesh" (or "body") and "spirit" pertains, in a thoroughly related way, to the contemplation of creation in general, to Christology, and to exegesis.[93] For Origen, the image of the Logos, present in all created things as their rational archetype, is not to be found at their surface but by "lifting up the eyes" in order to penetrate into their hidden nature (*In Jo.* 13.42).[94] One cannot attain to this hidden nature, however, without seeing the physical things themselves. In order to make himself known and thus in order to make God known, Christ must take human flesh, concretely, in history. He also must be "incarnate" in the words of Scripture:

> For just as he is cloaked by the flesh, so also he is clothed with the garment of these words, so that the words are that which is seen, just as the flesh is seen, but hidden within (the words) the spiritual sense is perceived, just as the flesh is seen and the divinity perceived. (*In Lev.* 1.1)[95]

The scriptural words, in their bodily sense, veil Christ even as they express him, make him known. One cannot attain their christological (spiritual) sense without the words themselves.[96]

---

93. See Torjesen, *Hermeneutical Procedure*, 124–38; and Behr, *Way to Nicaea*, 169–73.
94. See Torjesen, *Hermeneutical Procedure*, 109.
95. See ibid., 110.
96. Behr, *Way to Nicaea*, 175.

It is through the "stuff" of Jesus's flesh, in history, that we know him, and through him the Father. Likewise it is through the stuff of the scriptural words, in their plain sense, that we may ascend to their spiritual sense. And the "spiritual" content of both Christology and exegesis is the same: it is Christ, God's Word. This is our goal, and although we need the literal (fleshly or bodily) dimension in order to attain the spiritual sense, we must not remain at the literal level, for, in and of itself, the fleshly or bodily does not avail salvation. Many saw Jesus in the flesh and did not see his divinity. True, many who were not eyewitnesses of the incarnate Christ have come to know him as God's Word, but they relied on eyewitness accounts. Likewise many who read the Scriptures only in the fleshly sense read as if with a veil over their eyes. Removing the veil and ascending to the spiritual meaning is an ascent to the Logos; it is the encounter with Christ.

What, then, is the role of the "plain sense" of Scripture? As we saw, Origen believed that the narratives of Scripture, that is, its flesh, are in many ways broken and imperfect, and this by design. Compared with Greek and Latin classical literature, these narratives often appear in a crude style (Origen had to answer to Celsus for this at length).[97] They deliberately contain discrepancies (σκάνδαλα). The "garment" that is the body of Scripture was written by God's Wisdom, and a great many can be edified at this level, even if it is not the final purpose of Scripture. "[God's] intention was to make even the outer covering of the spiritual truths, I mean the bodily [σωματικόν] part of the scriptures, in many respects not unprofitable but capable of improving the multitude in so far as they receive it" (DP 4.2.8). Scripture was written in a basic language, sometimes taking the form of rustic stories so that it could reach the common people. But even the common people should not stop there. For both the basic nature of scriptural narrative and the σκάνδαλα embedded therein also ensure that exegesis does not stop with the fleshly, literal sense for either advanced devotees or the simple. Along those lines, Origen wrote regarding the Pentateuch:

> The fact that the description is filled with mysteries does not escape even an ordinary understanding. Indeed, the entire narrative, which seems to be written about weddings or the births of sons or different battles or whatever other stories one wishes, what else must it be believed to be than the forms and types of hidden and sacred matters? (DP 4.2.2)

And later:

> After they have once been introduced to Christianity they are easily able to aspire to grasp even deeper truths which are concealed in the Bible. For it is obvious even to an ungifted person who reads them that many passages can possess a meaning deeper than that which appears at first sight. (C. Cels. 7.60)

97. See C. Cels. 6.1–11; 7.59–61.

He thus describes the scriptural narratives as an intentional interweaving of things that happened, things that could or could not have, and things that in fact did not. And Origen says that it is precisely in this spirit of veiling that "the account of the visible creation is introduced, and the making and fashioning of the first man, and then his offspring" (*DP* 4.2.8). Adam, Eve, the trees, and paradise constitute a mixed narrative that serves the purpose of bringing us to Christ. Adam serves within Scripture (especially for Luke) and within Origen's exegesis as a genealogical starting point to ground the patriarchs and the incarnate Christ in the first-formed of all human beings, thus making Jesus truly one of the human race as well as of the line of David. But the stories and their human, animal, geological, and agricultural characters and details also serve as the shell, flesh, garment, and veil of meanings beyond themselves. They carry rich and rather self-evident moral and etiological lessons about the nature and vocation of the human person and the origin and consequence of sin. But they also carry deeper meanings that culminate in, and point toward, the divine Word himself. This once again is the destination point of all Scripture, and this, too, is where Origen—not as a systematician but as a Christian and pastoral exegete—sought to lead his readers. It is to this that he devoted his entire life.

Conclusions

Given that no human being was present during the six days of creation and no third-party observer was in the garden of Eden, a literal-historical interpretation of Genesis 1–3 presupposes a very particular concept of the divine inspiration of Scripture: Adam and Eve may have reported to their family about their exploits in the garden, and word may have come to Moses. But God was the only witness to the six days of creation and to the divine deliberation on creating the human person. Inspiration in this case must constitute the divine dictation of history and science to Moses as the amanuensis. Not many early Christian writers paused to consider these implications, but Origen did. He concluded that Scripture had indeed been dictated to Moses by the Holy Spirit, to the very last letter (see *Phil.* 2.4). Yet the Holy Spirit dictated not history but stories that contained complexities and difficulties, with the intention of inviting readers into the deepest and most serious engagement.

Already by Origen's day, Christians versed in cosmology were faced with a choice: either suspend their belief in nature as they observed it, or suspend their insistence on the literal or scientific interpretation of Genesis 1–3. Origen seemed to opt for the latter, yet his understanding of Scripture had never been wedded to a scientific interpretation in the first place, so he never felt forced to suspend anything. In his genealogical mode of thought on the matter, he probably conceived Adam and Eve as actual persons. But he saw it as sheer folly to hold that Genesis 2 described a physical garden planted by God, with trees from which one could pluck and eat.

It did not help his cause that he also offered an allegedly more far-fetched allegorical account of the Hexaemeron. This enterprise was so challenging to a particular mind-set that it damned Origen's whole enterprise, as we shall see in the next chapter. Somehow the Cappadocians, especially Gregory of Nazianzus, were able to elude similar castigation despite Nazianzen's own insistence (dependent on Origen) that we ought not take Genesis 2–3 literally. As we take up the Cappadocians now, we might bear in mind the aftershocks of Origen's teaching outside its parameters.

One important example is his teaching on the fall. However inconsistently Origen reckoned Adam and his legacy, he had a strong sense of human fallenness, which he attributed sometimes to the Adamic transgression and sometimes to God's preexisting ideas for humanity. This emphasis was taken up within the maelstrom of the Origenist controversy. Pelagius's teaching on the self-sufficient goodness of human nature was part of an anti-Origenist wave, and Augustine's anti-Pelagian stance could be seen as Origenist in the sense of retaining a strong doctrine of the human person as fallen. Yet given the condemnation of the alleged teaching of preexistent souls, Augustine placed the burden of human fallenness entirely on Adam.[98] This, of course, is another story. But it serves to emphasize that Origen dropped a very great stone in the water, and the waves were felt powerfully, if inconsistently, through the subsequent centuries. We experience them even to the present day.

---

98. This legacy is nicely summarized in Bammel, "Adam in Origen," 62, and worked out far more thoroughly in Clark, *Origenist Controversy*, 194–244.

5

Paradise, Whatever That May Mean

The Cappadocians and Their Origen

Origen's teaching, its distortions at the hands of detractors and supporters, and its encounters with a still nascent Christian orthodoxy had a powerful, if variegated, effect on the fourth century. Not that the line between Origen's friends and enemies could be so sharply drawn—the Cappadocians, for example, took up some aspects of his legacy, distanced themselves from others, and refuted yet others altogether. Even the precise nature of the criticism of Origen is not always easy to pinpoint. As Methodius of Olympus became a crucial figure in forming the enduring portraiture of a heretical Origenism, he simultaneously relied heavily on Origen's ideas, including the primacy of the spiritual sense of Scripture over the literal.[1] Methodius's main charge against Origen was his teaching that human intellects (pre)exist coeternally with God; this charge was based on Origen's insistence that God must always have had something over which to be almighty. But here again we encounter transmission problems, since much of this argument is available to us only as digested by later thinkers such as Photius.[2] Before studying each of the Cappadocian fathers—and their appropriation of Origen—this chapter briefly examines two who came before them, Cyril of Jerusalem and Athanasius of Alexandria.

1. Farges, *Idées morales et religieuses*, 224–38. Methodius also made use of the Adam-Christ typology, here perhaps following Irenaeus more than Origen; see Patterson, *Methodius of Olympus*, 76–79.
2. Patterson, *Methodius of Olympus*, 200–227.

Cyril of Jerusalem

The early-fourth-century Christian writers continued to follow a variety of exegetical approaches to Genesis 1–3. Typology reigned. Cyril of Jerusalem in *Cat.* 13, for example, retells Christ's passion with reference to relevant passages in OT Scripture, notably the paradise narrative. To wit, Jesus was buried in the earth to reverse the curse on the ground, and he cursed the fig tree for the sake of the fig leaves, which acted as types (13.18). He goes on in the same section:

> And since we have touched on things connected with Paradise, I am truly astonished at the truth of the types [τὴν ἀλήθειαν τῶν τύπων]. In Paradise was the fall, and in a garden was our salvation. From the tree came sin, and until the tree sin lasted. In the evening, when the Lord walked in the garden, they hid themselves; and in the evening the robber is brought by the Lord into Paradise. (13.19)

Adam is a type by contrast, not only for Christ but also for the thief. Cyril gives Christ the following words:

> Most swift was my condemnation of Adam; most swift is the pardon I grant you. Adam was told: "In the day that you eat of it, you shall die" (Gen. 2:17). As for you, today your faith has led to obedience, today is your salvation. Wood caused Adam to fall; wood leads you into Paradise. (13.31)

Adam and the other figures of paradise have become timeless elements in an ongoing story. Christ's words to the thief continue: "Do not be afraid of the serpent; he will not cast you out, for he has already fallen from heaven."

Athanasius of Alexandria

Cyril's contemporary Athanasius uses the Hexaemeron narrative to underline God's creation of the world out of nothing (*DI* 3; *Decr.* 3.13; *CA* 2.57). For him, creation ex nihilo signifies creation in perfect divine freedom, as distinct from the timeless begetting of the divine Son, which is a characteristic of the divine nature itself. (The concern radically to distinguish Creator from creature is definitive of Athanasius's thought.)[3] Regarding the paradise narrative, he too considers Adam a multivalent figure. At a few points Adam serves Athanasius's overarching anti-Arian concerns: Christ was not a created mediator or demiurge. God created Adam and all subsequent human beings without the agency of a created intermediary figure (*Decr.* 8) but, rather, with his coeternal Son (*CG* 46). It is in the image of this Son, Jesus Christ,

3. See Anatolios, *Athanasius*.

the divine Word, that the human person was made (*CG* 2). As was common, Adam continued to play a vital function as the beginning of the universal genealogy (we all descend from him) and of the particular lineage of Christ (*DI* 35). He was also the first sinner, although he did not determine the sin of subsequent generations.

But Athanasius also saw Adam as an indicator of the age to come in his pre-fallen purity. In one striking passage of *Against the Pagans*, Athanasius's depiction of Adam's purity, freedom, and absence of shame presents Adam as something of a mythical figure:

> The holy scriptures say that the first human to be created, who was called *'adam* in Hebrew, had his mind fixed on God in unembarrassed frankness, and lived with the holy ones in the contemplation of intelligible reality, which he enjoyed in that place which the holy Moses figuratively [τροπικῶς] called Paradise. (*CG* 2)

Elsewhere Athanasius writes, "The human person is perfected in the Logos and restored, as he was made at the beginning—nay, with greater grace. For on rising from the dead, we shall no longer fear death, but shall ever reign in Christ in the heavens" (*CA* 2.67). Subsequently, however, he seems to say that Adam before his transgression, indeed before he was placed in paradise, was bodiless and pure through no merit of his own but only through external grace (ἔξωθεν λαβὼν τὴν χάριν). He presents this condition as lamentable, only made worse through sin (*CA* 2.68). In *CG* 2 Athanasius suggested, in a positive light, that pre-fallen Adam had been free from sensual and bodily things, although he did not say that Adam was bodiless. Athanasius is anything but consistent in his concept and presentation of Adam.

The period between Origen and the Cappadocians featured several thinkers of profound importance to the development of Christian theology, perhaps none more so than Athanasius. Their concerns, which in many cases were bound up with the nascent legacy of Origen, were mostly subsumed under the controversy of Arianism, so that their main theological energy was directed toward defining the relationship of the divine Son/Logos to the Father. We might allude to Gregory of Nyssa's oft-cited lament that, whether on the streets or in the baths, people talked of nothing apart from that relationship (*On the Deity of the Son* [PG 46:557B]). Arianism had repercussions for (and origins in) matters that concern us here, such as scriptural exegesis and anthropology, but Genesis 1–3 was not critical to this period, though it would again become so for those who flourished in the last decades of the fourth century.

The main subject of this chapter is the three writers who come to be called the Cappadocian fathers—Saints Basil ("the Great") of Caesarea, Gregory ("the Theologian") of Nazianzus, and Gregory of Nyssa. They were related geographically and had family ties (Basil and Nyssen were brothers) and enjoyed deep friendship (especially Basil and Nazianzen), yet grouping them under one name is, in some ways, arbitrary and ought not be pressed, for their theological output and relationships to the church differed in as many respects as not. But they are treated together here as three towering theologians, whose anthropological conclusions taken from Genesis 1–3 had important and enduring influence and who worked, each in his own way, with the legacy of Origen.

Enshrining Origen: The *Philocalia*

Our first task here is to examine the *Philocalia,* an anthology of Origen's texts that was probably compiled by Basil and Gregory of Nazianzus. Although the legacy of Origen for the Cappadocians is a complex issue, the selection of texts found in the *Philocalia of Origen* provides some indication of what mattered to Basil and Nazianzen. The study-anthology was probably compiled during their monastic retreat in Pontus in the late 350s to early 360s,[4] but at any rate early in their ecclesiastical careers and before their theological writing. The evidence that they alone compiled the *Philocalia* is scarce, and it is not impossible that their participation in the anthology was limited to studying it closely (which they in any case did) rather than compiling it completely by themselves. The very least one can say is that these texts were profoundly meaningful to them and formative for their thinking.[5]

The collection is divided into twenty-seven chapters, with titles given by the compilers. To judge by the number of pages devoted to it there, Origen's understanding of Scripture is what captivated them more than anything else, perhaps an indication that they saw him primarily as an exegete. But it also means that when we listen to what these two fathers say about Genesis 1–3 and about Scripture in general, we must bear in mind their study of Origen—specifically of those very passages that set out his scriptural method and that led him into such trouble later on.

The *Philocalia* opens—significantly—with a selection from Origen's *On First Principles* (4.1.1–4.3.11), a fragment that is cut off before it sums up the doctrine of the Father, the Son, and the Holy Spirit, matters that seem not to have interested the anthologists as much as Origen's exegetical principles.[6] This section is followed in the *Philocalia* by several short passages from the Jeremiah homilies, the Psalms commentaries, and the Leviticus homilies, which reemphasize points already established: Scripture is divinely inspired, and although it contains σκάνδαλα, Origen advises the reader to "first believe, and you will

4. See Junod, "Remarques."

5. See Origen, *Philocalia of Origen* (Harl, *Philocalie 1–20,* introduction, esp. 19–41).

6. In the surviving text of *On First Principles,* 4.3 continues for four more sections that were preserved only in Latin in Rufinus.

find beneath what is counted a stumbling-block much gain in godliness" (*Phil.* 1.28). Referring to the threefold sense of Scripture, Origen exhorts his readers, "Let us search, not for the letter, but for the soul of what we are considering. Then, if we are able, we will ascend also to the spirit" (1.30).

After *Phil.* 1, which is devoted to the foundational elements of Origen's understanding of Scripture, the next several chapters serve to underscore and refine these principles. At the core of *Phil.* 2–8 is the message that Scripture—though through the agency of multiple human authors and in language both varied and at times crude—is a complete whole, inspired in its every word by God's exquisite design. *Philocalia* 9–12 is more specific about scriptural word choices and especially the apparently difficult passages; *Phil.* 13–15 therefore explains the specific principles governing the reading of Scripture that account for its stylistic idiosyncrasies. Subsequent chapters move on to other subjects.

In all this material, taken from a broad selection of Origen's writings from different years in his career, we do not learn a great deal more than we do from the passages examined in our previous chapter. Basil and Gregory had a clear sense of Origen's teaching on the multiple senses of Scripture and on which kinds of people would benefit from which kinds of exegesis. They were also acutely aware of the questions he posed about historicity, including his statement that many events recorded in Scripture did not happen within physical space and chronological time. *Philocalia* 15 contains the passage from *Against Celsus* (cited in chap. 4) that discusses the impossibility, in many cases, of ascertaining whether something (such as the Trojan War) actually happened. Although Gregory of Nyssa's dependence on Origen (or on Methodius of Olympus) will be shown in other ways, the *Philocalia* demonstrates the questions that Basil and Gregory of Nazianzus were grappling with before they began to form the theological positions they would articulate in subsequent decades. What the three Cappadocians develop from Origen's teaching in their own works is quite another question.

Basil of Caesarea

The life and work of this major figure of the church have been well documented.[7] Basil was born in 329 or 330 and baptized in the late 350s after secular training in rhetoric in Athens. Soon after his baptism, he began his period of monastic retreat at Annisa in Pontus, where he was joined by Gregory of Nazianzus. In the early or mid-360s, he began his prolific writing career with a commentary on Isaiah[8] and his treatise *Against Eunomius*. Over the next decade and a half,

7. See esp. the magisterial work of Rousseau, *Basil of Caesarea*. For a more concise chronology, see Fedwick, "Chronology."

8. See Lipatov, *Basil the Great*, which defends Basil's authorship of this text.

Basil produced a large corpus consisting of homilies, letters, ascetical writings and rules, and his treatise *On the Holy Spirit*, among other texts.[9] In 370 he was consecrated to the episcopate and began to mobilize the dioceses around him in a complex and politically fraught atmosphere. In 372 he forced the consecration of his friend Gregory, for which Gregory scarcely forgave him until his (Basil's) death, sometime between 377 and 379.

Our examination of Basil's treatment of Genesis 1–3 will take note of the degree that he adopts, rejects, or ignores Origen's exegetical principles. The precise nature and extent of Basil's involvement with the *Philocalia* is obscure, and it has been suggested that the work was mainly Gregory's.[10] If Basil almost never mentions Origen this is partly because, as a rule, the church fathers referred to each other by name only rarely. Moreover, people with a church career tended to distance themselves from the name of Origen, whose legacy was, to say the least, checkered. His posthumous role in the Arian controversy, which continued to rock the church of Basil's time, did nothing to simplify Basil's ties with Origen's name. He does mention Origen by name at least once, in the treatise *On the Holy Spirit* (29.73), with a mixed evaluation: Origen is not always to be trusted, but sometimes the force of tradition shines through in his works. This suggests that when Origen is correct, it is almost in spite of himself. Yet Basil surely also admired Origen, at the very least through the mediation of his beloved teacher Gregory Thaumaturgus.[11]

Basil on Scripture

To what degree does Basil, in fact, adopt Origen's principles of scriptural exegesis? This question does not allow an easy answer, and certainly not a fixed or consistent one. If the *Commentary on Isaiah* is indeed Basil's—his authorship was doubted in the Middle Ages[12]—it provides a few clues to where Basil stood early in his career on the interpretation of Scripture in general and Genesis 1–3 specifically. The commentary dates from just after the Pontic retreat, where Basil and Gregory studied Origen. Basil concludes his introduction to the commentary by echoing *DP* 4: "Along with every literal [historical] account is intertwined a mystical one" (ἑκάστου τῶν καθ' ἱστορίαν λεγομένων, καὶ τοῦ μυστικοῦ συγκαταπεπλεγμένων, *In Isa.* pref.7). This and his homiletic commentary on the Psalms are his only explicitly exegetical works, but his polemical treatises, orations, and ascetical works are peppered with scriptural reference. Scripture, for Basil, is polyvalent. Typical

9. For a listing of his works, see Fedwick, *Basil of Caesarea*, 1:xix–xxxi.

10. McGuckin, *Gregory of Nazianzus*, 102–4; see also McGuckin, "Patterns of Biblical Exegesis," 45.

11. On the nature of these interrelationships, see Rousseau, *Basil of Caesarea*, 11–14, with supporting notes.

12. Lipatov, *Basil the Great*, iii.

of the fathers, he uses Scripture either inside or outside its original context, interpreting it typologically or literally, and perhaps most often employs it paraenetically—to make a moral point. Indeed, Basil opens the Isaiah commentary as Origen always did when speaking of Scripture: affirming its divine inspiration. But he continues in his preamble by identifying different kinds of biblical writings: "The prophets, the historians, the law, give each a special kind of teaching, and the exhortation of the proverbs furnishes yet another." This understanding—that Scripture functioned in different ways in different contexts—pervades Basil's homilies on the Psalms.[13] It also recalls Origen's testimony to the multifaceted nature of Scripture in his own commentary on the first Psalm, found also in the *Philocalia* (2.3).

What about allegory? He may not have had an Origenistic concept of ascent to Scripture's mystical sense, yet that is what his friend Gregory saw in him. Nazianzen even referred to it in his funeral oration for Basil:

I will only say this of him. Whenever I handle his [commentary of the] Hexaemeron, and take its words on my lips, I am brought into the presence of the Creator, and understand the words of creation, and admire the Creator more than before, using my teacher as my only means of sight. Whenever I take up his polemical works, I see the fire of Sodom, by which the wicked and rebellious tongues are reduced to ashes, or the tower of [Babel], impiously built, and righteously destroyed. Whenever I read his writings on the Spirit, I find the God whom I possess, and grow bold in my utterance of the truth, from the support of his theology and contemplation. *His other treatises, in which he gives explanations* [ἐξηγήσεσιν] *for those who are shortsighted, by a threefold inscription on the solid tablets of his heart, lead me on from a mere literal or symbolical interpretation to a still broader view, as I proceed from one depth to another, calling upon deep after deep, and finding light after light, until I attain the highest pinnacle.* When I study his panegyrics on our athletes, I despise the body, and enjoy the society of those whom he is praising, and rouse myself to the struggle. His moral and practical discourses purify soul and body, making me a temple fit for God, and an instrument struck by the Spirit, to celebrate by its strains the glory and power of God. In fact, he reduces me to harmony and order, and changes me by a Divine transformation.[14]

This is more than a beautiful panegyric for a beloved friend. Gregory attributes to Basil a "threefold sense of Scripture" that leads, as this translation has it, from the "mere literal or symbolical." But what the Greek actually says is that Basil leads us away from seeing either *exclusively* literally or spiritually; he takes us further, from depth to depth.[15] The beauty of Basil's exegesis, then,

---

13. See Gribomont, "L'origénisme de saint Basile," 1:286–87.
14. Gregory of Nazianzus, *Or.* 43.67; translation from *NPNF*[2] 7:417–18, emphasis added.
15. μὴ μέχρι τοῦ γράμματος ἵστασθαι μηδὲ βλέπειν τὰ ἄνω μόνον, ἀλλὰ καὶ περαιτέρω διαβαίνειν, καὶ εἰς βάθος ἔτι χωρεῖν ἐκ βάθους.

is not that it moves from the literal to the allegorical but that it shuns the exclusivity of either. To that extent, he sounds much like Origen.

But do Gregory's words really describe Basil? Modern commentators say not. They often refer to a passage in the ninth Hexaemeron homily where Basil, speaking of Genesis 1, seems to decry allegory:

> I know the laws of allegory, although I did not invent them of myself, but have encountered them in the works of others. Those who do not admit the common [κοινάς] meaning of the scriptures say that water is not water, but some other nature, and they explain a plant and a fish according to their opinion. They describe also the production of reptiles and wild animals, changing it according to their own notions, just like the dream interpreters, who interpret for their own ends the appearances seen in their dreams. When I hear "grass," I think of grass, and in the same manner I understand everything as it is said, a plant, a fish, a wild animal, and an ox. "Indeed, I am not ashamed of the gospel" [Rom. 1:16]. And, although those who have written about the world have argued much about the shape of the earth, whether the earth is a sphere, or a cylinder, . . . I shall not be persuaded to say that our version of the creation is of less value because the servant of God, Moses, gave no discussion concerning the shape and did not say that its circumference contains one hundred and eighty thousand stades, nor measured how far its shadow spreads in the air when the sun passes under the earth, nor explained how, when this shadow approaches the moon, it causes the eclipses. . . . Shall I rather give glory to Him who has not kept our mind occupied with vanities but has ordained that all things be written for the edification and guidance of our souls? This is a thing of which they seem to me to have been unaware, who have attempted by false arguments and allegorical interpretations to bestow on the Scripture a dignity of their own imagining. But, theirs is the attitude of one who considers himself wiser than the revelations of the Spirit and introduces his own ideas in pretense of an explanation. Therefore, let it be understood as it has been written. (*In Hex.* 9.1)

The problem with citing these words out of context—or worse, isolating certain sentences from the whole passage—is that they sound like an attack on allegory in general and perhaps Origen in specific. This, at any rate, is how the passage has been read by many commentators.[16] Although Origen did work in "spiritual" ways with the Hexaemeron narrative, how much he did so is not evident to us.[17] Whatever the date of Basil's homilies, he wrote them around the time Epiphanius was making his catalog of heresies, which included the charges against Origen's alleged allegorization of Genesis 1. But Epiphanius's charges—and again we cannot know their accuracy—concerned primarily the

16. See R. Lim, "Politics of Interpretation," 365n1.

17. Recourse to the *Commentary on Genesis* of Didymus, for whom Origen's lost commentary was the principal source (see Nautin and Doutreleau's translation, *Sur la Genèse*, 1:22–24), cannot provide a conclusive answer, for even if Origen put many of the words into Didymus's mouth, it does not mean he was always Didymus's sole source or influence.

alleged allegorization of the stars, the waters, and paradise itself, which Basil does not single out. To interpret this passage as anti-allegorical either makes Basil sound positively hypocritical or misrepresents him. For elsewhere he either acknowledges multiple senses of Scripture or is seen making extensive (if sometimes only implicit) allegorical use of it—for example, in order to arrive at his teaching on the Holy Spirit.[18]

> The one who has been empowered to look into the depth of the meaning of the law, and, after passing through the obscurity of the letter, as through a veil, to arrive within things unspeakable, is like Moses taking off the veil when he spoke with God. He, too, turns from the letter to the Spirit. So with the veil on the face of Moses corresponds the obscurity of the teaching of the law, and spiritual contemplation with the turning to the Lord. He, then, who in the reading of the Law takes away the letter and turns to the Lord. (*DSS* 21.52)

Could the Basil of *In Hex.* 9.1 be the same Basil who said that in the book of Isaiah, "along with every literal [historical] account is intertwined a mystical one"?

The fact is that Basil's chief annoyance is less with allegory than with the completely arbitrary or translational exercise of it, where the original word bears no perceptible relationship to its alleged true (spiritual) meaning. Basil targets "excessive allegorization of details such that the moral import of the text's overarching *skopos* loses itself in a welter of secondary details," which, we might add, lead ultimately to heretical teachings.[19] It was precisely this kind of allegory that was practiced by the Manichaeans, the probable referents not only here but earlier in the Hexaemeron homilies as well, at *In Hex.* 2.2. There Basil speaks of "counterfeiters of truth, who do not teach their minds to follow Scripture, but distort its meaning according to their own will," the result of which is the refutation of the teaching of creation out of nothing. Basil's reaction may be attributed to a cumulative effect: when enough people start saying that nothing in the Bible is what it really seems to be, it is natural to return to literalism. Basil's frustration in this passage—"Grass is grass! A fish is a fish!"—calls to mind Freud's: "Sometimes, gentlemen, a cigar is just a cigar."

Some scholars have suggested that Basil's rant against arbitrary allegory in *In Hex.* 9 was a response to his audience's dissatisfaction with an earlier, overly literal approach to Genesis 1:6.[20] This is quite possible, given that these homilies were presented extemporaneously[21] and at points engendered

18. See Pelikan, "'Spiritual Sense' of Scripture"; also McGuckin, "Patterns of Biblical Exegesis," 46–47.
19. McGuckin, "Patterns of Biblical Exegesis," 45.
20. This point is made by R. Lim at the close of his essay. See "Politics of Interpretation," 370n79.
21. See Basil, *Hom.* 350 (Way, ix).

a spirited exchange between Basil and his listeners.[22] But who were these listeners, and what effect might they have had on the character of his remarks? Basil refers to his audience frequently. At the beginning of the third sermon, he addresses the artisans among his hearers, who work hard for a living. He professes worry about detaining them too long from their livelihood. He speaks of God's "workshop" in the creation of the world, in canny homage to them.[23] At the end of the seventh and eighth homilies, he exhorts his hearers to discuss these issues at the dinner table and worries that many will go out from the church and return to the gaming tables. Gregory of Nyssa describes Basil's audience for these homilies in his own "further explanation" of the Hexaemeron:

> He spoke to a large audience present in this church and made provision for them to receive his message. Among the many listeners were some who grasped his loftier words, whereas others could not follow the more subtle train of his thought. Here were people involved with private affairs, skilled craftsmen, women not trained in such matters together with youths with time on their hands; all were captivated by his words, were easily persuaded, led by visible creation and guided to know the Creator of all things. Should anyone assess the words intended by the great teacher, no doubt he would not omit a single one. They were unfamiliar with senseless controversy concerning the matter under discussion, nor were they entrapped by questions; instead, a simpler explanation sufficed so that they could attend to his words with uncomplicated minds.[24]

As Gregory notes, Basil tailored his exegesis to his audience. We know of his familiarity with Origen's *DP* 4 and his threefold sense of Scripture, surely Basil was acutely aware of his listeners and the level of exegesis that would most suit them. (In the *Philocalia*, Origen's different senses of Scripture correspond to the different levels of its hearers.)[25] In some of these same passages, Origen remarks that even "ordinary minds" are aware of the deeper senses of Scripture and should not stop at the literal.[26] But Basil throughout the Hexaemeron homilies expounds on the basic, literal sense, simultaneously alluding to the deeper meaning by reiterating that Moses's account was not about physical science. As he says in *In Hex.* 9, God's intention, through Moses, is "not [to keep] our mind occupied with vanities, but [rather He] has ordained that all things be written for the edification and guidance of our souls" (9.1).

22. "How much trouble you caused me in my previous lectures, demanding the reason for the invisibility of the earth . . . !" (*In Hex.* 4.2).

23. This point is made in McGuckin, "Patterns of Biblical Exegesis," 45.

24. Gregory of Nyssa, *In Hex.* (PG 44:66). R. Lim, "Politics of Interpretation," 362, refers to this passage.

25. R. Lim, "Politics of Interpretation," 362–63, points to other ancient writers who paid attention to matching particular audiences with different levels of interpretation.

26. Origen, *DP* 4.2.2 (*Phil.* 1.15); *C. Cels.* 7.60 (*Phil.* 15.10).

Basil deemed that the edification in these homilies would best be served by a down-to-earth presentation. McGuckin writes of modern analyses of Basil's fine-tuning of his rhetoric:

> Like his audience of craftsmen workers, Basil knows that the *teleology* is the fundamentally important thing. If a table does not have sturdy and equal legs, it hardly matters how well it has been carved. . . . [Basil] delivered these remarks right at the end of his discourses, as if he were apologizing for the 'plainness' of his series of lectures on providence within cosmology. These are graceful but highly rhetorical remarks that have been taken far too literally by subsequent commentators.[27]

In sum, although he was nowhere near as rigorous as Origen in either the identification or the application of exegetical principles, he followed several of Origen's main trajectories. He was alert to different genres and functions within biblical books, and different registers according to which each may be understood. Owing as much to his reading of Origen as to his pastoral sense, he was acutely aware of his audience, whether he was writing or preaching, and he interpreted more literally, typologically, practically, or allegorically depending on his hearers and on the needs of the moment, whether these be theological correction, edification, or ascetical and moral guidance.

Writings

How does Basil apply these principles to the reading of Genesis 1–3? Most of the fathers up to Basil were more interested in Adam, Eve, and paradise than in the six days of creation. By contrast, the Hexaemeron is of far greater importance to Basil, and not only in the homilies devoted to it. Stanislas Giet attributes Basil's interest in Genesis 1 to the influence of the tradition of Genesis commentaries and to the pagan fascination with the constitution of the world.[28] One may question how large the "tradition" of Genesis commentaries really was by his day while not discounting Basil's anti-Arian interest in establishing God's creation of the world out of nothing. At any rate, we hear little from him regarding Genesis 2–3. He shows little interest in Adam. At one point near the end of the Isaiah commentary (*In Isa.* 300), he notes the etymology of Adam's name, much as Origen often did. *In Isaiah* has two other references to Adam, both relating him to Christ: the first Adam's formation not through intercourse but from the earth typifies the second Adam's bodily formation in the virgin womb (201). Following this assertion, Basil likens Adam's pre-fallen state to Christ's childhood: both were ignorant of evil. The difference lay in what each did when he came to know evil: Adam succumbed but Christ

---

27. McGuckin, "Patterns of Biblical Exegesis," 45–46, emphasis added.
28. See Basil, *In Hex.* (Giet, 49).

rejected it (202). Elsewhere Basil mentions Adam only rarely. In the ascetical works, he uses Adam a few times to warn against sins of greed and of the stomach; in other works, he is again the type for Christ. Christ took on our flesh, the same as Adam's; otherwise "we who died in Adam would not have been made to live in Christ. . . . And what need was there of the Holy Virgin, if the God-bearing flesh was not to be assumed from the material from which Adam was molded?" (*Ep.* 261).

In his homilies on the Psalms, Basil makes the parallel between the creation of the human person (ἄνθρωπος, not Αδαμ) in Genesis 2:7 and the re-creation in Christ. Commenting on Psalm 33:9 ("For he spoke, and it came to be; he commanded, and it stood firm"), he suggests that "perhaps 'they were made' [ἐγενήθησαν] is spoken in the case of the first begetting of the human, and 'they were created' [ἐκτίσθησαν] in the case of the second regeneration through Christ" (*Hom.* 350.6).

The anti-Arian character of Basil's interest in Genesis 1 appears briefly in his three books against Eunomius. He distinguishes the creation of the world in Genesis 1:1 from the eternal begetting of the Son (*C. Eun.* 2.2). But here, too, we find an important and recurrent emphasis in Basil's thinking: that the information given in Genesis 1 about the world is strictly limited to its having been created in an ordered way by God. The details are less important than the fact of divine creation ex nihilo and divine ordering. He returns to this theme, especially in the Hexaemeron homilies, but here is how he expresses it in *Against Eunomius*:

> The one who explicated creation for us taught only this: 'In the beginning God created the heavens and the earth, the earth was invisible and unformed' [Gen. 1:1–2 LXX]. He deemed it sufficient to make known the one who created and ordered it, refusing to examine out of curiosity the question of its essence [οὐσία], as this would be vain and useless. (*C. Eun.* 1.13)

Likewise, commenting on Psalm 33:4 ("all his work is done in faithfulness"), Basil enumerates created things, averring that this verse really means to say that the heavens and the earth and the wondrous order in them are testimony to the Craftsman: "We have perceived the invisible God through visible things" (*Hom.* 350.3). With a tacit reference to Origen—the emphasis on the need for the visible (and literal) as a way upward to the spiritual—Basil stresses what matters in the Hexaemeron account. This does not prevent him from drawing evidence from the exact sequence of days as presented in Genesis 1, as he does when he refutes the Eunomian concept of time by referring to the creation of the luminaries on the fourth day (*C. Eun.* 1.21). But the overall weight of Genesis 1 for him rests on the divinely arranged creation.

ON THE HEXAEMERON

The influence Basil's homilies on the Hexaemeron had was considerable even in his own day. Ambrose of Milan drew on them extensively for his own Hexaemeron sermons, Rufinus translated them into Latin, and Jerome and Socrates Scholasticus praised them.[29] Their content is rich and varied; they also expand on themes found in other of his treatises. These homilies are tied together by a moral and soteriological concern: all the points Basil draws out from the biblical account lead him to contemplate the awesome glory of creation (and therefore of the Creator) as well as how to live rightly and attain to salvation.[30] Although he follows the six-day sequence in detail—as a rule, quite literally, drawing implications for what can be seen empirically[31]—he insists at the beginning that neither his homilies nor the scriptural account are about science. Instead, the details of the narrative show that "the world was not devised at random or to no purpose, but to contribute to some useful end and to the great advantage of all beings, if it is truly a training place for rational souls and a school for attaining the knowledge of God" (*In Hex.* 1.6). Basil closes his first homily by returning to what he says in *Against Eunomius*: there is no need to discuss the substance or essence (οὐσίας) of creation in its scientific sense. It is enough to say "God created the heavens and the earth."

Just as Origen had done in his commentaries on the letter to the Romans—a work Basil knew well—Basil investigates (*In Hex.* 1.2–6) the many senses of the word "beginning." The fact of a beginning is crucial, especially in arguing against the pagans ("vain heathens") who contested that God shaped preexisting matter (1.2). Positing a beginning also indicates that there will be an end. There is nothing new here until 1.5, when Basil raises the stakes: whereas there was a clear beginning to creation, there was a certain "condition older than the birth of the world, . . . beyond time, everlasting," wherein God perfected his works. Creation already existed, therefore, in God's mind or ideas. As already seen, this is probably what Origen meant as well, rather than the doctrine of concretely preexisting intellects that was (and still is) commonly ascribed to him. To Basil, this is what Paul means when he says, "in him all things . . . were created" (Col. 1:16). Basil conceives a pretemporal, conceptual creation in God. Later in *In Hex.* 3.10, he will compare God to "the artist [who], even before the combination of the parts, knows the beauty of each and approves them individually, directing his judgment to the final aim."

His next sermon, *In Hex.* 2, begins with an investigation of the invisibility of the first-created world, for Genesis 1:2 as translated in the LXX reads

29. See Basil, *Hom.* 350 (Way, viii).

30. The comments of Rousseau, *Basil of Caesarea*, 318–49, on these homilies are extremely insightful.

31. His interest in the natural world and its workings is particularly evident in *In Hex.* 6–9. As the footnotes in Way's translation of the homilies (*Saint Basil*) regularly attest, Basil's ideas about the natural world are often dependent on Aristotle.

that the earth was "invisible [ἀόρατος] and unformed." The thrust here is to reemphasize that there was no preexisting matter out of which God created. The world was invisible because there was yet no light and no human person to behold it. Basil held that those who teach preexistence were confused because, in the world we know, the material exists before the artisan works with it, even before the art itself is developed. But it is different with God. Here, too, the allegorizations of Marcionites, Manichaeans, and Valentinians (in this instance Basil calls them by name) are shown to be responsible for terrible misunderstandings of what *light, darkness,* and *deep* mean: not opposing deities, good and bad. Instead, they are what they say they are: light, darkness, deep water (2.4). Basil (in 2.5) then raises the question of evil and alludes to the classical Greek doctrine that evil has no existence in itself. He aims to steer our focus away from contemplating evil as a substance and toward our own choices: "Each person must recognize him/herself as the first author of the vice that is in them. . . . So, you yourself are master of these actions; do not seek elsewhere their beginnings, but recognize that evil, properly speaking, has no other origin than our voluntary falls." Basil's rejection of fate recurs strongly throughout the homilies.[32]

In 2.8 Basil shares the perplexity of several early commentators as to how a day in Scripture could be identified, especially before there was even a sun. The inquiry continues the discussion of light and darkness but also touches on the circular nature of time.[33] Eternity, says Basil, operates cyclically; it "turns back upon itself never to be brought to an end." The cyclical character of our chronological days mirrors that of eternity. He appears to take for granted that the days of creation were twenty-four-hour periods, yet he follows with a discussion of ages and eras:

> Therefore, whether you say "day" or "age" you will express the same idea. If, then, that condition should be called "day," it is one and not many, or, if it should be named "age," it would be unique and not manifold. In order, therefore, to lead our thoughts to a future life, he called that day "one," which is an image of eternity, the beginning of days, the contemporary of light, the holy Lord's day, the day honored by the Resurrection of the Lord.

The crux, at least for this first "day," is on its being named "day one," which to him clearly refers to the day of Christ's resurrection.

His third homily, about God's creation of the firmament, begins with the observation that God's "saying," "Let there be . . ." is not a spoken word in the sense of breath passing through vocal chords; rather, "the divine will, joined with the first impulse of his intelligence, is the Word of God." This

---

32. See *In Hex.* 5.8; 6.5; 7.5; 8.7; 9.4. On Basil's "optimism" regarding the fall and human freedom, see Rousseau, *Basil of Caesarea,* 336n112.
33. See also Ambrose, *Hex.* 10.36–38.

is a tacit indication of the only-begotten Son, the coworker by whom God creates. Furthermore, the words "Let there be . . ." draw us deliberately into a mystery and are placed in Scripture to give us the joy of plumbing it (3.2), which is a recurring theme in Basil: in *In Hex.* 6.2 he states, "Theological teachings are scattered as mystical seeds throughout the historical account" (πανταχοῦ τῇ ἱστορίᾳ τὸ δόγμα τῆς θεολογίας μυστικῶς συμπαρέσπαρται); and in *De creat.* 1.4 he writes, "Behold history in the [biblical narrative's] form, and theology in its meaning" (ὅρα ἱστορίαν μὲν σχήματι, θεολογίαν δὲ δυνάμει). We are not far from Origen's concept of the scriptural interweaving of history and mystery, even of σκάνδαλα that would goad us to the pleasure of further pursuit.

At any rate, Basil does not have an easy time explaining what the newly created firmament is exactly. But he is cautious about allegorizing; it was precisely the allegorizing of the stars and the waters that led Origen into trouble with Epiphanius and the other heresy hunters. Basil says on this score:

> And if they tell you that the heavens mean contemplative powers, and the firmament active powers which produce good, we admire the theory as ingenious but we will not concede that it is altogether true. For in that case dew, the frost, cold and heat, which in Daniel are ordered to praise the Creator of all things, will be intelligent and invisible natures. But this is only a figure, accepted as such by enlightened minds, to complete the glory of the Creator. (*In Hex.* 3.9)

Who are these "enlightened minds"? They are the scriptural authors and their enlightened readers, who understand *rightly* that when Daniel speaks of the heavens' praise of God, he is not talking about intelligent beings but about the things of nature, such as the deep and the tempest. As he does in his homily on Psalm 32 (see *Hom.* 350.3), he closes *In Hex.* 3 by invoking the natural theology of Romans 1:20.

Basil continues to develop his theme in the beginning of *In Hex.* 4: the glory of creation bespeaks the Creator. For him, the primary message of creation in all its beauty and order is that the Craftsman is great beyond measure; furthermore, he has creation under his complete control and providential care, an idea well stated later in *In Hex.* 7.5:

> I have heard it said that the sea urchin, a little contemptible creature, often foretells calm and tempest to sailors. . . . No astrologer, no Chaldaean, has ever communicated his secret to the urchin: it is the Lord of the sea and of the winds who has impressed on this little animal a manifest proof of his great wisdom. God has foreseen all, he has neglected nothing. His eye, which never sleeps, watches over all. He is present everywhere and gives to each being the means of preservation. If God has not left the sea urchin outside his providence, is he without care for you?

The secondary message of creation is rhetorical and moral. Basil likens the gathering of the waters—good in the sight of God—to the even more beautiful gathering of men, women, and children in the church where he is speaking (4.6). Natural phenomena frequently invite comparison with human situations and bring moral lessons. When we look at the plants, we are to recall that "all people are grass, their constancy is like the flower of the field" (5.2, citing Isa. 40:6). God wants us to embrace our neighbors as would a vine's tendrils, climbing heavenward toward lofty teachings (5.6). The shining of the sun is like the dispelling of ignorance by the saints of old (6.2). The cycles of the moon resemble the waxing and waning of human endeavors (6.10). And in *In Hex.* 7–9 the habits of sea creatures and land animals, about which Basil knows a great deal, are positively brimming with moral lessons. He shows us the creatures whose examples we should either shun or emulate. Bees, for example, receive high marks in 8.3–4, as do widowed turtle doves for spurning second marriage (8.6). He generally esteems land animals and believes that they possess souls, however irrational. Unimpressed by aquatic animals and their capacity for memory or training—though a visit to a modern marine-mammal show might have caused him to rethink—Basil observes that many land animals clearly have memories, experience and express joy and grief, and feel separation from their companions (8.1).

Given how much he focuses in the Hexaemeron homilies on the moral and doxological potential of the created world, we ought not to be surprised by his apparent anti-allegorical outburst at the opening of *In Hex.* 9. These homilies, for this audience, are about God's greatness as testified by the glory of creation, in both its general ordering and its minute details. This greatness and these lessons are visible to us only when we adopt the simple (ἁπλόος) reading of Scripture that shuns arbitrary allegory. Basil finds the greatest joy and inspiration in the literal, visible, tangible physicality of the world. *On the Hexaemeron* 6–9 acts as a guided tour of the created world—a fourth-century National Geographic documentary, as it were—so that Basil can demonstrate that Genesis 1 is about God and about how we should live.

On the Origin of Humanity

Basil may never have finished the task he set himself in this series of homilies. The ninth Hexaemeron homily closes with a very brief mention of the creation of the human person, what the first person plural of Genesis 1:26 means, and what image and likeness signify. Basil promised to continue the work "later," and Gregory of Nyssa presented his *On the Making of Humanity* as the fulfillment of this task. Yet we have two homilies *On the Origin of Humanity*, whose attribution to Basil was long categorized as dubious or spurious but is lately accepted. These homilies were not preserved with the nine on the Hexaemeron and their style differs considerably. But arguments for seeing them as Basil's own are strong, especially as they seem to have been written at a later time and under different circumstances.[34] At any rate, the author, whom I accept as Basil, presented them as the continuation of the Hexaemeron homilies and makes a typically Basilian reference to his audience: "The church assembled here does not expect a lecture on paradoxical concepts but seeks the resolution of problems with a view to edification" (*De creat.* 2.8).

The first homily picks up where *In Hex.* 9 left off. Citing "an old debt" (having talked about all those beasts, fish, and birds) to discuss more fully the creation of the human person, it revisits themes from *Hex.* 9, developing each a little further: Genesis 1's use of the first person plural of "Let us make" to show the Father talking to the Son and the Holy Spirit (*De creat.* 1.3–4) and the meaning of "image and likeness." "Image" is associated with the rational soul, the outward instrument of which is the body (1.5–7). "Likeness," carefully distinguished from "image," describes the human vocation to become truly like God, in all freedom, following the command "Be perfect, therefore, as your heavenly Father is perfect" (1.15–18, citing Matt. 5:48).[35] Basil was perhaps first among the Christian fathers to call attention to the equality of male and female with reference to the concept of image and likeness: "Nobody may ignorantly ascribe the name of human only to the man. . . . The natures are alike of equal honor, the virtues are equal, the struggles equal, the judgment alike," after which Basil enumerates some of the classically feminine qualities that are unmatched by anything men can offer (1.18).

In the second of these homilies, Basil discusses Genesis 2:7 and raises the question of how it relates to Genesis 1:26–27. He follows the teaching by some that the "making" of Genesis 1:27 refers to the soul and the "fashioning" of Genesis 2:7 refers to the body (2.3–4). Basil's innovation is his observation that Genesis 2:7 constitutes the sole instance where it is not simply said that "God made" but it is shown *how* God made, that is, deliberately and painstakingly. He omits any mention of the drama of paradise and the fall. But he does speak—rather in passing—of the age to come as a restoration (ἀποκατάστασις) of the first creation, where "the human being will come again to his original condition, rejecting evil, . . . [and] will return to that life in paradise unenslaved to the passions of the flesh, free, intimate with God, with the same way of life as the angels" (2.7). He seems to envisage pre-fallen paradise as a state of angelic perfection, even if he is not doctrinaire or consistent in this teaching: this mention

---

34. In their translation of these homilies, Smets and Esbroeck (*Sur l'origine de l'homme,* 13–126) argue for Basilian attribution. Rousseau, *Basil of Caesarea,* 318n1, concurs completely, citing them as the tenth and eleventh Hexaemeron homilies, admitting stylistic inconsistency, and suggesting that Gregory of Nazianzus performed some posthumous editing. See Harrison's translation in *Saint Basil the Great,* 14–15, and also Gribomont, "Notes biographiques," esp. 33–34.

35. On the image-likeness distinction in these homilies, see Rousseau, *Basil of Caesarea,* 341–46, who shows how it is also borne out elsewhere in Basil's work, notably in *On the Holy Spirit.*

of restoration takes place in the context of talking about what foods would have been eaten in paradise compared to what we eat now. He does not feel compelled to press a particular vision of paradise, even if he does subscribe to a concept of eschatological restoration that necessarily posits an ideal protological state.

These homilies on the Hexaemeron and on the origin of humanity represent the efforts of a great theologian and churchman to edify a working-class audience whom he respected and loved. Although he fed them somewhat rudimentary content, based on a practical, down-to-earth approach to Scripture and a deep-seated awe of the created world, he cannot but periodically reveal (the sometimes Origenistic) elements of his theological pedigree. Giet may maintain that Origen had less of an influence than Theophilus of Antioch on Basil.[36] But even if his approach tended toward the literal, Basil was light-years removed from Theophilus's Christ-bereaved literalism. No, throughout them Origen's concepts are to be found: from the preexistence of creation in God's mind, to the mysteries interwoven into Scripture's histories, to a preoccupation with "the beginning." There is even a text-critical moment in *In Hex.* 4.5 that may well be dependent on Origen's *Hexapla.* Let us now focus on Basil's thinking—or lack thereof—on Adam.

"Adam, Where Are You?"

Basil's lack of interest in the person and plight of Adam continues in *On the Origin of Humanity*, although the title would suggest him as an ideal subject. Instead, we hear about anything but Adam. We are invited to meditate on why our head is round and sits on a neck and why we have two eyes; the second of the two homilies trails off on that note. Indeed, these two homilies, as well as the nine on the Hexaemeron, are strikingly similar in orientation with the treatises on providence by Theodoret of Cyrus and John Chrysostom that would appear some decades later, essays that similarly enumerated the marvels, both great and small, of the created world. In Basil's homilies on the origin of humanity, Adam is only mentioned once: in an incongruously long discussion of Scripture's use of the number seven and its multiples, Basil notes the seventy-seven generations between Adam and Christ (2.9). In Basil's *Hom.* 336, *On Why God Is Not the Cause of Evil*—a question for which Adam and Eve and the serpent were commonly brought into service by other theologians—Adam and paradise merit but a brief mention. Adam, as protoplast, as protosinner, does not engage Basil. The reason can probably be found in Basil's preoccupation with personal freedom and responsibility and in his rejection of any kind of determinism, whether astrological or genealogical.[37] Or as he says, "Evil has no other origin than our voluntary falls. . . . Each of us is the first author of his own vice; . . . you are the master of your actions"

---

36. See Basil, *In Hex.* (Giet, 51–56).
37. See citations above, in n. 32.

(*In Hex.* 2.5). So strong was his sense of human free choice that Basil did not even consider an action sinful unless it was done consciously and voluntarily.[38] He thus has no interest in blaming Adam for our sin, because freedom—a part of the divine image itself—trumps all determinism.

We can see most clearly what Adam meant to Basil in his liturgical anaphora. This anaphora is almost certainly Basil's own, even if it makes use of kernels of preexisting text.[39] It consists mainly of a recital of God's economy in creating and saving the human person and culminates by describing an Adam-Christ relationship firmly grounded on Romans 5:12–18 and 1 Corinthians 15:21–22. It is worth quoting at length:

> With these blessed [angelic] powers, O Master who loves mankind, we sinners also cry aloud and say: Holy are you—truly most holy—and there are no bounds to the magnificence of your holiness. You are gracious in all your deeds, for you have ordered all things for us with righteousness and true judgment.
>
> When you created the human being by taking dust from the earth, and honored him with your own image, O God, you set him in a paradise of delight, promising him eternal life and the enjoyment of everlasting blessings in the observance of your commandments. But when he disobeyed you, the true God who had created him, and was deceived by the guile of the serpent, he became subject to death through his own transgressions. In your righteous judgment, you, O God, sent him forth from paradise into this world, returning him to the earth from which he was taken, yet providing for him the salvation of regeneration in your Christ himself.
>
> For you did not turn yourself away forever from your creature, whom you had made, O Good One, nor did you forget the work of your hands. Through the tender compassion of your mercy, you visited him in various ways: you sent prophets; . . . foretelling to us the salvation which was to come; you gave us the law as a help; you appointed angels as guardians.
>
> And when the fullness of time had come, you spoke to us through your Son himself, by whom you also made the ages; who, being the radiance of your glory and the image of your person, upholding all things by the word of his power, thought it not robbery to be equal to you, the God and Father. He was God before the ages, yet he appeared on earth and lived among people, becoming incarnate of a holy Virgin; he emptied himself, taking the form of a servant, being likened to the body of our lowliness, that he might liken us to the image of his glory. For as by a human sin entered into the world, and by sin death, so it pleased your only-begotten Son, who was in the bosom of you, the God and Father, who was born of a woman, the holy Theotokos and ever-virgin Mary, who was born under the law to condemn sin in his flesh, that those who were dead in Adam might be made alive in your Christ himself.[40]

38. See Amand de Mendieta, *Ascèse monastique*, 167–68.
39. See Fenwick, *Anaphoras of St. Basil and St. James*, 19–30. We even see fragments from the anaphora in his other works, e.g., *Longer Rules* 2 and *Ep.* 261.
40. Codex Barberini gr. 336, at f. 15. For ease of reading, I have omitted indication of the copious references to Scripture throughout this prayer.

For Basil, then, Genesis 1–3 was the story of the world's creation out of nothing and its ordered establishment by the almighty Creator. The paradise narrative's significance lay not in its details but along its broadest contours, which carry profound soteriological significance. The first-created ἄνθρωπος was placed in paradise. Not immortal but promised eternal life, he allowed himself to be deceived and fell. Thus ends Genesis 1–3 in the strict chronology of its narrative, but this is not the end of the story. Although Basil adds nothing significant to these most rudimentary elements of the narrative, this was all he needed from Genesis 1–3 to nourish his teaching on Jesus Christ, the Trinity, and the personal and communal life of the Christian. He uses the creation account as a springboard to show God leading ἄνθρωπος to salvation through a process culminating in Jesus Christ—by whom the world was made in the first place.

Gregory of Nazianzus

Basil was barely fifty years old when he died. Gregory of Nazianzus, his contemporary and close friend, outlived him by just over a decade, dying circa 390.[41] These extra years saw him go through difficult times, including his presidency over the 381 Council at Constantinople (the Second Ecumenical Council), an event that is difficult to romanticize after reading Gregory's account of it. But he also produced some of his most important work during these years, including the *Theological Orations*, for which he is perhaps best known. Sermons constitute his most significant theological output. Although he wrote a few crucial theological letters against Apollinarius and a collection of theological and autobiographical verse, he did not compose treatises or exegetical commentaries; he preached his theology.

Gregory's appropriation of Origen is, like Basil's, not easy to discern with precision. We must consider the contemporary church-political situation: anti-Nicene theologians were availing themselves of Origen's legacy more than their pro-Nicene counterparts, so that waving the Origenist flag would have been ill advised. Gregory's involvement in compiling the *Philocalia*, which was likely greater than Basil's, had been a subtle bid to resuscitate Origen's name by drawing attention to the great Alexandrian's exegetical principles and, through them, his spiritual genius.[42] We must presume that Gregory, even more than Basil, is deeply invested in Origen's way of interpreting Scripture to yield an orthodox Christian theology and spirituality.

41. For the chronology of Gregory's life and works, see McGuckin, *Gregory of Nazianzus*, vii–xi.
42. See ibid., 102–4.

ADAM, EVE, AND GENDER

In Gregory we have one of the few early fathers to devote serious reflection to questions of gender,[45] informed by Genesis 1–3. In his funeral oration for his sister Gorgonia, Gregory praises her as an example of "the nature of woman overcoming that of man in the common struggle for salvation" and as one who "demonstrates that the distinction between male and female is one of body not of soul" (*Or.* 8.14). In so saying, he addresses a serious anthropological issue, but he takes the subject no further.[46] In some ways Gregory was a product of his day, which saw both physical and moral strength and courage as the province of masculinity; even the word for these traits, whether describing men or women, was ἀνδρεία. But regarding moral strength, he was convinced that masculinity and femininity as purely bodily characteristics—however dualistic—implied the need to reconsider what really makes a man "manly" or a woman "womanly." He presents Gorgonia as an example that one's sex does not ultimately determine one's personal characteristics and that stereotypes can be overcome.

Whatever he may have said periodically about "feminine weakness," Gregory's sensitivity to the plight of women in daily life and their equality with men in the face of God was unusual for his time. Nowhere is this awareness more apparent than in *Or.* 37, where in the most sustained biblical exegesis in his corpus he discusses Matthew 19:1–12, in which Jesus confronts the Pharisees' question about marriage. At one point Gregory questions why women suffer the brunt of divorce laws while men get off scott-free. The laws, drafted by men, are sexist and as such unacceptable (37.6). He moves immediately to the subject of Eve, so frequently scapegoated in ancient discussions of women's dangerous weakness. Gregory—still concerned with moral double standards—intends to show the men in his audience that they are no better than women and that Christ saves both:

> How then do you demand chastity, when you do not observe it yourself? How do you demand that which you do not give? How, though you are equally a body, do you legislate unequally? If you inquire into the worse: the woman sinned, and so did Adam. The serpent deceived them both; and one was not found to be the stronger and the other the weaker. But now consider the better: Christ saves both by his Passion. Was he made flesh for the man? So He was also for the woman. Did he die for the man? The woman also is saved by his death. He is called of the seed of David; and so perhaps you think the man is honored; but he is born of a Virgin, and this is on the woman's side. The two, he says, shall be one Flesh; so let the one flesh have equal honor. (37.7)

He brings us a long way from the Eve-centered misogyny of Sirach and some patristic texts.

45. Gregory of Nyssa did likewise. See Harrison, "Male and Female."
46. Harrison takes up this matter in "Maleness of Christ," 122–23.

A Genealogical Anthropology

When Gregory does turn his attention to Adam, he focuses on him as the first-created human, the one from whom we are all descended. In *Or.* 14.25 he discusses the freedom in which Adam was created, and this freedom (which "consisted simply in observing the commandments") was given "to the rest of the human race as well, through the single seed of our first ancestor." Elsewhere Gregory expresses this same idea by placing "us" in paradise (as he frequently does, making all of humanity the collective actor in the garden), saying that "we were entrusted with Paradise. . . . We received a commandment. . . . [God] had laid down the law of free will" (*Or.* 45.28).

Adam is therefore a galvanizing figure used to indicate the unity of human nature by being its single point of origin. But this unity is still further realized in the second Adam, who himself—as fully human—can also be traced back to the first. Gregory discusses the "backward genealogy of Luke," going back to Adam in *Or.* 41.4. He brings his ideas on Adam's significance together in *Or.* 33.9, enumerating what human beings share:

> We all have this in common: reason, the Law, the Prophets, [and] the very sufferings of Christ by which we were re-created. For all partake of the same Adam, and were led astray by the serpent and slain by sin, and are saved by the heavenly Adam and brought back by the tree of shame to the tree of life whence we had fallen.

That is—and here we have a crucial and consistent feature of Gregory's portrayal of the first human—Adam is us.

Adam and Us

Gregory's rule of faith (or catechetical guide) in the baptism oration has already provided a clue to what he draws from Genesis 1–3. Focusing on Christ and salvation, he begins by identifying the creation of all things ex nihilo, creation governed by the providence of God. That first creation, writes Gregory, "will receive a change to a better state," here implying what he will state outright in *Or.* 38: the first-created state is not one of perfection but is rather a work in progress. He goes on to speak of the nonexistence of evil as such—a staple of Greek philosophical and Christian thought. This teaching points out that evil is "our work, and the evil one's," the result of "our heedlessness." We cannot blame Adam, for the sin is existential: it is *ours*. He then discusses only Christ and closes with an exhortation to do good works "on the foundation of this dogma."

When speaking of sin elsewhere, Gregory may invoke Adam but not outside the primary context of one's own personal sin: Christ, he writes, "gathered me to himself as he mounted the cross that he might crucify my sin, triumph over the serpent, sanctify the tree, vanquish pleasure, redeem Adam, and restore our fallen image" (Or. 24.4). When Gregory speaks of the paradise episode, the main character is as often "me" or "us" as it is "Adam": the serpent constantly seduces us (14.26) and "I came to know my nakedness and clothed myself in a garment of skin, and fell from the garden" (19.14). We will see more of this logic below in the discussion of 38.12, but here is an excellent summation, expressed entirely in the first person plural:

> We were created that we might be made happy. We were made happy when we were created. We were entrusted with Paradise that we might enjoy life. We received a commandment so that we might obtain a good repute by keeping it; not that God did not know what would take place, but because he had laid down the law of free will. We were deceived because we were the objects of envy. We were cast out because we transgressed. We fasted because we refused to fast, being overpowered by the tree of knowledge. For the commandment was ancient, coeval with ourselves, and was a kind of education of our souls . . . , so that we might recover by keeping it that which we had lost by not keeping it. We needed an incarnate God, a God put to death, that we might live. We were put to death together with him, that we might be cleansed; we rose again with him because we were put to death with him; we were glorified with him, because we rose again with him. (45.28)

Gregory universalizes and existentializes the paradise narrative as he also did gender and genealogy, partly because of the rhetorical and oratorical character of his theology. Not only does it talk about the enormous practicality of Adam, Eve, and paradise; it bypasses any idea that we can blame the person of Adam for our sin or that we inherit his guilt.

ADAM AND THE TRINITY

On several occasions, Gregory uses Adam to help his audience understand the relationship of the divine Son (and the divine Spirit) to the Father as part of his anti-Eunomian argument. Gregory argues that differentiating between the natures of the Father and the Son, as Eunomius does, would be as absurd as differentiating between the natures of Adam and Seth. As in the Trinity, one is unbegotten and one is begotten, yet both are the same nature (Or. 30.20; 39.12). In Or. 31.11, in the fifth Theological Oration, Gregory uses Adam to explain the consubstantiality or codivinity of the Holy Spirit. Here the crux is not Adam's unbegottenness but his having "generated" both Eve and Seth, though in different ways. Both Eve and Seth are "derived from" Adam, one as "a portion [τμῆμα] of Adam," the other as his offspring. Yet both are human beings sharing his same nature, a hope that illustrates the begetting of the Son and the procession of the Spirit from the Father to yield an identity of natures.[47]

---

47. See also Carm. 1.1.3, lines 37–43. For Basil's use of Adam against Eunomius, see DSS 18.47.

ADAM AS TYPE

Gregory frequently discusses the relationship between the paradise and the gospel narratives, primarily as a rhetorical method. In one oration early in his career, Gregory speaks of salvation, the restoration of the divine image, in terms of Christ, "who was superior to and beyond the reach of sin, because of Adam, who became subject to sin" (*Or.* 2.24). He elaborates the types involved:

> This is why the new was substituted for the old, why he who suffered was for suffering recalled to life, why each property of his, who was above us, was interchanged with each of ours, why the new mystery took [the] place of the dispensation, due to loving kindness which deals with him who fell through disobedience. This is the reason for the generation and the virgin, for the manger and Bethlehem; the generation on behalf of the creation, the virgin on behalf of the woman, Bethlehem because of Eden, the manger because of the garden, small and visible things on behalf of great and hidden things.

He gives us not so much a case of type and fulfillment as a focus on the particular elements of salvation and what best represents their *necessity*. Because Eve fell, we needed the Virgin. Because of the fiasco in Eden, we needed Bethlehem. This same kind of logic is also found in a much later oration. In 45.13 Gregory explains some of the imagery used for Christ and details about his person. Christ is a lamb because of his innocence and vulnerability. He is a perfect victim, not only being divine but having divinized his humanity. Gregory calls attention to Christ's maleness—a rarity in patristic reflection[48]—according to three principles: Christ was male "because offered for Adam," because maleness denotes strength (Gregory even notes that Christ "burst the bonds of the Virgin mother's womb with much power"), and because maleness fulfilled the Isaianic prophecy.

Likewise, in *Or.* 2.25 Gregory once more spells out all the elements of paradise that foreshadow their respective fulfillment in the redemptive work of Christ. Here he contrasts the tree of the cross with the tree in the garden, the hands of Christ—stretched out in generosity and fixed by nails—with the hand of Adam, stretched out in self-indulgence and unrestrained. Christ is lifted up to atone for the fall, is given gall instead of Adam's fruit, dies for Adam's death, and is raised so that Adam may be raised.

Despite the Adam-Christ connection, Gregory does not employ typology in the strict sense; instead he indicates different kinds of connections between Christ and that which preceded and either necessitated or foretold him. Our study now follows Gregory's logic through a more sustained passage, which may shed further light on the nature of his typology.

---

48. The maleness of Christ is scarcely ever mentioned by the fathers, even if the fact is implicit in seeing the church as his bride. See Harrison, "Maleness of Christ."

ORATION 38: A TOTAL VISION

We have dealt piecemeal with a variety of contexts in which Adam plays a part. In *Or.* 38 Gregory produces a more sustained treatment of the creation of the human person vis-à-vis redemption. This oration on the Feast of the Theophany, particularly from 38.9 onward, is a tour de force in which Gregory sets out his understanding of creation and redemption.[49] Here, too—although implicitly—Gregory distinguishes between teachings and images that are fundamental and salvific and ideas and images that are provisional in nature. Regarding the latter, at several points Gregory uses qualifiers such as "perhaps" and "by my interpretation," and when he first mentions paradise, he adds the amazing qualifier "whatever this Paradise was!" Let us explore this passage and its context.

The Feast of the Theophany in Gregory's day was celebrated together with Christ's Nativity; the occasion inspired Gregory to tell his hearers about the coming of Christ into the world, an advent that constituted the world's being made anew. But in order properly to understand the re-creation (ἀναπλάσις), one needs first to understand the creation (πλάσις), especially of the human person. So Gregory sets out to discuss God's being, which is beyond time and boundless (38.7–8): since self-contemplation was not enough for God, so God (in the Word and in the Spirit) created the world. Gregory makes clear the sequence of creation: first the angelic or intelligible realm, then the material or sensible (38.9–10). He tentatively presents the nature of the angelic world (as morally "movable" or "immovable") but gives his understanding of the sequence—intelligible, sensible, and then human—unhesitatingly. God then creates material things—and here Gregory makes plain that the material world is good and beautiful, particularly as an ordered whole. True, the angelic realm, being intellectual, is more closely related to God than the material, for the uncircumscribable God is foreign to materiality. But the visible world is "praiseworthy for the natural excellence of each of its parts, but still more praiseworthy for the proportion and harmony of all of them together." In all, God brings together a single, ordered universe (38.10). Although Gregory does not refer here to the Hexaemeron narrative, the sense of ordered material creation (albeit not the angelic) that characterizes that narrative—and Basil's beloved homilies on it—might have informed his thinking.

He uses this as a buildup to his exposition of the creation of the human person (38.11), an exposition that focuses on the concept of microcosm.[50] Until humans entered the picture, the intelligible and sensible realms had no meeting point; each remained within its respective boundaries. (Animals, being material yet sensory—but not rational—receive a passing reference in 38.10.) From the outset of his

---

49. The translation of Daley (*Gregory of Nazianzus*, 117–27), used in this chapter, shines as none before.

50. See also *Or.* 28.22; 40.8; *Carm.* 1.1.8, 61–69.

description of the human being's creation, Gregory makes implicit reference to the paradise narrative, beginning with Genesis 2:7. The meeting of immaterial and rational nature with the material is expressed in terms of God's exhaling into the material body. Gregory describes this breath as the rational soul, which is God's image. Although a certain dualism lurks behind Gregory's anthropology, he accounts consistently (here and elsewhere) for the thorough intermingling of body and soul and uses mixture language (μίξις, κρᾶσις) inherited from the Stoics (14.7; 27.7; 28.3; 28.22; 32.9).[51] So the human person is "a second world, great in its littleness: another kind of angel, a worshipper of mixed origins . . . king of things on earth and yet ruled from above" (38.11). Gregory here alludes to the human vocation: "as the final stage of the mystery, [to be] made divine by his inclination toward God [πρὸς θεὸν νεύσει θεούμενον]."

By what path will the human person attain to that final mystery? Gregory suggests an answer in the next section (38.12):

> This creature God placed in Paradise—whatever this Paradise was!—and honored him with free choice,[52] so that the Good might belong to him by choice (no less than it belonged to the one who provided the seeds).[53] He was the cultivator of immortal plants—divine thoughts, perhaps . . .

Paradise, however one wants to understand it (and Gregory implies that there are a variety of acceptable ways), is the space within which the human person begins to till not the physical earth but the realization of God's seed ideas for all of creation.

> He was naked in his own simplicity, his life free from artifice, and needed no covering or defense. This is the way the original man was meant to be. And God gave him a law, as matter for his free choice. Now the law was a command concerning which plants he was allowed to partake of, and which one he was not to touch.

The human person was simple, but this God-intended simplicity was not actualized until God had first made matters more complex. For paradise is also the space where the human person, endowed with free will, is given the substrate over which to exercise that freedom.

> This latter [the tree not to be touched] was the tree of knowledge; it was not originally planted with evil intent, nor prohibited out of ill-will . . . but was a

51. Gregory also makes clear that the body and the soul together share in the passions, that they are fellow servants and partners. See *Or.* 2.17; 14.6; *Carm.* 2.1.1, 465.

52. Daley (*Gregory of Nazianzus*) translates this as "self-determination," which renders αὐτεξουσία more literally but in this context less helpfully.

53. The following sentence suggests that these seeds are probably God's eternal ideas; see ibid., 227n384.

good thing, if partaken at the right time. For this plant was, by my interpretation, contemplation—something which may only safely be attempted by those who have reached perfection in an orderly way. So it was not beneficial for those still in a state of immaturity, greedy in appetite, just as mature food does not profit those who are still infants, still in need of milk.

What exactly "the tree of knowledge" represents is not a matter of dogma to Gregory; the idea that it was "contemplation" (θεωρία) is a matter of Gregory's own "interpretation" (θεωρία), one that he imposes on no one. What is important for him is that it was something good and intended for human partaking, only at the right time. Here is one of the clearest articulations after Irenaeus of the pre-fallen human as a work in progress, a child.[54] True, in this homily (at 38.16) and in 39.2, Gregory mentions that our goal is to become perfect, "as we once were," in "the first condition of Adam." With this he hearkens back to a lost purity rather than reversing his clear teaching that Adam was not perfect but childlike—pure but still unable to chew real food. In 38.11, describing the original creation of the human person, Gregory has no illusions of a perfected state: God gives the human person a body "in order to suffer, so that he may come to his senses and be corrected from his ambitions of grandeur." The text in 38.12 continues, speaking of the transgression:

> And when, by the envy of the Devil and by his bullying of the Woman—something she suffered because she was weaker, and something she passed on because she was more persuasive; alas for my weakness! for my ancestor's weakness is my own—he forgot the command that had been given him, and was overcome by that bitter food.

Many points emerge from this passage. First is the idea of the devil's envy, found especially in later Jewish thinking as directed toward the human's being made in God's image.[55] Second is the agency of the woman (note that neither Adam nor Eve is named in this passage). Gregory sees her as being both more susceptible to bullying and more persuasive, whether as stereotypical "woman" or simply as this particular woman. In either case (see the feminist Gregory of 37.6–7), far from gloating or passing blame, he brings her transgression, and the man's, back to existential and personal reality, identifying in (and claiming for) *himself* the weakness of the ancestors. (Earlier in the oration, he likewise states that "a taste of fruit has brought judgment on *us*," *Or.* 38.4, emphasis added.) Last, in accordance with the long tradition identified throughout this study, Gregory plays down the transgression to portray it not as a defiance of God but as a mere "forgetting" of the command.

54. See also *Or.* 2.25; 39.7; *Carm.* 1.1.7, 101–11.
55. See Anderson, *Genesis of Perfection*, 25–37. Also *Or.* 36.5.

Then he was banished, all at once, because of his wickedness, from the tree of life and the Paradise and God; he was dressed in tunics of skin—coarse, mortal and rebellious flesh, perhaps. So this was the first thing he came to know: his own shame; and he hid himself from God. But even here he drew a profit of a kind: death, and an interruption to sin; so wickedness did not become immortal, and the penalty became a sign of love for humanity. That, I believe, is the way God punishes!

The "tunics of skin" are another matter for Gregory's provisional speculation (hence the "perhaps"), and death—already understood by Irenaeus, Theophilus, and others as a "mercy"—is a gain, a profit, an advantage, even a sign of divine love, given by God so that sin would have a terminus.

In this way Gregory has set out his explication of the paradise episode as but a part (albeit a crucial one) of a longer narrative, beginning with the creation of the human person as a mixture of natures, passing through human transgression and expulsion from paradise—"whatever that was"—and culminating in the coming of Christ (Or. 38.13), who is seen as "the new mixture" (ἡ καινὴ μίξις). Like the human person, Christ is a mysterious blending of natures.[56] The coming of Christ "establishes a second communion" (δευτέραν κοινωνεῖ κοινωνίαν)—the first being the divine image in the human person, the second being the enfleshment of the divine Son. Summing up, Gregory reverts to the first person singular: "I had a share in the image and I did not preserve it; he took on a share in my flesh, so that he might both save the image and make the flesh immortal" (38.13). Gregory therefore presents us with a large tableau that uniquely and profoundly describes the relationships of identity between Adam and us (in our capacity for sin) and of contrast between Adam and Christ (who is everything that Adam failed to be). The words "type and fulfillment" scarcely do justice to the intricacy and holism of Gregory's vision.

Adam and History

Gregory's phrasing often indicates his openness to how details of the narrative may be understood. Specifically, these concern the human vocation of "cultivation," the first commandment (which in Or. 40.6 he considers to be "light"), the tree of knowledge, the garments of skin, and—lest we forget—paradise itself. Centuries after his death, at least one major Christian commentator, Gregory Palamas, expressed discomfort at how people might understand Nazianzen's exegesis of the tree. Not that Palamas cares, in this instance, about the trees in paradise: he wants to show that the light of the transfiguration on Mount Tabor was both symbolic and real. His interest, therefore, is in symbols:

56. Gregory takes his place in the trajectory of christological terminology that would become enshrined at Chalcedon. See Bouteneff, "Gregory Nazianzen."

In analogical and anagogical theologies, things that are said to have (and do have) a proper existence are called "symbols." It is in this sense that Maximus calls [the light of Tabor] a "symbol," and why he has cannily titled his works "Contemplation" [θεωρία]. So Gregory the Theologian likewise named the tree of the knowledge of good and evil "contemplation" [θεωρία]. For he considered it—in his own contemplation—a symbol of that contemplation which is to raise us upward. But it does not follow that he conceives an illusion or a symbol without proper existence [ἀνυπόστατος]. In a like manner, Moses and Elias [at the transfiguration] are symbols of judgment and of providence, says the divine Maximus! Does this mean that—though they are not really present—they are symbolic inventions? [57]

Palamas then asks whether, if Peter is a symbol of faith, James a symbol of hope, and John a symbol of love, they were acting as mere symbols at the transfiguration. Palamas, following Maximus, needs to call the Taboric light a symbol. But he also needs to affirm its concrete reality so that it would not become a mere image.

Regarding Gregory of Nazianzus, although we rarely find an obvious reference to Origen, we do well to recall his close study of the Alexandrian and of *DP* 4.3 specifically. He cannot but be mindful of the "interweavings" of historical and allegorical narrative within Scripture, specifically within the paradise narrative. He doesn't feel pressed to establish Adam, Eve, the tree, and the serpent as concretely existing phenomena or to categorize them as symbolic. For Gregory as for Origen, the genealogical function of Adam is perhaps the only one that referred (implicitly) to the concreteness of his person. For the rest, the scriptural narrative gave Gregory all he needed to read with the eyes of a Christian who was utterly compelled by the gospel and the desire to explain it to the people of his time.

Adam proved useful to Gregory in a particular set of contexts. He and Eve served as a focus of reflections on gender and sex. He was a genealogical point of origin for all humans and led to Christ; in this way Adam indicates Christ's genuine humanity. Gregory illustrated trinitarian theology in his sermons against both the Eunomians and the pneumatomachians by drawing on Adam's unique condition in having been formed by God rather than born, and in having both offspring (Seth) and something akin to a clone (Eve). Primarily, however, Adam, Eve, and paradise are a collective reference point for human creation and sin, although always with primary reference to the responsibility of each individual human. This, together with the speculative character of the Theologian's exegesis of the paradise narrative, serves to underscore what really mattered to Gregory in this complex and beautiful biblical narrative. Paradise and Adam are ultimately about us and our sin, a story that has its fulfillment in our re-creation in Christ, the second Adam.

57. Gregory Palamas, *Tri.* 2.3.22.

Gregory of Nyssa

Gregory of Nyssa was a member of a large and illustrious family that included his brothers Basil the Great and Peter of Sebaste (the addressee of many of his treatises) and his sister Macrina (a moral and theological teacher of Basil and Gregory alike). He produced much of his work during the same period that Gregory of Nazianzus flourished—the early 380s—but continued to write into the 390s after Nazianzen's death. It was during this late period of his career that he wrote his allegorical works *On the Life of Moses* and the *Homilies on the Song of Songs*, works that also give us useful insight into his understanding of Scripture.

Exegesis

Gregory of Nyssa was keenly aware that Scripture is not self-interpreting: the inspired reading of Scripture is as vital to the Christian enterprise as is its inspired composition. Borrowing from the opening lines of Origen's Exodus homilies, Gregory likens the scriptural word to a seed: its proper exegesis is the resulting tree, on whose branches (viz., dogmas) birds (viz., sublime souls) may safely alight (*In Hex.* 64AB). The forms that proper exegesis may take are widely varied depending on context. Both within and outside the books that he devoted to the allegorical interpretation of scriptural events and persons, he worked to articulate a sense of the nature and use of allegory. At one point, while making a moral example of symbols in Abraham's life, he states that when, "in the lofty spirit of the Apostle," he exegetes Abraham allegorically, he is "penetrating to the inner sense of the history, [while] manifestly retaining the historical truth."[58] Later in the same anti-Eunomian context, he sounds more like Origen, suggesting that the "historical" narrative might act like a veil that needs to be removed. He says that the inspiration of Scripture (2 Tim. 3:16) is not available to just anyone, for "the divine intention lies hidden under the 'body' of the narrative, as it were under a veil." This body may consist of "some historical narrative being cast over the truths that are contemplated by the mind." In such cases, "the obvious interpretation" may indeed "kill" (*C. Eun.* 3.5.8–10 [GNO 2:163] citing 2 Cor. 3:6).

He takes up this logic again in the prologue to his *Homilies on the Song of Songs*. It is his most interesting and complete discussion of allegory and thus serves well as a case study. Acknowledging that multiple readings may be appropriate—he advocates "searching the divinely inspired Scriptures with every means at our disposal" (*In Cant.* prol. [GNO 6:4])—Gregory emphasizes the particular importance of spiritual exegesis, to which he refers with words that all suggest the same thing: αἴνιγμα, ὑπονοία, and ἀλληγορία and

---

58. ἀλλάξαντα τὴν φωνὴν ἀλληγορικῶς τὸν τοῦν τῆς ἱστορίας κατανοῆσαι, μενούσης δηλαδὴ καὶ τῆς ἱστορικῆς ἀληθείας (*C. Eun.* 2.85 [GNO 1:251]).

the adjectives τροπικός and πνευματικός. In his prologue he discusses the ways in which events or persons may carry moral lessons, represent different spiritual states, or foreshadow the cross as a "type"; these literary terms are all a package. He cites 2 Corinthians 3:6 to say that the literal sense, taken entirely on its own, might be "mortal"; it is the "veil" that must be removed (GNO 6:6–7). Unless the scriptural words are "worked over by a more subtle contemplation, [they] are food for irrational beasts rather than for rational human beings" (GNO 6:12). The literal and the symbolic must work together: "Both lead to knowledge of the mysteries and to a pure way of life for those who have diligent minds" (GNO 6:5). He does not spell it out as did Origen (to whose own Song of Songs commentary he refers in the same prologue) to say that the events recorded as history may not have actually occurred. But he is emphatic that "what really happened" is not the most important thing and may, in fact, be quite beside the point. After all, Paul himself, citing the Deuteronomic proscription on muzzling an ox, says that God does not care about oxen; rather, the law was written for *our* sake (1 Cor. 9:9–10, cited in GNO 6:6).[59]

Still, he was puzzled about certain scriptural accounts that would seem to be physically or otherwise untenable, notably the trees in paradise. Twice he discusses the impossibility of locating both of the trees in the "center" of the garden. Both in the prologue (GNO 6:10–11) and in the twelfth homily (GNO 6:348–52) he reveals his frustration: how can they both be in the middle? There was only one garden, and there is technically one center to any circle. So only one tree can occupy the exact middle! To Gregory this can mean only that in such cases we must contemplate the truth of the story "through philosophy" (διὰ φιλοσοφίας), or else the text will "either be incoherent or a fable [ἀσύστατον ἢ μυθῶδες]" (GNO 6:11). Genesis 3:3 in the LXX is easy enough to interpret in terms of two trees "in the midst," or even "in the middle," of the garden;[60] surely, Gregory was simply seeking the excuse to treat the trees spiritually. He found a "stumbling block" to lead us, as Origen said it would, deeper into the meaning of Scripture.

According to Gregory's resulting exegesis (GNO 6:348–52), the story confirms that the responsibility for death and sin lies with the human person and not God. This was the other Gregory's point as well, but Nyssen differs from Nazianzen on the meaning of the trees. For him, they are life-giving and death-dealing, respectively. In effect, therefore, given the geometrical dilemma Gregory poses, the tree of life truly occupies the center of the garden whereas the tree of death is only symbolic, having no real roots (for evil has no genu-

---

59. Origen, *DP* 4.2.5, cites the same passage to make the same point.

60. καὶ τὸ ξύλον τῆς ζωῆς ἐν μέσῳ τῷ παραδείσῳ καὶ τὸ ξύλον τοῦ εἰδέναι γνωστὸν καλοῦ καὶ πονηροῦ.

ine existence). By partaking of the tree of death, Adam and Eve gave it real existence; it was their choice that "placed" it in the center of the garden.

Gregory's exegesis of the paradise narrative is idiosyncratic and inconsistent; the details of the story remain a veil of the deeper meaning. To make a point about the nonexistence of evil, he fixes on the detail of the two trees' ostensibly occupying the center; on the other hand, he completely ignores several of the narrative's more obviously vital features. For him, the lethal tree represents sin and death, which are "good and evil" together (because sin only *seems* good).[61] The scriptural account describes no such thing, identifying it as the tree of the *knowledge* of good and evil. Still, what Gregory has made of the paradise story does not remain at the level of protology and the privation of an ostensible once-possessed immortality. The point for him is that, just as the primordial couple exchanged life for death, we too constantly have the option—only in our case of exchanging death for life. But eternal life requires another kind of death: death to sin, death to a mortally conditioned life (GNO 6:351). Genesis 2–3 finally teaches us about our own lives, for "whoever dies to good lives for evil, and he who dies to evil lives for virtue" (GNO 6:351–52).

For Gregory, history and allegory do not reside within airtight compartments. They are interpenetrating ways to look at the scriptural narrative. Once again, although Gregory does not suggest discarding the basic historical narrative, in his reading it takes second place or at least requires a different kind of analysis to be understood rightly. As we have seen, he is liable to adjust or ignore even some of the narrative's basic details. He fixates on the geometry of the trees of Eden and ignores the component of "knowledge" so central to the scriptural account.

We will return to Gregory and paradise after examining his reading of the Hexaemeron.

The Hexaemeron

Gregory devoted two texts to elaborating or completing the homilies on the Hexaemeron by his brother Basil, whom he calls "our father" and who had probably only recently died. One of these texts was the treatise *On the Making of Humanity*, which will be explored later. The other was the *Apologia to His Brother Peter on the Hexaemeron*. It is, in many respects, a puzzling text: from the outset, Gregory addresses his brother Peter, with periodic reference to Basil's homilies, to testily defend himself against charges—never specified—that Peter had leveled against him regarding his teaching about the six days of creation. The biblical Hexaemeron narrative held an especially sacred place for the Cappadocians—especially Nyssen and Basil. Origen had highlighted the Jewish proscriptions against casual or uninformed discussion of the *ma'aseh*

---

61. See also *In inscript.* 2.13.190 (GNO 5:139).

bereshit, the "work of the beginning."[62] Nyssen echoed that position: "The fact of creation we accept; but we renounce a curious investigation of the way the world was framed as a matter altogether ineffable and inexplicable" (*Or. cat.* 11). Likewise in his Hexaemeron treatise, Gregory asserts that his task is "not to fathom those matters which appear contradictory." What he proposes is "not dogma giving occasion for calumny" (PG 44:68D).[63] He reminds us (*In Hex.* 65B) that the audience Basil addressed for his own treatment of the subject was also unfamiliar with the "senseless controversy" about the Hexaemeron and was better served by a "simpler explanation." Nyssen was writing for a different audience: he therefore allowed himself a more technical and scientific level of discourse, but however willing he was elsewhere to turn to allegory for a text's deeper meaning, he was not about to do so with the Hexaemeron.

First, he establishes God as the One who forms all things from matter, which God himself creates on the basis of his own immaterial ideas (44:69CD). Like Origen and Basil, Gregory contemplates what "the beginning" might be, taking note that his Greek translation of the first words of Genesis reads Ἐν κεφαλαίῳ, which we might render, "in the culmination of things." Both "the beginning" and "the culmination" are of use to Gregory, for the "beginning" is not to be understood temporally, without the interval of time (διάστημα); the "culmination" indicates to him that "everything was created together" (72A). Indeed, later in the text Gregory identifies "one impulse of creation, for [God's] power seminally contained every created being and came into existence through one initiative" (77D).

Gregory surmises that the sequence of days of creation "instruct us about God's wisdom, which preordained all things, and which follow a determined order of sequence" and that nothing has occurred either by chance or by its own authority or power (76BC). (Ἀκολουθία ["succession" or "order"] for Nyssen represents a key to the whole divine economy and appears multiple times in this treatise and *On the Making of Humanity*.)[64] Gregory develops an idea latent in Basil's homilies[65] to form one of his signature doctrines, namely, that the days refer simultaneously to creation on two planes of being: "Who does not know that creation is twofold, one spiritual and the other perceptible, which the lawgiver presents at once? Moses does not refer to those things which the mind perceives, but he manifests them by visible reality to the senses which adorn them" (76D). For Gregory, the bringing of things from nonexistence into being is first a matter of the instantaneous realization of God's ideas in an invisible, spiritual, intelligible manner and, subsequently,

---

62. Origen, *In Cant.* prol.1.7.
63. There is as yet no critical edition since PG 44, which has no chapter delineations. The column numbers in PG 44 are used henceforth in this section to cite passages of Gregory's treatise on the Hexaemeron.
64. See Alexandre, "Théorie de l'exégèse," 95–100.
65. See Basil, *In Hex.* 1.5; 3.10.

(over a period of "diastemic" or chronological time) the endowment of that invisible creation with sensible attributes and materiality.[66] Finally, Gregory sees the days as a sequence of "cycles," self-contained units, each occasioning our great wonderment at the Creator (85CD).

The rest of the treatise, established on Gregory's ideas about the two stages of creation and the then-current principle of four elemental substances, might just as well be entitled *On Fire, Light, and Especially Water*. It consists of page after page (fifteen columns in PG 44) of speculation about water, vapor, ice, and more water, and only then a (considerably shorter) discussion of light. At initial reading, it seems odd to squander the largest part of a treatise concerning the six days of creation on the question of water. This focus may stem from the condemnations of Origen's treatment of the waters, which had allegedly allegorized them beyond recognition. "Spiritualization" of the waters may also have constituted a part of Peter's charges to which Gregory is responding;[67] at any rate, he seems compelled to assure his reader(s) that he is talking of real, material water, the very stuff that freezes, vaporizes, and is found in oceans, lakes, rivers, rain, and mist. And whereas "the wise Moses did not speak as one versed in science about our natural elements" (88C), Gregory is pleased to.[68] Furthermore, he makes explicit his literal treatment, indicating that he has "not changed anything into figurative allegory" (121D) but, rather, desires "to guard the letter of the text and the consideration of nature that agrees with it" (123B). This apologia for the literal reading may seem striking in view of his use of allegory in his other works (albeit he is here writing at least a decade before his allegorical treatises on the Song and on Moses's life). But Gregory—here carrying the legacy of Basil's homilies—is not arguing that the Hexaemeron is a scientific account that is to be taken literally in all its dimensions. He is saying only that it refers to actual water, light, earth, and stars, the things we see, and not to elements in some unseen angelic realm.

There are other more specific points Gregory also seeks to address here. One is the precise nature of the "firmament," for he, like any of his learned contemporaries, has to account for the change in cosmology from the time of the authorship of the Hexaemeron to his own day. In his discussion, Gregory, in a manner of speaking, does spiritualize the waters above the firmament, pointing out that these are not visible to the eye and are not composed of matter (84C–85A). But more broadly, he—as we know from the rest of his work—is interested in *change*. At the climax of his discussion of water and

66. This understanding of creation will be more important in Gregory's discussion of the creation of the human person. Its treatment in the treatise on the Hexaemeron is the subject of Alexandre, "Exégèse de Gen. 1, 1–2a." Balthasar, *Presence and Thought*, 27–45, remains helpful.

67. Peter seems to have been uneasy with aspects of Basil's Hexaemeron homilies. See Alexandre, "Exégèse de Gen. 1, 1–2a," 159n1.

68. On Gregory's use of science, see Young, "Adam and Anthropos."

the other elements, he asks, "What is the nature of things? The Creator of the elements did not endow them with constancy and permanence. That is, all things are subject to change. . . . This change is unceasing among the elements and by necessity they pass into other things, undergo alteration, and change again" (108AB). This discussion constitutes a part of his explanation of creation's initial days, which involve the genesis and separation (change) of land masses, waters, and lights (113AD).

Nyssen's work on the Hexaemeron, much like Basil's, is not a simple walk-through of the days, what happened, and what it means. Both works are very much shaped by their contexts and, perhaps first and foremost, by the condemnations of Origen's idea and allegorization of the same. The two brothers strove strenuously to avoid being seen as suggesting that the waters were anything other than H_2O. From this starting point, each could take off on his preferred trajectory: Basil marvelling at the providentially ordered, intricate, and beautiful creation, Gregory explaining God's two-tiered work of creation.

Nyssen's Paradise

What, then, did Gregory understand from Genesis 1:26–27; 2:7 and the paradise narrative? We already have had some hints. We now must plumb deeper into the treatises *On the Making of Humanity, On the Soul and the Resurrection*, and the *Catechetical Oration.*[69]

The most interesting and important anthropological conclusion Gregory of Nyssa draws from Genesis 1–3 is the distinction he identifies between an essential image-bearing human nature conceived by God outside diastemic time and the existential humanity we experience in the world. This teaching, which he elaborates further in *On the Making of Humanity* and *On the Hexaemeron*[70] (written about the same year), is rightly distinguished from a Philonic (or Platonic) "double creation" in that Gregory does not envisage two created realms, one copying the other, but two stages—or, better, two *aspects*—of the same creation. For Gregory, the initial moment of creation was purely conceptual, as distinct from its being realized in substance. He may indeed be closer to Origen, although he distances himself from the allegedly Origenist teaching of preexisting souls (see *DHO* 28 [PG 44:229B–33C]).

Gregory was driven by two interrelated problems, which might best be expressed as questions. One concerns theodicy: how can God have created a humanity that suffers and sins and still be considered good, all-knowing, and all-powerful? The other concerns the divine image: how can the human

---

69. All three treatises date from the same time period, what Daniélou calls the second phase, or middle period, of Gregory's career: *On the Making of Humanity* in 379, *On the Soul and the Resurrection* in 380, and the *Catechetical Oration* in probably 381 (see Daniélou, "Chronologie des oeuvres"). The last is an adjustment of Daniélou's dating; see May, "Chronologie."

70. On the continuity of these teachings, see Zachhuber, *Human Nature*, 154–74.

person, who is mortal, passionate, and gendered, be said to be in the image of the immortal, dispassionate, and genderless God?[71] His answer to each question varies in some significant ways within the three treatises under review, but the main contours remain: The image-bearing humanity of God's conception *is* immortal. It is free from passions. It is even, probably, without gender distinction. But in God's dispensation for humanity and for creation, he sees fit to add all these characteristics to human nature, thus arriving at the human person, who is genuinely image-bearing as well as a microcosmic summation of spiritual, animal, and material creation. All three treatises distinguish between essential, image-bearing humanity, and the existential, alloyed humanity. Where *On the Making of Humanity*, *On the Soul and the Resurrection*, and the *Catechetical Oration* vary is in *what* is added to human nature and *when* and *why* it is added.

On the Making of Humanity

Gregory devotes the most attention to this matter in *On the Making of Humanity*, especially in the second half of the treatise, DHO 16–22. These chapters have received considerable scholarly attention either in isolation from or in relation to the rest of Gregory's work.[72] Our analysis will focus on how his presentation there relates to those in *On the Soul and the Resurrection* and the *Catechetical Oration* and how each draws on Genesis 1–3. As few scholars have failed to point out, Gregory prefaces his treatment in *On the Making of Humanity* with words of qualification. Before presenting his idea of the nature of human sex distinction, he says that although it is "only for the ministers of the Word" to know what really is the case,

> we, as far as possible, imagining the truth by guesses and images, do not expose that which comes to mind *categorically* [ἀποφαντικῶς], but will set it forth as in an exercise [ὡς ἐν γυμνασίας εἴδει] for those who consider *charitably* [εὐγνώμοσι] what they hear. (*DHO* 16.15, emphasis added)

One must take care to render and understand this passage correctly. One scholar, adopting an unlikely translation, has suggested that Gregory was here signaling to his readers that the subsequent paragraphs would be "enigmatic" or "ironic," that is, that he was about to say things that he did not really mean.[73] But Gregory means exactly what he says; he only wishes to emphasize that he is not categorical about it, that he is setting out ideas, a

---

71. God is also bodiless yet the human person has a body, but Gregory does not mention this explicitly. For his solutions to this problem, see Bouteneff, "Essential or Existential."

72. A useful bibliography appears in Behr, "Rational Animal," 221n5, to which can be added Smith, *Passion and Paradise*; and Zachhuber, *Human Nature*.

73. Behr, "Rational Animal," 222–23. This approach does not prevent Behr from making several useful conclusions about *On the Making of Humanity*.

theoretical speculation for his readers' charitable consideration, about matters that ultimately are a mystery. He makes the same point in *DHO* 17.2, with reference back to 16.15, and uses the same formulation in *On the Soul and the Resurrection* (PG 46:57C) with not the slightest suggestion that he is speaking "enigmatically."

What are these ideas that Gregory so cautiously proposes? They constitute nothing more than the consistent application of his lines of inquiry concerning the nature of the divine image and of the two-stage creation. They are controversial because they pertain to human sex distinction, but their logic is clear. Since there is no gender or sex in the God in whose image we were created, there must, in some sense or in some aspect of our creation, be no gender in us either; otherwise we could not properly be said to be in God's image. Aside from the logic of the argument alone, Gregory puts great stock in Genesis 1:26 as distinct from 1:27. At two points in *On the Making of Humanity*,[74] he points out that the first verse, "Let us make humankind in our image, according to our likeness," refers to a point where "Adam yet was not," for the reference here is to the humanity conceived by God. It is this "universal nature" that is made purely in the image of God. The second passage (Gen. 1:27) refers to the temporal stage, where humans come into being, at which one can say, "male and female he created them." This latter is "outside the Prototype: for 'in Christ Jesus there is neither male nor female' [Gal. 3:28]" (*DHO* 16.7). We are not very far from Philo's "two men" idea, in *Opif.* 134–35.[75]

Gregory thus shows how humanity might conform to his rather exact and literal understanding of "divine image." But why did God add sex distinction to humanity, which otherwise would have remained "purely" in his image? Gregory stresses two reasons, one practical, the other cosmological. Practically speaking, we must procreate. God, says Gregory, knows that humans endowed with free will "fall away from the angelic life" and turn toward—and appropriate themselves to—a mode of living akin to irrational animals, and therefore he gives us our (animal) mode of procreation (*DHO* 17.4–5 [PG 44:189C–192A]) so that we may in time reach the full number (πλήρωμα) originally conceived by God. Gregory emphasizes that this addition to human nature is not punitive;[76] what is more, it is an aspect of our mode of life that should be used in a holy and good manner.[77] He never suggests that there ever was a "time" when humans did or would reproduce in any other ("angelic") manner, as sexless spirits.

74. *DHO* 16.7–8 (PG 44:181AB); 22.3–4 (PG 44:204C–205B).
75. See pp. 28–30 above.
76. Balthasar, *Presence and Thought*, 78, has it wrong. Gregory himself never presented this addition as punishment and in *Or. cat.* 28 distinctly refuted his (Apollinarian) opponents who taught otherwise.
77. See Harrison, "Male and Female," esp. 469.

Gregory's other reason for the addition of gender distinction is that the distinction between the image-bearing hypothetical humanity and the gendered existential humanity is purely conceptual. The humanity that we know as male and female *is* humanity as God intended it. For it is not just about the sexual mechanics of procreation. Gregory takes it as nothing less than a "great and lofty dogma of Scripture" that God created the human person as "the midpoint [μέσον] between the divine and incorporeal nature and the irrational and bestial life" (*DHO* 16.9 [PG 44:181BC]). This is but one of the ways in which Gregory articulates the view, so common in the Greek fathers (drawing on the pagan philosophers), that the human person is a microcosm of the spiritual and the material.[78]

Gregory seems to want it both ways. On the one hand, he makes a value judgment about human sexuality, seeing it as a characteristic borrowed from the irrational ("bestial") animal creation, given (in foreknowledge of our fall) to us so that we can procreate. If this is all he were to say on the subject, it would sound as if sex distinction were something provisional and unnecessary, even if he never suggests that it is in any way sinful.[79] On the other hand, this same blending of the animal qualities with the divine and more obviously "image-bearing" qualities serves to make of the human person what God wants it to be: a unique God-ordained midpoint between the divine and the earthly, a being who, by virtue of the intellect (νοῦς), may even make use of what is taken from the animal realm in order to lead a godly life. Even if humans remain liable to "appropriate themselves" to the animal dimension and turn away from God, they cannot be microcosmic mediators without that dimension. Sex distinction is nonessential (from the point of view of the divine image) and yet essential (from the point of view of the human vocation in and for the world). Gregory never fully resolves the tension between these views,[80] and it seems that he knows it and thus clearly acknowledges the mystery of the underlying truth and the provisional nature of his speculation.

On the Soul and the Resurrection

Gregory sets *On the Soul and the Resurrection* as a dialogue between himself and his sister Macrina on her deathbed. In this format, he sets out

78. In *DHO* 8.5, 14–15, Gregory shows at length and with precision that the exact composition of the human person—body, soul, intellect—is the summation and fulfillment of the whole of creation.

79. In *DHO* 17.2 Gregory seems indeed to suggest even that the resurrection will be a return to the "angelic" state, but it is not entirely clear whether this means a sexless state or merely one where we "neither marry nor are given in marriage" in an earthly, utilitarian way. Behr, "Rational Animal," 241, believes it to be the latter.

80. Smith overstates the case when he asserts that, for Gregory, "gender is not an essential or ultimately meaningful component of human nature" (*Passion and Paradise*, 41), though he correctly says that Nyssen is simply not fully consistent with himself (p. 17).

teachings on human nature, the person, and the relationship of soul to body—especially at the resurrection. In *On the Making of Humanity* Gregory emphasized the physical additions to the conceptual image-bearing humanity. In *On the Soul and the Resurrection*, however, he concerned himself almost exclusively with the psychic additions—the passions of the soul. The discussion sets out the same fundamental presupposition underlying *On the Making of Humanity*:

> [The scriptural teaching that] the soul is a likeness of God has proclaimed that everything which is alien to God is outside the definition of the soul, for the likeness would not be preserved if there were differences. Therefore, since clearly no such thing [as desire or anger] appears in the divine nature, logically one would suppose that these are not essentially united with the soul either. (PG 46:52AB)[81]

The passions, distilled to the classical dyad of θύμος ("zeal") and ἐπιθυμία ("desire"), cannot be essentially united (συνουσιοῦσθαι) to image-bearing humanity. Nor can they be considered definitive of human nature; they are not of its essence (53AD). They are like warts, Macrina tells Gregory in the dialogue, which only seem to be an integral part of a thing because they grow on it but are in fact external to it. Here, exactly as Gregory had it in *On the Making of Humanity*, Macrina says that these ideas are set out "as in a lecture hall [ὡς ἐν γυμνασίῳ], so that it may avoid the abuse of those who listen in order to criticize" (57C).

Gregory and Macrina now explore the various reasons how and why the passions were introduced into the human composition. There is the microcosm factor: passions enter by virtue of sense perception, and the human being cannot "encompass every form of life" without his or her senses. The dialogue here pauses to stipulate that the passions are, in fact, neutral capacities, which may be turned upward (serving our journey to God) or downward (toward sin), just as a blacksmith can make a sword or a plow from the same steel (61B). Both desire and zeal are necessary for attaining to the divine. If desire were rooted out of us, Macrina asks rhetorically, then "what is there which would raise us towards the union with the heavenly? Or if love [ἀγάπη] is taken away, in what manner will we be joined to the divine? If zeal is quenched, what weapon will we have against our adversary?" (65AB).

In *On the Making of Humanity*, Gregory views sex distinction as both a "blending of the bestial with that which is divine" and a happy and God-intended addition to human nature. In *On the Soul and the Resurrection* he describes a similarly ambiguous condition, though perhaps more pessimistically. God certainly intended us to have passions: indeed, they are the only way that

---

81. The column numbers in PG 46 are used in this section to cite passages of Gregory's *On the Soul and the Resurrection*.

human beings can strive to attain union with him.[82] But they are warts nonetheless, to be tolerated provisionally. The above-cited passage continues: "The
farmer leaves the bastard seeds in us ['Εφίησι τοίνυν τὰ νόθα τῶν σπερμάτων
ἐν ἡμῖν ὁ γεωργός], intending not that they should permanently dominate the
more honorable sowing, but that the field itself [viz., the heart], through reason,
should dry up one part of the plants and render the other part fruitful and
thriving." So it is clear that in the age to come, we will have shed our passions,
as he later explains, "for attainment will replace desire" (89C).

    In contrast to *On the Making of Humanity*, *On the Soul and the Resurrection*
makes no reference to God's foreknowledge of the fall. Gregory does, however—
though not until the very end—refer to God's conception of pure human nature
outside diastemic time (156A–160C). Yet Gregory is not chiefly concerned with
the pretemporal/temporal distinction here but with the fall. "Human nature was
a divine sort of thing before humanity started on the course of evil" (148A). It
was "a divine sort of thing," therefore, even with the neutral, provisional passions. The fall represented only their down-turning. The consequences, then,
are the "garments of skin," which Gregory and Macrina interpret as "sexual
intercourse, conception, child-bearing, dirt [ῥύπος], lactation, nourishment,
evacuation, gradual growth to maturity, the prime of life, old age, disease and
death" (148C–149A). These, too, are not sinful in themselves (Christ himself,
as Gregory notes elsewhere, partakes of many of them).

    But whereas his focus in *On the Making of Humanity* is more etiological,
in *On the Soul and the Resurrection* he sets his sights on the eschatological
and is therefore more concerned with what is extraneous to human nature
and therefore will be shed in the age to come. Telling us at several points that
the resurrection will be a restoration (ἀποκατάστασις) of our nature to its
original (image-bearing) state, he thus also says that we may be sure that any
characteristics not definitive of essential human nature will be shed in the
age to come. He closes the treatise promising that all will be purged in fire
and what will be left will be "incorruptibility, life, honor, grace, glory, power,
and whatever else of this kind we recognize in God himself and in his image,
which *is* our human nature" (160C, emphasis added). We find him here once
again ambivalent about God's additions to "essential" humanity. They are
provisional ("warts") but also an integral part of what we are in the sensible
and the intelligible worlds.

THE CATECHETICAL ORATION

    The *Catechetical Oration* is what the title suggests: a broad instructional
work. Gregory covers a great expanse of material; anthropology is but one

---

82. As Rowan Williams notes concerning this treatise, "Paradoxically, [human spirituality
or intellectuality] can do what it is meant to do only in the hybrid *phusis* which is humanity as
we actually know it" ("Macrina's Deathbed Revisited," 235–36).

important component among a broad range of topics. He makes no disclaimers here about speaking "as in an exercise" because in eschewing the kind of detail in the texts above, he avoids some of the controversial dimensions of his now customary solutions. He continues to present humanity in two modes—one "before" and one "after"—but draws the line of demarcation more simply, without recourse either to the two-stage creation of the world or to God's foreknowledge of the fall.

The underlying questions are by now familiar. The relevant section in the *Catechetical Oration*, like that in *On the Making of Humanity*, explains how the good God could have made humanity, which sins and suffers, and how this humanity can be said to be in God's image. "Where is the soul's likeness to God? Where is the body's dispassion? Where is eternal life?" (GNO 3.4:18).[83] Humanity as we know it can hardly be said to be the image of the immortal and dispassionate God. Here, however, Gregory does not explore the precise character of the image of God; he says only that God endowed us with his image so that we—and, through us, all of creation—could share in his goodness. Humanity was created good, endowed with characteristics of the divine nature, namely life, reason, wisdom, immortality, and free will (17–18). Evil, as Gregory frequently reminds us here and elsewhere, does not of itself originate with God, nor does it even have any existence other than as a privation of good. He (at least in this one instance) takes the matter out of the primordial and into the existential: "He made your nature independent and free. The cause [of your present woes] is rather your thoughtlessness in choosing the worse instead of the better" (20).

He does not explain how and why the human person has his or her current composition with any reference to a rarefied essential humanity. Instead, Gregory centers his argument in cosmology. God blended the human person from the sensible and the intelligible (this is how Gregory reads Gen. 2:7), since the world itself is a "harmonious coexistence" of these two. Because of the human person's composition, neither the sensible nor the intelligible will fail to share in the divine κοινωνία ("communion"/"participation"); the sensible will be raised up to the intelligible in its participation in the divine life. This microcosmic mingling has nothing to do either with divine prevision of the fall or with the two stages of creation; it is God's intention for the human person and for the cosmos. Gregory places his chief emphasis on what God adds to humanity "after" the fall—an "event" that Gregory sees as chiefly influenced by the fallen angels.[84]

As his explanation progresses, Gregory does introduce the idea of divine foreknowledge, only to stress that, even if God foreknew the fall, God was

83. The page numbers in GNO 3.4 are used henceforth in this section to cite passages of Gregory's *Catechetical Oration*.
84. "Before," "after," and "event" should all be placed in quotation marks because, as shown in the following paragraphs, Gregory does not have a linear, temporal understanding of the paradise narrative.

not therefore responsible for it: "If someone in broad daylight, of his own free will, closes his eyes, the sun is not responsible for his failure to see" (28). Later Gregory also notes that God's prescience of the fall did not prevent him from making humanity, for God also foreknew its restoration (34).

Now on the subject of the fall, Gregory can speak of the garments of skin that God gave in response to it. (Gregory notes that Moses gives us this image as an allegory, "by means of a story, in a veiled manner" [29–30].)[85] The list of additions represented by the garments is here greatly simplified: the garments simply represent *mortality*. The human being was created for immortality, but as a response to our freely willed fall, God grants us something borrowed from the irrational animals: death. As Gregory muses:

> I am sure the skins mean the attribute of death. This is the characteristic mark of irrational nature; and in his care for humanity, he who heals our wickedness subsequently provided it with the capacity to die—but not to die permanently. For a suit [of skins] is an external covering for us. The body is given the opportunity to use it for a while, but it is not an essential part of its nature. Mortality, then, . . . provisionally [οἰκονομικῶς] clothed the nature created for immortality. It enveloped its outward, but not its inward, nature. (30)

Gregory does not envisage a historic pre-fallen immortal state;[86] although he posits Adam as the beginning of human genealogy (as well as Christ's), he alludes twice in the *Catechetical Oration* to the fact that Moses is speaking through a story, or an allegory. The implication of this is that God's addition of mortality is a part of his creation of humanity from the beginning, in foreknowledge of the *ongoing* fall. However, Gregory does not care to make this plain here. Nor does he ever develop a portraiture of an idealized pre-fallen Adam or Eve who would not have been subject to death and all that it entails for human life. As far as this treatise is concerned, what is important is that we bring together the sensible and the intelligible before God, that we are essentially immortal, and that—because we fall—we are given mortality as a provisional dimension to our life.[87]

Summary

Three influences converged in Gregory to yield his reading of Genesis 1–3: a profound sense of divine providence, an inclination to think in terms of universals, and the ability to distinguish between God's timelessness and created

---

85. τὸ δὲ τοιοῦτον δόγμα ἱστορικώτερον μὲν καὶ δι' αἰνιγμάτων ὁ Μωϋσῆς ὑμῖν ἐκτίθεται, πλὴν ἔκδηλον καὶ τὰ αἰνίγματα τὴν διδασκαλίαν ἔχει.

86. Behr ("Rational Animal," esp. 237) and Balthasar (*Presence and Thought*, esp. 72) agree on this point.

87. We find the same basic schema also in *On the Premature Death of Infants* (GNO 3.2:77–78).

diastemic (chronological) time. These and his concern to separate God from the responsibility for evil joined his all-or-nothing concept of what it means to be in the divine image. The result was that Gregory interpreted the creation narrative to show that God conceived the sum total of creation in an instant and then brought it into being over time until that fullness was realized. This interpretation is not entirely unique to him. It can be found in Philo and in Origen (provided Origen's understanding of preexistence is qualified along the lines of ideas rather than concrete substances) and later would be developed considerably in the Logos theology of Maximus the Confessor. In any event, in Gregory's work it came into service, though only in *On the Making of Humanity* and *On the Soul and the Resurrection*, to explain the evident discrepancy between humanity as God's perfect image and humanity as we experience it—namely, a blending of spiritual and physical, rational and irrational. In the former treatise, the main emphasis is on sex distinction; in the latter, it is on the passions and then, after the fall, the further addition of all the characteristics that have to do with mortality.

In all three treatises examined here, Gregory retains the conviction that the admixture of that which is in the divine image with that which is of the animal world is part of God's plan for the whole world, for God thereby makes of the human person a creature that epitomizes that world, giving it a principle of coherence and a means of return to God. But as Gregory emphasizes in *On the Soul and the Resurrection* and in the *Catechetical Oration,* since human beings turn away (or "fall") from God and toward their animal nature, God adds something further: mortality and the entire mortal mode of being.

Gregory also maintained that certain elements that have been added to humanity are provisional, temporary; he conceived of resurrection as a restoration to the original state.[88] He was not entirely clear or consistent about what might have constituted the original state of humanity or which provisions were absent from it. In *On the Soul and the Resurrection* and in the *Catechetical Oration* he states that the "garments of skin" will not be with us in the age to come. He suggests still less emphatically and less consistently—but suggests nonetheless—that we will also shed some of the very things that make us the microcosmic beings that we are, namely, sex distinction,[89] zeal, and desire.[90] He expressed these ideas in the early 380s. Later in his career, when he had more thoroughly developed his concept of *epektasis* (our continued

88. This is suggested by Basil as well in *De creat.* 2.7.

89. This may be the implication of *DHO* 17.2, and it is certainly the sense when Gregory says that in the resurrection "there will be neither male nor female" just as "there is no male or female in God" (*In Cant.* 7 [GNO 6.213]).

90. In *On the Soul and the Resurrection*, Gregory writes that when, in the age to come, "the soul will be joined with the divine through its purity, . . . there will no longer be a need for the impulse of desire to lead us toward the beautiful. . . . Attainment will replace desire" (PG 46:89C).

movement, growth, and progress in the age to come) he came to believe that we will always be propelled forward by something like the passions—a "dispassionate eros."[91]

The assets and liabilities of this anthropology, its consistencies and significant inconsistencies, can no longer detain us here. We may note, however, that not only in the *Catechetical Oration* but also in treatises other than the three we have looked at—written at other time periods and focusing less on anthropology—Gregory is prone to draw the line of distinction at the fall rather than between a conceptual "essential" humanity and a diastemic existential one.[92] These later treatises also find him adamant about the necessity of allegorical interpretation—not as an arbitrary displacement of meaning but as a way to approach the things lying beneath the veil of historical narrative that are rightly contemplated by the mind.

Gregory's grounding of these ideas in the Genesis narratives is sketchy and infrequent. True, his ideas about sex distinction in *On the Making of Humanity* rely on distinguishing Genesis 1:26 and 1:27, and his emphasis on the blending of the intelligible with the sensible refers to Genesis 2:7. But the person of Adam does not loom large in any of his explanations. Gregory alludes to the etymology of *'adam*, who was taken from the earth (*'adamah*) (DHO 22.3), and identifies him as the beginning of the realization of what was at first the divine conceptual creation. In other treatises he mentions only rarely the sin of the first couple as prompting the "garments of skin." Adam does not even play much of a genealogical role, nor do we hear much about him as a type for Christ. Gregory takes after Nazianzen in illustrating the consubstantiality of the Father and the Son by means of Adam's common οὐσία with his offspring (C. Eun. 3.1.74–75 [GNO 2:30]). Adam appears for a moment at the end of *On the Soul and the Resurrection* to further illustrate a metaphor: Adam was like a fully formed ear of wheat that through sin split into a multitude of bare seeds, each of which was planted in the soil, eventually to become a whole field of wheat ears. Adam thus represents an idealized, perfected, and single beginning that through corruption multiplied and through redemption and resurrection returned to idealized (but still multiplied) perfection.

Conclusions

The Cappadocians had three disparate, yet related, voices. All three manifested a clear awareness both of the interweavings in Scripture of history and story and of the necessity of multiple exegetical approaches in order to understand what Scripture is telling us at any given point. Although multilayer exegesis was

91. See Smith, *Passion and Paradise*, 202–16.
92. See, e.g., *De beat.* 1 (GNO 7.1:80–81).

nothing new, the Cappadocians' willingness, however cautious, to reconsider the exact historicity of scriptural narrative surely is part of Origen's legacy.

Although Nazianzen and Basil were more closely linked in their rhetorical education, their common monastic retreat, and their erstwhile close friendship, it is Nyssen and Basil who share the most in their approaches to Scripture and what they glean from the creation narratives. Each was manifestly cautious in his interpretation of the Hexaemeron narrative, for fear of being implicated in the radical allegorization for which Origen had been assailed. But they spurned only the seemingly arbitrary kind of allegory that turns a narrative into an obscure code; thus they emphasized that "water is water." Yet each (Basil most obviously) also applied Origen's view that different levels of exegesis were appropriate for different audiences. Nyssen and Basil also shared the doctrine of the nonexistence of evil as well as convictions about creation and ontology, in particular the idea of a pretemporal, seminal, conceptual creation in God of all that exists as distinct from its realization in time and space.[93] Both, too, saw salvation in the age to come as a restoration to original perfection.[94] Basil, however, never pursued these doctrines very far; it was Nyssen who made the most of them in his reading of Genesis 1–3, pressing them to a sometimes unwonted degree.

A pattern applies to many areas of their theological reflection, whether about Christ, the Trinity, creation, or the human person. Basil wrote first, wielding only lightly the brush of Origen's insights. Nyssen applied some of the same ideas as Basil but was more thorough—in some cases to the point of obsession—and more systematic. His very thoroughness forced him to make statements that (at least at face value) contradicted each other, statements that can be held together only through a patient and thorough engagement with Gregory's entire corpus. In effect, the disclaimers we find in *On the Making of Humanity* and *On the Soul and the Resurrection*, where he begs patience and compassion on the part of his readers as he works out his thoughts, are justified.

Gregory of Nazianzus, with his preached theology, gravitated naturally toward formulations and approaches that avoided controversy and unnecessary complexity. We see this in his treatment of Genesis 1–3. He had no particular interest in the Hexaemeron, and so he neatly sidestepped the problem of its allegorization. He brought an open mind to the paradise narrative and found that an allegorical and paraenetic reading was most conducive to his evincing of the dual (though not dualistic) nature of the human person. This understanding was not unique to him—nor was his sense that Adam and Eve were like children, works in progress simply unready for the tree

93. These, in turn, are related to the doctrine of the nonexistence of matter, not discussed in this chapter. See, e.g., Armstrong, "Theory of Non-existence of Matter."
94. In Basil this is clearest in *De creat.* 2.7.

of knowledge—but he gave it a fresh and potent expression that resulted in a holistic and self-consistent treatment, even if less thoroughgoing and less philosophically influenced than Nyssen's.

All three Cappadocians exulted in the glory and mystery of the created world and its microcosmic summation in the human person; they saw in creation the clear signs of an all-loving, all-wise Creator who providentially orders and oversees his work. Especially Basil and Nyssen grounded these observations in Genesis 1. But in their reading of the whole of the creation narratives, all three also retained what became the common patristic emphasis on the paraenetic teaching, and the clear focus on Christ, the center of one's rule of faith. The christological lens periodically yielded an anti-Arian refraction, particularly where Nyssen and Nazianzen used Adam and his offspring as examples to illustrate the consubstantiality of the Trinity. But it also took the form of an argument that can be called typological—if this means far more than merely rehearsing the slogan "Adam is a type for Christ." Basil (especially in his liturgy), Nazianzen (particularly in his thirty-eighth oration), and Nyssen (notably in his *Catechetical Oration*, the books against Eunomius, and his late exegetical work) were so focused on the work of the Savior that their teaching on creation and on the generation of humanity was narrated exclusively through the lens of *re*generation, or restoration, in Christ.

6

These Are the Generations

Concluding Observations

This study has traced a journey through several beginnings. We have looked at the narratives that described the origins of the world, and how they began to be recited and eventually codified into written form as Scripture. We then focused on how these narratives first appeared in the two centuries before Christ with the creation of the Septuagint. Then came the New Testament authors, representing the first Christian interpretations of the creation texts. We ended our journey in the late fourth century, in a world very different from that of any of these beginnings.

The interpreters studied here emanated from a variety of contexts spanning six centuries, even as they, for the most part, shared the Greek language and the LXX text. Their diverse contexts dictated a concomitant diversity of interests and concerns and therefore of approaches to the texts. Yet there are also points of remarkable unity, especially from the first century, where our journey takes on a Christian character.

Scripture and Exegesis

The nascence of the Christian exegesis of Scripture (i.e., of the OT) coincided with the start of a concept of canonicity, the codification of Old and New Testaments and their contents, and the wider availability and dissemination of collections of Scripture in new formats. As a "Bible" was being identified, it became necessary to defend not only its precise contents but also the nature of its coherence—in particular how the two testaments worked together and made sense of each other. The idea of type and fulfillment (or, when it became more elaborated, recapitulation) formed a large part of this early reflection but would have been insufficient without the identification of a genuine underlying sense and meaning (ὑπόθεσις). Scripture made sense as a whole only when it was understood along the lines of its principle of coherence, its rule of faith, its canon of truth—which the early writers consistently identified with the Father, the Son, and the Holy Spirit, with particular emphasis on the Son, Jesus Christ. It followed, then, that Genesis 1–3 was read in terms of the Trinity (e.g., in the use of the first person plural at Gen. 1:26) and even more in terms of Christ. This rule of faith, which our writers identified as something made known through the apostolic witness, was both the hermeneutical key and the treasure sought through early patristic exegesis, whether served through literal, typological, or allegorical readings or through combinations thereof. Indeed, all modes of reading were placed at the service of discerning and elaborating the rule, and the rule, in turn, served as the filter through which the scriptural colors could be seen truly.

The Hexaemeron

Whatever the reasons for the lack of scriptural reference to the Hexaemeron after the book of Exodus, the sense of its sacredness, testified by the talmudic proscriptions that were known by Origen and others, helps explain why it was not the focus of extensive analytical attention by the early Christian writers. But this proscriptive factor is not as important as the simple fact that, for both the NT authors and the fathers, the particulars of the narrative paled in significance to its broader message. The writers who did reflect on the Hexaemeron at any length tended not to analyze it verse by verse; even when some (such as Basil and Ambrose) did so, it was only in the service of deriving its broader lessons. Our writers emphasized that the Hexaemeron was not about science: it did not narrate God's technology. Origen and especially the three Cappadocians were versed in the science and medicine of their day and enjoyed engaging it for its own sake, but not primarily to reconcile it with the scriptural account of creation, although, given the evolution of cosmology, they did periodically pause to consider, for example, the precise nature of the "firmament." Their excursuses into science served only to amplify their sense of wonder at the intricacy of creation and the glory of God. More than anything else, all Christian commentators on the Hexaemeron were taken by what the creation told us about the Creator.

The de-stressing of science did not forbid the early writers from asking what the "days" actually were—whether they were six twenty-four-hour periods, whether they were eras, millennia (for "with the Lord one day is like a thousand years, and a thousand years like one day" [2 Pet. 3:8]), or even how there could be said to be a morning, an evening, or a day before there was a sun. These questions admitted a variety of solutions, some of which yielded theological conclusions. "The beginning" could refer to Jesus Christ, who is the Alpha and the Omega, and the first day could be seen as a type for the day of the Lord's resurrection. Some took the seventh-day Sabbath as foreshadowing the Sabbath of Holy Saturday, when Christ's body lay in the tomb. But to our writers, the days—whether chronological or not—testified most importantly and most consistently to the omnipotent, ordered, and providential (saving) character of God's creative act. The Hexaemeron, together with the way the Bible itself operated as a book of old and new covenants, testified to divine providence. This, too, is why the longer reflections on the Hexaemeron, especially at the hands of Basil of Caesarea and Gregory of Nyssa, so resembled (in form and content alike) the treatises on providence that proliferated from the fifth century onward. Providence, indeed, was central to the early fathers' understanding of the Bible as a whole. Their identification of types in the OT—or, more broadly, their understanding of the OT in the light of Christ—testified to their conviction that God's love for the world was expressed in a thorough, providential ordering of the world through history, though outside the constraints of chronological time.

Basil summarizes the overall priorities of the writers considered here. The six days do not tell us about science but about God:

> If we undertake now to talk about [the competing theories of scientists], we shall fall into the same idle chatter as they. Let us rather allow them to refute each other. And let us stop talking about the substance, since we have been persuaded by Moses that "God created the heavens and the earth." Let us glorify the Master, and from the beauty of the visible things let us form an idea of Him who is more than beautiful. From the greatness of these perceptible and circumscribed bodies let us conceive of Him who is infinite and immense and who surpasses all understanding in the plenitude of His power. (*In Hex.* 1.11)

By and large, whether or not the fathers were literal in their understanding of "days" and of the precise nature of the unfolding of creation, they were adamant that when the Hexaemeron spoke of water, it meant water, and likewise for the stars, the sun, the moon, the animals, the plants, and humanity. Their insistence on this was in part a reaction to the plight of Origen's commentaries. But apart from this, the definitive perspective of divine providence would have been distorted had this creation account been about realities separate from the natural physical world that surrounds us. Basil and Gregory of Nyssa are particularly adamant on this point: if "allegory" means that a text does not refer to what it seems to and that everything in it means something else, then one cannot allegorize the Hexaemeron. These same authors saw perfectly well that not all allegory is of a translational character, which meant that they could and did allegorize other texts or stories, such as Moses's ascent on Sinai or the Song of Songs or even, as we saw, the seven days themselves.

Some of our writers, especially in the second century, predicated their arguments for Christianity on the antiquity of their Scriptures, which surpassed that of the Greek foundational texts. Yet only a few were concerned with the implications for the actual dating of the origins of the world. It was chiefly Theophilus of Antioch who, perhaps because he failed to account for any christological or eschatological perspective on the creation narratives, felt it vital to establish in a precise way the years between the origins of the world and his own day. A few other writers did so later on, notably Eusebius. He had no difficulty with naming Jesus Christ and reading the Scriptures typologically, but he did apply his obvious interest in history, chronology, and divine providence to every dimension of his reading of the world and of Scripture. It is not impossible that his strict dating of the creation of the world was also a bid to play down his pro-Origenist associations.[1]

Three final points about the fathers on the Hexaemeron: First—dating questions aside—many writers shared a fascination with the idea of "the beginning" and what this word could mean. For all of them, Genesis 1 served as a decisive affirmation that God created the world out of nothing, that contrary to pagan assertions there was no preexisting matter that God might have used as a substrate, nor was creation an emanation of God. This, in turn, underscored for them something that would become increasingly explicit in subsequent centuries: the critical line of demarcation between "created" and "uncreated." Second, regarding what "the beginning" might have meant, Theophilus and Origen also supposed that it referred to Christ (the beginning and end of all things). But even aside from this particular association, our writers saw Genesis 1–3 as supporting the NT assertions that the Son was the chief agent of creation.[2] And third, the writers consistently concluded from the Hexaemeron that the human person is the center and the coherence-principle of creation. In some cases, they did so by elaborating what was meant by the divine image. This concept was barely ever mentioned before Irenaeus but saw a thorough development by the end of the fourth century, perhaps

---

1. Eusebius's *Chronicle* is lost in its original, but it was so popular as to be cited frequently in antiquity and was partly translated by Jerome. By the fifth century, Byzantine calendars based in part on Eusebius's calculations were in place, dating the creation of the world 5,509 years before Christ. The date of the world's origins would vary depending on whether one was calculating on the basis of the Hebrew text or the LXX. This was noticed by Augustine, who was keenly interested in dating creation, especially since he realized that if all the numbers are correct, Methuselah would have outlived the flood (*City of God* 15.9–14).

2. E.g., John 1:3; 1 Cor. 8:6; Heb. 1:2.

nowhere more than by Gregory of Nyssa. In other cases (here drawing more on Gen. 2:7), they built on the classical understanding of the human person as a microcosm of creation and, if a microcosm, then a mediator between all of creation and God.

Paradise

Neither before nor after the aftershocks caused by Origen did the Hexaemeron lend itself to a great variety of exegetical approaches. Aside from raising a few questions concerning the "days" and the "beginning," the fathers saw it as basically narrating God's wondrous act in bringing the cosmos into coherent existence. Ironically, it was Theophilus of Antioch who, alongside his unusually explicit chronological and scientific literalism, wandered into some rather far-fetched allegorical and typological interpretations of the days and the activities on each (*Autol.* 2.14–15). But the paradise narrative was another matter. The fathers evidently saw it as having a different character: from the start, it was the subject of a wide range of readings undertaken without particular regard or concern for their compatibility with each other. From the Second Temple literature onward, paradise was occasionally read either as a historical and physical space or as a parahistorical reality, but (more usually) it was left unspecified. The lack of precision and consistency in this regard stemmed, in great part, from a widely fluctuating sense of the nature of history and its relation to story—to the extent that these words could be fully distinguished from each other—likewise the relationship between truth and historical facticity. Regardless of the exact means of interpretation, and even of the presuppositions about the physical reality of the paradise described, our writers' conclusions about the human person, sin, and death were in fundamental harmony with each other, although they featured different accents emerging from the writers' respective concerns.

'Adam

Its early interpreters recognized the paradise narrative as decisively anthropocentric. They generally linked the formation of *'adam* in Genesis 2:7 and 2:22 with the creation of the human person described in Genesis 1:26–27. The LXX translation played a role in smoothing the differences between the Hexaemeron and paradise narratives;[3] its solutions to the problem of translating the Hebrew *'adam* are particularly significant. These translation choices enforced the tendency to conflate the male "Adam" of Genesis 2 with the generic *'adam* of Genesis 1:26–27. Whether or not our writers took note of the etymological significance of *'adam* as some did, they identified one of the functions of Adam

3. Loader, *Septuagint, Sexuality*, 30–32.

as standing for universal humanity, both as its genealogical point of origin and as an emblem and originator of the transgressive patterns of human behavior.

Genealogy

No matter how open many of our writers were to the fictive or poetic character of much of Scripture, including Genesis 1–3, when it came to human genealogy, they tended to put Adam at the beginning of it. This function uniquely established Adam as a real person in the fathers' minds. This is the case, too, for Scripture itself. With the important exception of some of the Pauline writings, Adam's function in the Bible outside Genesis 1–3 is exclusively genealogical.[4] Genesis 5 serves to ground the pivotal figure of Noah in Adam's line; likewise 1 Chronicles 1 traces the patriarchs back to him. Luke 3, narrating the lineage in reverse, does the same for Christ; unlike Matthew's, the Lukan genealogy shows Christ to be not only in the line of David and Abraham but in the line of universal humanity. For the scriptural authors as well as for some of the Second Temple writers examined here, Adam played the role alternately of first patriarch and, more commonly, of first human— and, as such, of symbol of "human nature."

The latter concept—nascent, at most, in the Bible—grew in significance as the early Christian writers elaborated on Adam as forefather. Yet still more than being identified as originator and therefore symbol of humanity, Adam—now not so much as genealogical forebear but as a kind of emblem—comes to stand for *fallen* humanity. (The same patriarchal climate that put Adam at the center of genealogical enumeration also identified him as the protosinner, although, in another mode of thinking, the early writers also focused on the importance of Eve's sin and influence.) But Adam acquires this symbolism for the first time in Paul and solely against the relief of Jesus Christ. From Paul onward—even if the Gospel authors did not fully catch on—Adam represents humanity of the old dispensation; he is the old man that is to be put off in order to put on the new man, Christ. The earliest of the Christian authors, like their Jewish predecessors, continued to reckon Adam's sin as mild in comparison with Cain's and other subsequent human falls, but he was still first.

This also meant that any "glory of Adam" tradition that may have originated with some of the Second Temple texts and survived in later Jewish material had no shelf life in Christian tradition.[5] True, the fathers had different

---

4. Although the Matthean recital of Christ's ancestors notably features several women, genealogies of the period under review were overwhelmingly patriarchal in character, which meant that Eve had essentially no genealogical significance either for Scripture or for the early Christian writers.

5. The absence of a "St. Adam" or a "St. Eve," until they were tentatively introduced into some calendars in the medieval West, testifies both to the lingering ambiguity regarding their concrete existence and to their status as primordial sinners. In their traditional orthodox icono-

ways of reckoning prelapsarian Adam and Eve—though never more than in passing mention. To some, notably Irenaeus and Gregory of Nazianzus (and also Ephrem the Syrian), Adam and Eve, naked and unashamed, were like children unready for the knowledge of good and evil that is part and parcel of mature, image-bearing humanity. To others, their unashamed nakedness, together with the vocation of naming created things, represented the perfection to which humanity will be restored in the age to come. Yet most of the patristic emphasis on "restoration" does not envisage anything described in the book of Genesis, and the perfection to which humanity will be restored is generally not understood as ever having been realized in human history, "prelapsarian" or otherwise. When Gregory of Nyssa referred to humanity's original "immortality," he was not speaking of any time in history; likewise Basil wrote of humanity's being created with the *promise* of immortality. More generally, humanity before the fall simply did not loom large in patristic reflection. In patristic and liturgical expression alike, "Adam," as a term taken on its own, primarily signifies fallen humanity redeemed in Christ.

Sin and Its Transmission

All this leads back to the issue of genealogy: Adam and Eve are the human forebears, but even more important, they are the progenitors of sin and, through sin, death. Yet none of the writers, scriptural or otherwise, whom we examined here understood human beings as born guilty of the sin of Adam. With Paul, they interpreted Genesis 3 as illustrating, among other things, the link between sin and death. Death was not a punishment for sin, however, but its natural consequence and (from Theophilus onward) even a mercy on the part of God to deliver humanity from an existence eternally bound to the spiraling cycle of sin. With Paul, too, they understood that everyone sins, but even if this is a semblance of Adam, it is not a sin "in Adam" or a perpetuation of Adamic guilt. The consistent emphasis in our authors was on human freedom: the sins people commit in semblance of Adam are sins committed of their own volition; one is culpable only for one's own sins. Here again, however, all thinking about Adam's sin and its legacy found its roots in, and developed from, the perspective of Christ.

Adam and Christ

Paul's counterposition of Adam and Christ made the very basic point that both of these figures, through their actions, had a universal effect. But going further, Adam's status as the old man or the old dispensation comes from understanding Christ as the new man, the new covenant. Adam as the sinner is the antitype of Christ as the glorious; indeed, the Jewish tradition that saw

---

graphic depiction, e.g., in the icon of the resurrection in which they are being pulled from Hades, they have no halos.

Adam as a priest, a patriarch, and a king, was utterly transformed in early Christian thinking, which saw Adam as failing in all these vocations and Christ as fulfilling them. The glory of Adam became the glory of Christ. The modern word "typology"—expressing this relationship and so many of the characters and features of the OT with those of the NT—hardly does justice to the transformative thrust of Christian thinking.

Identifying OT features as types or antitypes has to do with the early Christians' need to affirm, against Marcion, the unity of the Bible. But even the earliest examples of typology signified more than biblical intertextuality as such and more than God's providential placing of hints and figures into history. Typology, as the early fathers used it, was nothing less than a completely new understanding of history based on a general (and profound) sense of divine providence as realized most sharply and significantly in salvation in Christ. All the gleanings of Scripture that identify Christ as the agent of creation itself and as its eternal principle of coherence conspire with the ways in which the persons and events of the creation narratives are recapitulated—summarized and fulfilled—in those of the gospel. One of the fullest expressions of this thinking came from Irenaeus, who interpreted the Lukan genealogy together with Romans 5:14 to mean that Christ joins the end to the beginning, recapitulating in himself all nations, languages, and generations. Irenaeus concluded—amazingly—that Adam came into being *as a result* of Christ and his passion, that Adam was made in the image of the incarnate Christ, who himself is the beginning and the end. This trajectory of thinking, which cannily stands temporal chronology on its head, was definitive for the patristic era and right on through the fourteenth century in Nicholas Cabasilas, who puts it this way:

> It was for the New Man that human nature was created at the beginning. . . .
> It was not the old Adam who was the model for the new, but the new Adam
> for the old. . . . For those who have known him first, the old Adam is the
> archetype because of our fallen nature. But for him who sees all things before
> they exist, the first Adam is the imitation of the second. (*The Life in Christ*
> 6.91–94)[6]

"Typology" must be understood against the backdrop of this reconfiguration of history, which, then, began not in some calendrically datable time five thousand, six thousand, or even 13.7 billion years ago, but with Christ and his incarnation and, even more, with his passion. Indeed, to the extent we dwell with the fathers in this perspective, the significance of the age of the world is entirely limited to the sphere of science and bears no theological significance whatsoever.

6. Cited in Behr, *Mystery of Christ*, 110. See the epilogue of Behr's book for a clear exposition of this perspective on Christ and chronology.

Allegory, Type, Myth, and History

Many ancient writers treated allegory and typology as synonymous, and there are broader and narrower definitions of each of these terms. Indeed, at several instances our investigation has pointed to their limitations, as anachronistic and as doing injustice to the exegetical approaches that fall between the cracks they create.[7] Certainly, these terms must be reconceived and deepened when we study patristic exegesis. As another stage in this reconception let us now explore the relationships between a type and its fulfillment and between a symbol and that to which it points.

Allegory

Two factors have alarmed allegory's critics both ancient and modern. One is its potentially arbitrary character: when an author asserts that the "two swords" that Christ sanctions in Luke 22:38 signify the papacy and the empire, on what is the author basing his interpretation, and what authority can the interpretation bear? The other is allegory's potentially translational character: can it genuinely be asserted that the allegorical meaning of any narrative is the only correct one, and does it then supersede or even supplant the literal meaning? Origen came under fire on both counts. As noted, in the fourteenth century, Gregory Palamas was intent on safeguarding Gregory Nazianzen from the translational peril; he assured his readers that even if the forbidden tree represents "contemplation," the tree could still have physically existed. A generation ago, G. W. H. Lampe echoed patristic concerns by asserting that all allegory consists of arbitrary interpretations, which "depend on the belief that the scriptures are an assortment of oracles whose meaning is revealed to those who have the insight to discern it and apply it to the contemporary scene." He warned (now about typology, apparently) that in the face of the "assumption that events in the past may have occurred simply because they were providentially intended to illustrate events in the distant future, history as such loses all value."[8] Although Lampe seriously underestimated the patristic concept of providence, especially in the pervasively christological terms that we have described above, he nonetheless gave voice to time-honored—and, in some cases, warranted—suspicions.

The kind of allegory we encounter in the fathers often shows us nothing less than an entire worldview. Allegory was part and parcel of how the fathers understood God's way of working in history and in Scripture. Their perspective

---

7. Frances Young's important study on biblical exegesis, even as it persists in wrestling with allegory, typology, and other such terms, finally proposes alternate schemata and nomenclatures that may better accommodate what the fathers do. See Young, *Biblical Exegesis*, esp. 202–13. One of the overarching theses is that paraenesis is the dominant motivator of all patristic exegesis.

8. Lampe, "Exposition and Exegesis," 159.

did not safeguard the practice of allegory from arbitrary and inappropriate use; we must distinguish the practice itself from its abuse. This practice expressed the patristic conviction, articulated increasingly clearly in the early centuries, that Scripture operates on a number of levels and that it contains implicit spiritual meanings.

Bearing this in mind, then, one must also distinguish between different intentions on the part of the allegorizer. In some instances, the exegete does indeed assert that the genuine meaning of the narrative lies elsewhere than in its plain sense; in others, he embarks on a parallel track of interpretation that does not deny the validity of a passage's prima facie meaning. Two examples can be seen when Gregory of Nyssa takes Moses's ascent on Sinai as an "allegory" of any soul's ascent to the "dazzling darkness" of divine encounter—or for that matter when Paul sees Abraham's two wives as "two covenants" in Galatians 4:24. Neither claims to be uncovering *the* hidden meaning that necessarily renders the original pointless; each is only pointing to an additional layer of interpretation.

But there is a kind of "in-between allegory" absent from superficial analyses, and Origen's practice is a useful test case. On the one hand, he believes that the Holy Spirit "clothes" mysteries in the ordinary words of a story and that God even inserts "stumbling blocks" into Scripture to awaken readers to deeper meanings. For example, the six stone jars at the wedding in Cana are not physical amphorae; rather, they represent "those who are placed in this world to be purified" (*DP* 4.2.5). Yet although he tells us that Scripture does not describe paradise as a place in the physical world, he does not suggest interpretations to replace the story's features or its dramatis personae. Like virtually everyone else discussed in this study, regardless of whether they exercise the different "senses of Scripture," he brings out the story's *paraenetic* character. The writers—who see it as historical, those who do not, and the majority who do not bother to ask the question—all see the paradise narrative outlining realities that do not stop at the garden's angelically guarded boundaries. It limns an "event" as well as the patterns of our lives, in which we constantly transgress in lesser or greater ways. "Event" here needs to be in quotation marks precisely because its concrete historical facticity has no bearing on its function as a description simultaneously of etiology and of existential reality.

Allegory therefore can be used either intentionally to supersede literal meaning or to retain it. Translational allegory can be seen in Origen's supposedly saying that "the waters above the heavens" are not waters but angelic powers. Parallel allegory appears when Origen avers that the firmament dividing the waters above and below *also* represents our inner firmament, which must discern the heavenly things from things below (*Hom. in Gen.* 1.2). Paraenesis, the moral, didactic, and etiological dimension of the narrative, causes the difference between the translational and parallel modes of allegory to be blurred.

This may especially be the case in an account such as the paradise narrative, which intentionally builds in a metaphorical dimension by identifying the "tree of knowledge" and "the tree of life." As a result, Gregory of Nazianzus felt free to manifest such an openness about Eden, "whatever that Paradise was," and its features. The story of the garden, as he constantly reminds his hearers, is about *us*.

Typology

Typology, as the allegorical practice that specifically relates the OT to the NT, carries with it a similar set of questions. Here, too, one may query what happens to the τύπος when it has been "revealed" or "fulfilled" in that which it was prefiguring. Among the authors treated in this study, two raised the question. Melito of Sardis, working from rhetorical as well as liturgical and poetic sensibilities, spoke consistently of the obsolescence of the type. It "is destroyed," "becomes useless," "yields to what is the true image" (*PP* 37). Tertullian's view was exactly the opposite: "Something used figuratively to express some other thing must have a prior existence for itself" (*De res.* 30). Types "must necessarily arise from existing, not from non-existing things" (*Herm.* 34).

As with other kinds of allegory, however, typology was so widely applied—to things general and specific, to narratives in prose and poetry—that types evidently do not have to exist concretely even if they often do. An important example appears in Basil's liturgy. At the anaphora, the bread and the wine are called antitypes (ἀντίτυπα) of the body and blood of Christ. They are thus designated as elements that are awaiting their fulfillment in what they are to become. While they are "shown" (the verb is ἀναδεῖξαι) to be the body and blood, they remain bread and wine.[9] At that point the bread and wine no longer matter, for they are revealed for what they genuinely are in their fulfilled character. Other types can be found in entirely fictional persons and events, even characters in parables. And in the liturgical and prayer life of the church, figures from historical chronicles often exist side by side with manifestly fictional ones. A fourth-century prayer attributed to Basil and used in the Orthodox Church to this day features the line "Receive me, O Christ, who loves all, as you received the prostitute, the thief, the publican, and the prodigal."[10] The first two appear in the NT as participants in Christ's earthly life; the second

---

9. Orthodox theology has not traditionally espoused transubstantiation; the uses of this term in seventeenth-century confessional statements (such as that of Dositheos of Jerusalem) were seen by later Orthodox commentators as "Latinized" reactions to the Calvinist confession of Cyril Lukaris. Orthodox writers who have used the term since then do so with both reluctance and care. For a useful summary, see Ware, *Orthodox Church*, 283–85.

10. Prayer in preparation for Holy Communion. Cf., e.g., *A Manual of Eastern Orthodox Prayers* (London: SPCK, 1945; Crestwood, NY: St. Vladimir's Seminary Press 1983), 64–65.

two are characters in his parables. But they are invoked together in one breath, playing identical roles in evoking a single attitude of prayer.

Tertullian's insistence on the concrete historicity of the type was unique up to his time. It found further expression later among the Antiochene exegetes, notably Diodore of Tarsus and Theodore of Mopsuestia, who were concerned with the validity of the OT on its own terms and not solely as a collective prefiguration of Christ. These thinkers denied neither allegory nor typology; they rejected only the translational variety, which they saw as threatening the importance of ἱστορία, or the coherent narrative of Scripture.[11] They thus maintained, for example, that even if the serpent in Eden represented Satan, there had still existed an actual serpent.[12] Generally, however, the insistence on the concrete was nearly always a *reactive* tendency, whether against Origen, as we find, for example, in Eustathius, or against other trends. (It is not clear whether the so-called Antiochene reaction arose against an exaggerated concept of Alexandrian allegory or against the emperor Julian's assertion that Christianity was mere *mythos*.)[13] Yet in the end, the perceived necessity of the type's (or symbol's) concreteness is, as it were, a recessive gene in the Eastern Christian's DNA. It is certainly not reflected in the church's liturgical dimension. Young summarizes patristic exegesis (including that of the Antiochenes) thus: "It is not the 'historical event' as such which makes typology what it is; it is the sense of recapitulation, the 'impress' of one narrative or symbol on another, 'fulfilling' it and so giving it meaning."[14]

The need for a symbol or type to be concrete is hardly a foregone conclusion. As typology functions, the type is, at any rate, fulfilled and given its true sense in the person, thing, or event that it typifies. With allegory the situation is more variable. Genesis 1, however its details are interpreted and however one translates them (or not) into science and history, concerns the physical earth, water, flora, and fauna that we know. The Song of Songs, however, derives its entire significance as a story of God's love for us rather than as a Canaanite wedding hymn.

Myth

"Myth" is a word we have scarcely encountered in this study, but it may be fruitful to examine it by way of a retrospective conclusion to the fathers' reading of Genesis 1–3. The word has a broad and elastic meaning in any age, depending on who is defining it. Whatever the characteristics that are brought into play in the definitions given myth by modern folklorists, literary theorists, theologians, or nonscholars, the presumption has always been

11. Young, *Biblical Exegesis*, 169–76.
12. See Hill, "His Master's Voice," 53n43.
13. I owe this suggestion to a conversation with John Behr.
14. Young, *Biblical Exegesis*, 152.

that myths do not describe events that happened in the physical and temporal world. (This is, in part, because most myths are explicitly set *in illo tempore*, "in that time," outside history.) As a result, two perceptions have arisen in antiquity and in modernity: some consider myths to be "false fictions" or lies; others see them as "true fictions," stories capable of bearing truth. Plato was ambivalent. He saw *mythos* as, at best, something with which to educate children but, generally, a pale imitation of *logos*. Similarly, no early Christian would use the word *mythos* to describe anything in Sacred Scripture; even Origen did not give this name to the scriptural passages that he considered not to have happened but nonetheless expressive of truth. Myths, to the ancients, were indeed lies. Religious Greek pagans did not speak of their stories as "myths," but Christians reserved this term precisely for the fanciful and false pagan tales that effectively constituted a competing and contradictory worldview to their own.

Yet the classical Greeks and the Christians alike (not to mention Philo) were well aware of the truth-bearing power of parable or other narrative constructs. Aristotle saw poetry as an art higher than history. Despite his caution about *mythos*, Plato presented his entire philosophy through fictional, hypothetical dialogues (some today even assert that Socrates himself was a fictional character); he composed his own cosmogenic myth in the *Timaeus*. Historians, especially from early to late antiquity, openly acknowledged the need to weave in invented details to satisfy the requirements and expectations of historiography, which has always been bound up with explaining the *present* as much as the (ultimately ungraspable) past.

Myth, then, was both a loaded and an ambiguous term. The same Julian who accused Christianity of resting on *mythos* sought to reassert the value of Greek mythology. Under his influence, Sallustius asserted myth's truth-bearing potential, even as he admitted its fictive basis in his famous dictum "A myth never was, but always is."[15] Yet in the NT Epistles, the μῦθοι of unbelievers are sharply contrasted with the ἀλήθεια of the gospel (2 Tim. 4:4; Titus 1:14; also 1 Tim. 4:7; 2 Pet. 1:16). Even in our own day the term "myth" is something of a two-edged sword. We distinguish "the (real) man from the (exaggerated) myth," considering the latter to be "*mere* myth" because it is false. Yet we are plainly aware of the enormous potency and truth-bearing capacity of myth.

Insofar as we today are able to define myths as fictions that can tell the truth about God and the world, can the Hexaemeron and paradise narratives be described as mythical? Not without grave consequences in most Christian circles. In a wide variety of settings, academic and popular, conservative and liberal, this question is met by sharply differing reactions. Some say that, since Scripture is inspired by God and myths are fiction, if we call these narratives

---

15. This dictum is also translated, "These things never happened, but always are." See Sallustius, *On the Gods and the World*, in Murray, *Five Stages of Greek Religion*, 195.

myths, then we are saying that God lied. Others say that if they are etiological myths, they are the uniquely true ones, whose composition and redaction were indeed inspired by God. Individuals in the latter category may argue that, just as the mythological figures of the Greeks commonly appeared in historical genealogies, so the scriptural authors related all of their most significant figures to Adam. Those in the former category maintain that genealogies were grounded in Adam because all human lineage ultimately descends from him.

Part of this disagreement stems from the presumed intentions of the narrator in each case: when Jesus told parables, everyone recognized them as true fictions, but when the biblical narrator says, "And the Lord God planted a garden in Eden, in the east; and there he put the man whom he had formed," he meant it as historical. But the disagreement also has something to do with a resistance to analysis. Once we categorize the creation narratives as myths (or even as "factual history") their character is changed. They become like a fugue whose beautiful melody has been analyzed into banality.

Aside from their revulsion at the word "myth," the ancient Christian writers reviewed here did not dwell on the poetic character of the narratives. In some cases they were not interested in this kind of analysis; in others they could not be assured of the sensibilities of their audiences. But finally they were also averse to possibly disrupting the coherence of the biblical narrative, the coherence realized through the sum total of the exegetical approaches the fathers brought to bear on the narratives in order to show them as revealing the gospel of Christ.

The One Thing Needful

The introduction to this study signaled that we would be addressing the question of historicity. The conclusions here about allegory, typology, and myth, pointing as they do toward the paraenetic and christological focus of early patristic exegesis of the creation narratives, hold clear implications for this question, perhaps even stripping the historicity question of significance. The introduction also alluded to three stages corresponding to three different time periods: that of the scriptural author/redactors, that of the early Christian exegetes, and our own. I suggested that the main break comes between the first and the second stage, for it is there that the questions begin to be asked about how one can speak of "days" and whether everything written in Scripture "happened" as it was written. Yet the difference between the early patristic era and our own cannot be underestimated either. Unlike many Christians in our day, for example, the fathers generally did not doubt Adam and Eve's historic existence; Adam was, after all, the root of the key scriptural genealogies. Unlike us, they had no scientific reason to doubt them as the first physical parents of humanity. Thinkers such as Origen, especially, took the literary cues of the biblical narratives as indicating an interweaving of fictive and historical material and pointed out that the "historical" tends to be completely beyond our means either to access or to prove. Yet even he, like the other fathers, when speaking genealogically, looked back to Adam. Taking this for granted, the fathers approached the narratives on the allegorical, typological, and moral levels, milking each for truth and meaning. Whatever their different conclusions about the details and historicity, they saw the narratives as telling the truth about God and created reality, about human sinfulness and the need for redemption, and ultimately about the person and work of Christ, the Son of the Father, anointed by and proclaimed in the Holy Spirit.

The point is not, then, whether the fathers took the seven "days" or Adam to be historical. For the fathers, as for us, the historicity question has much more to do with how narrative, and scriptural narrative specifically, works to convey its message—something that both the fathers and we understand in a variety of ways. As to the end result, however, none of the fathers' strictly theological or moral conclusions—about creation, or about humanity and its redemption, and the coherence of everything in Christ—has anything to do with the datable chronology of the creation of the universe or with the physical existence of Adam and Eve. They read the creation narratives as Holy Scripture, and therefore as "true." But they did not see them as lessons in history or science as such, even as they reveled in the overlaps they observed between the scriptural narrative and the observable world. Generally speaking, the fathers were free from a slavish deference to science. Rather their theological and paraenetic approach to the creation narratives left them free to enjoy an unprejudiced scientific inquisitiveness.

That being the case, those of us who seek fidelity to the fathers should likewise refrain from overly conflating Scripture with science, in order to bring realistic expectations to each. This means that we would have no reason to manipulate or ignore scientific findings that do not appear to accord with the Genesis accounts, since they operate on a different register. This separation is important for us because, unlike the fathers, we do have data that would make a sheerly scientific and historical interpretation of Genesis 1–3 well nigh impossible, despite some modern authors' best efforts. Yet the ever-unfolding data about the size, layout, and probable age of the created world—which goes so far beyond what the fathers knew about it—can give us the same exuberance as it did the early Christian writers: a joyous wonder in mystery and divine providence, and even, at times, a recognition of overlaps with aspects of the scriptural narratives.

If we follow the fathers, we will see the Genesis creation accounts as God's uniquely chosen vehicle to express his truth about cosmic and human origins and the dynamics of sin and death, all recapitulated and cohering in the person of Christ. However we might reckon the narratives' relationship to the unfolding of events in historical time, our gaze will be fixed decidedly on the New Adam.

Appendix

Genesis 1–3 and Genesis 5:1–5

I have <u>highlighted</u> each occurrence of the Hebrew word *'adam* (אָדָם or הָאָדָם)
in the Greek and English translations so that each <u>highlighted</u> word renders
the Hebrew *'adam* or its cognate.

LXX Greek	LXX English (NETS)	NRSV
Chapter 1		
1 Ἐν ἀρχῇ ἐποίησεν ὁ θεὸς τὸν οὐρανὸν καὶ τὴν γῆν.	1 In the beginning God made the heaven and the earth.	1 In the beginning when God created the heavens and the earth,
2 ἡ δὲ γῆ ἦν ἀόρατος καὶ ἀκατασκεύαστος, καὶ σκότος ἐπάνω τῆς ἀβύσσου, καὶ πνεῦμα θεοῦ ἐπεφέρετο ἐπάνω τοῦ ὕδατος.	2 Yet the earth was invisible and unformed, and darkness was over the abyss, and a divine wind was being carried along over the water.	2 the earth was a formless void and darkness covered the face of the deep, while a wind from God swept over the face of the waters.
3 καὶ εἶπεν ὁ θεός Γενηθήτω φῶς. καὶ ἐγένετο φῶς.	3 And God said, "Let light come into being." And light came into being.	3 Then God said, "Let there be light"; and there was light.
4 καὶ εἶδεν ὁ θεὸς τὸ φῶς ὅτι καλόν. καὶ διεχώρισεν ὁ θεὸς ἀνὰ μέσον τοῦ φωτὸς καὶ ἀνὰ μέσον τοῦ σκότους.	4 And God saw the light, that it was good. And God separated between the light and between the darkness.	4 And God saw that the light was good; and God separated the light from the darkness.
5 καὶ ἐκάλεσεν ὁ θεὸς τὸ φῶς ἡμέραν καὶ τὸ σκότος ἐκάλεσεν νύκτα. καὶ ἐγένετο ἑσπέρα καὶ ἐγένετο πρωί, ἡμέρα μία.	5 And God called the light Day and the darkness he called Night. And it came to be evening and it came to be morning, day one.	5 God called the light Day, and the darkness he called Night. And there was evening and there was morning, the first day.

LXX Greek	LXX English (NETS)	NRSV
6 Καὶ εἶπεν ὁ θεός Γενηθήτω στερέωμα ἐν μέσῳ τοῦ ὕδατος καὶ ἔστω διαχωρίζον ἀνὰ μέσον ὕδατος καὶ ὕδατος. καὶ ἐγένετο οὕτως.	6 And God said, "Let a firmament come into being in the midst of the water and let it be a separator between water and water." And it became so.	6 And God said, "Let there be a dome in the midst of the waters, and let it separate the waters from the waters."
7 καὶ ἐποίησεν ὁ θεὸς τὸ στερέωμα, καὶ διεχώρισεν ὁ θεὸς ἀνὰ μέσον τοῦ ὕδατος, ὃ ἦν ὑποκάτω τοῦ στερεώματος, καὶ ἀνὰ μέσον τοῦ ὕδατος τοῦ ἐπάνω τοῦ στερεώματος.	7 And God made the firmament, and God separated between the water that was under the firmament and between the water that was above the firmament.	7 So God made the dome and separated the waters that were under the dome from the waters that were above the dome. And it was so.
8 καὶ ἐκάλεσεν ὁ θεὸς τὸ στερέωμα οὐρανόν. καὶ εἶδεν ὁ θεὸς ὅτι καλόν. καὶ ἐγένετο ἑσπέρα καὶ ἐγένετο πρωί, ἡμέρα δευτέρα.	8 And God called the firmament Sky. And God saw that it was good. And it came to be evening and it came to be morning, a second day.	8 God called the dome Sky. And there was evening and there was morning, the second day.
9 Καὶ εἶπεν ὁ θεός Συναχθήτω τὸ ὕδωρ τὸ ὑποκάτω τοῦ οὐρανοῦ εἰς συναγωγὴν μίαν, καὶ ὀφθήτω ἡ ξηρά. καὶ ἐγένετο οὕτως. καὶ συνήχθη τὸ ὕδωρ τὸ ὑποκάτω τοῦ οὐρανοῦ εἰς τὰς συναγωγὰς αὐτῶν, καὶ ὤφθη ἡ ξηρά.	9 And God said, "Let the water that is under the sky be gathered into one gathering, and let the dry land appear." And it became so. And the water that was under the sky was gathered into their gatherings, and the dry land appeared.	9 And God said, "Let the waters under the sky be gathered together into one place, and let the dry land appear." And it was so.
10 καὶ ἐκάλεσεν ὁ θεὸς τὴν ξηρὰν γῆν καὶ τὰ συστήματα τῶν ὑδάτων ἐκάλεσεν θαλάσσας. καὶ εἶδεν ὁ θεὸς ὅτι καλόν. —	10 And God called the dry land Earth and the systems of the waters he called Seas. And God saw that it was good.	10 God called the dry land Earth, and the waters that were gathered together he called Seas. And God saw that it was good.
11 καὶ εἶπεν ὁ θεὸς Βλαστησάτω ἡ γῆ βοτάνην χόρτου, σπεῖρον σπέρμα κατὰ γένος καὶ καθ' ὁμοιότητα, καὶ ξύλον κάρπιμον ποιοῦν καρπόν, οὗ τὸ σπέρμα αὐτοῦ ἐν αὐτῷ κατὰ γένος ἐπὶ τῆς γῆς. καὶ ἐγένετο οὕτως.	11 Then God said, "Let the earth put forth vegetation of the pasture, seed propagating according to kind and according to likeness, and fruit-bearing tree producing fruit of which the seed is in it according to kind, on the earth." And it became so.	11 Then God said, "Let the earth put forth vegetation: plants yielding seed, and fruit trees of every kind on earth that bear fruit with the seed in it." And it was so.

LXX Greek	LXX English (NETS)	NRSV
12 καὶ ἐξήνεγκεν ἡ γῆ βοτάνην χόρτου, σπεῖρον σπέρμα κατὰ γένος καὶ καθ' ὁμοιότητα, καὶ ξύλον κάρπιμον ποιοῦν καρπόν, οὗ τὸ σπέρμα αὐτοῦ ἐν αὐτῷ κατὰ γένος ἐπὶ τῆς γῆς. καὶ εἶδεν ὁ θεὸς ὅτι καλόν.	12 And the earth brought forth vegetation of the pasture, seed propagating according to kind and according to likeness, and fruit-bearing tree producing fruit of which the seed is in it according to kind, on the earth. And God saw that it was good.	12 The earth brought forth vegetation: plants yielding seed of every kind, and trees of every kind bearing fruit with the seed in it. And God saw that it was good.
13 καὶ ἐγένετο ἑσπέρα καὶ ἐγένετο πρωί, ἡμέρα τρίτη.	13 And it came to be evening and it came to be morning, a third day.	13 And there was evening and there was morning, the third day.
14 Καὶ εἶπεν ὁ θεός Γενηθήτωσαν φωστῆρες ἐν τῷ στερεώματι τοῦ οὐρανοῦ εἰς φαῦσιν τῆς γῆς τοῦ διαχωρίζειν ἀνὰ μέσον τῆς ἡμέρας καὶ ἀνὰ μέσον τῆς νυκτὸς καὶ ἔστωσαν εἰς σημεῖα καὶ εἰς καιροὺς καὶ εἰς ἡμέρας καὶ εἰς ἐνιαυτοὺς	14 And God said, "Let luminaries come into being in the firmament of the sky for illumination of the earth, to separate between the day and between the night, and let them be for signs and for seasons and for days and for years,	14 And God said, "Let there be lights in the dome of the sky to separate the day from the night; and let them be for signs and for seasons and for days and years,
15 καὶ ἔστωσαν εἰς φαῦσιν ἐν τῷ στερεώματι τοῦ οὐρανοῦ ὥστε φαίνειν ἐπὶ τῆς γῆς. καὶ ἐγένετο οὕτως.	15 and let them be for illumination in the firmament of the sky so as to give light upon the earth." And it became so.	15 and let them be lights in the dome of the sky to give light upon the earth." And it was so.
16 καὶ ἐποίησεν ὁ θεὸς τοὺς δύο φωστῆρας τοὺς μεγάλους, τὸν φωστῆρα τὸν μέγαν εἰς ἀρχὰς τῆς ἡμέρας καὶ τὸν φωστῆρα τὸν ἐλάσσω εἰς ἀρχὰς τῆς νυκτός, καὶ τοὺς ἀστέρας.	16 And God made the two great luminaries, the great luminary for rulership of the day and the lesser luminary for rulership of the night, and the stars.	16 God made the two great lights—the greater light to rule the day and the lesser light to rule the night—and the stars.
17 καὶ ἔθετο αὐτοὺς ὁ θεὸς ἐν τῷ στερεώματι τοῦ οὐρανοῦ ὥστε φαίνειν ἐπὶ τῆς γῆς	17 And God set them in the firmament of the sky so as to give light upon the earth	17 God set them in the dome of the sky to give light upon the earth,
18 καὶ ἄρχειν τῆς ἡμέρας καὶ τῆς νυκτὸς καὶ διαχωρίζειν ἀνὰ μέσον τοῦ φωτὸς καὶ ἀνὰ μέσον τοῦ σκότους. καὶ εἶδεν ὁ θεὸς ὅτι καλόν.	18 and to rule the day and the night and to separate between the light and between the darkness. And God saw that it was good.	18 to rule over the day and over the night, and to separate the light from the darkness. And God saw that it was good.
19 καὶ ἐγένετο ἑσπέρα καὶ ἐγένετο πρωί, ἡμέρα τετάρτη.	19 And it came to be evening and it came to be morning, a fourth day.	19 And there was evening and there was morning, the fourth day.

LXX Greek	LXX English (NETS)	NRSV
20 Καὶ εἶπεν ὁ θεός Ἐξαγαγέτω τὰ ὕδατα ἑρπετὰ ψυχῶν ζωσῶν καὶ πετεινὰ πετόμενα ἐπὶ τῆς γῆς κατὰ τὸ στερέωμα τοῦ οὐρανοῦ. καὶ ἐγένετο οὕτως.	20 And God said, "Let the waters bring forth creeping things among living creatures and birds flying on the earth against the firmament of the sky." And it became so.	20 And God said, "Let the waters bring forth swarms of living creatures, and let birds fly above the earth across the dome of the sky."
21 καὶ ἐποίησεν ὁ θεὸς τὰ κήτη τὰ μεγάλα καὶ πᾶσαν ψυχὴν ζῴων ἑρπετῶν, ἃ ἐξήγαγεν τὰ ὕδατα κατὰ γένη αὐτῶν, καὶ πᾶν πετεινὸν πτερωτὸν κατὰ γένος. καὶ εἶδεν ὁ θεὸς ὅτι καλά.	21 And God made the great sea monsters and every creature among creeping animals, which the waters brought forth according to their kinds, and every winged bird according to kind. And God saw that they were good.	21 So God created the great sea monsters and every living creature that moves, of every kind, with which the waters swarm, and every winged bird of every kind. And God saw that it was good.
22 καὶ ηὐλόγησεν αὐτὰ ὁ θεὸς λέγων Αὐξάνεσθε καὶ πληθύνεσθε καὶ πληρώσατε τὰ ὕδατα ἐν ταῖς θαλάσσαις, καὶ τὰ πετεινὰ πληθυνέσθωσαν ἐπὶ τῆς γῆς.	22 And God blessed them, saying, "Increase and multiply and fill the waters in the seas, and let birds multiply on the earth."	22 God blessed them, saying, "Be fruitful and multiply and fill the waters in the seas, and let birds multiply on the earth."
23 καὶ ἐγένετο ἑσπέρα καὶ ἐγένετο πρωί, ἡμέρα πέμπτη.	23 And it came to be evening and it came to be morning, a fifth day.	23 And there was evening and there was morning, the fifth day.
24 Καὶ εἶπεν ὁ θεός Ἐξαγαγέτω ἡ γῆ ψυχὴν ζῶσαν κατὰ γένος, τετράποδα καὶ ἑρπετὰ καὶ θηρία τῆς γῆς κατὰ γένος. καὶ ἐγένετο οὕτως.	24 And God said, "Let the earth bring forth the living creature according to kind: quadrupeds and creeping things and wild animals of the earth according to kind." And it became so.	24 And God said, "Let the earth bring forth living creatures of every kind: cattle and creeping things and wild animals of the earth of every kind." And it was so.
25 καὶ ἐποίησεν ὁ θεὸς τὰ θηρία τῆς γῆς κατὰ γένος καὶ τὰ κτήνη κατὰ γένος καὶ πάντα τὰ ἑρπετὰ τῆς γῆς κατὰ γένος αὐτῶν. καὶ εἶδεν ὁ θεὸς ὅτι καλά. —	25 And God made the wild animals of the earth according to kind and the cattle according to kind and all the creeping things of the earth according to their kind. And God saw that they were good.	25 God made the wild animals of the earth of every kind, and the cattle of every kind, and everything that creeps upon the ground of every kind. And God saw that it was good.

LXX Greek	LXX English (NETS)	NRSV
26 καὶ εἶπεν ὁ θεός Ποιήσωμεν **ἄνθρωπον** κατ' εἰκόνα ἡμετέραν καὶ καθ' ὁμοίωσιν, καὶ ἀρχέτωσαν τῶν ἰχθύων τῆς θαλάσσης καὶ τῶν πετεινῶν τοῦ οὐρανοῦ καὶ τῶν κτηνῶν καὶ πάσης τῆς γῆς καὶ πάντων τῶν ἑρπετῶν τῶν ἑρπόντων ἐπὶ τῆς γῆς.	26 Then God said, "Let us make **humankind** according to our image and according to likeness, and let them rule the fish of the sea and the birds of the sky and the cattle and all the earth and all the creeping things that creep upon the earth."	26 Then God said, "Let us make **humankind** in our image, according to our likeness; and let them have dominion over the fish of the sea, and over the birds of the air, and over the cattle, and over all the wild animals of the earth, and over every creeping thing that creeps upon the earth."
27 καὶ ἐποίησεν ὁ θεὸς **τὸν ἄνθρωπον**, κατ' εἰκόνα θεοῦ ἐποίησεν αὐτόν, ἄρσεν καὶ θῆλυ ἐποίησεν αὐτούς.	27 And God made **humankind**, according to the divine image he made it, male and female he made them.	27 So God created **humankind** in his image, in the image of God he created them; male and female he created them.
28 καὶ ηὐλόγησεν αὐτοὺς ὁ θεὸς λέγων Αὐξάνεσθε καὶ πληθύνεσθε καὶ πληρώσατε τὴν γῆν καὶ κατακυριεύσατε αὐτῆς καὶ ἄρχετε τῶν ἰχθύων τῆς θαλάσσης καὶ τῶν πετεινῶν τοῦ οὐρανοῦ καὶ πάντων τῶν κτηνῶν καὶ πάσης τῆς γῆς καὶ πάντων τῶν ἑρπετῶν τῶν ἑρπόντων ἐπὶ τῆς γῆς.	28 And God blessed them, saying, "Increase and multiply and fill the earth and subdue it, and rule the fish of the sea and the birds of the sky and all the cattle and all the earth and all the creeping things that creep upon the earth."	28 God blessed them, and God said to them, "Be fruitful and multiply, and fill the earth and subdue it; and have dominion over the fish of the sea and over the birds of the air and over every living thing that moves upon the earth."
29 καὶ εἶπεν ὁ θεός Ἰδοὺ δέδωκα ὑμῖν πᾶν χόρτον σπόριμον σπεῖρον σπέρμα, ὅ ἐστιν ἐπάνω πάσης τῆς γῆς, καὶ πᾶν ξύλον, ὃ ἔχει ἐν ἑαυτῷ καρπὸν σπέρματος σπορίμου—ὑμῖν ἔσται εἰς βρῶσιν—	29 And God said, "See, I have given to you all sowable herbage, propagating seed that is atop the whole earth, and every tree that has in itself fruit of sowable seed—you shall have it [or "them"] for food,	29 God said, "See, I have given you every plant yielding seed that is upon the face of all the earth, and every tree with seed in its fruit; you shall have them for food.
30 καὶ πᾶσι τοῖς θηρίοις τῆς γῆς καὶ πᾶσι τοῖς πετεινοῖς τοῦ οὐρανοῦ καὶ παντὶ ἑρπετῷ τῷ ἕρποντι ἐπὶ τῆς γῆς, ὃ ἔχει ἐν ἑαυτῷ ψυχὴν ζωῆς, πάντα χόρτον χλωρὸν εἰς βρῶσιν. καὶ ἐγένετο οὕτως.	30 and to all the wild animals of the earth and to all the birds of the sky and to every creeping thing that creeps on the earth, that has in itself the animating force of life, even all green herbage for food." And it became so.	30 And to every beast of the earth, and to every bird of the air, and to everything that creeps on the earth, everything that has the breath of life, I have given every green plant for food." And it was so.

LXX Greek	LXX English (NETS)	NRSV
31 καὶ εἶδεν ὁ θεὸς τὰ πάντα, ὅσα ἐποίησεν, καὶ ἰδοὺ καλὰ λίαν. καὶ ἐγένετο ἑσπέρα καὶ ἐγένετο πρωί, ἡμέρα ἕκτη.	31 And God saw all the things that he had made, and see, they were exceedingly good. And it came to be evening and it came to be morning, a sixth day.	31 God saw everything that he had made, and indeed, it was very good. And there was evening and there was morning, the sixth day.

Chapter 2

1 Καὶ συνετελέσθησαν ὁ οὐρανὸς καὶ ἡ γῆ καὶ πᾶς ὁ κόσμος αὐτῶν.	1 And the heaven and the earth were finished and all their arrangement.	1 Thus the heavens and the earth were finished, and all their multitude.
2 καὶ συνετέλεσεν ὁ θεὸς ἐν τῇ ἡμέρᾳ τῇ ἕκτῃ τὰ ἔργα αὐτοῦ, ἃ ἐποίησεν, καὶ κατέπαυσεν τῇ ἡμέρᾳ τῇ ἑβδόμῃ ἀπὸ πάντων τῶν ἔργων αὐτοῦ, ὧν ἐποίησεν.	2 And on the sixth day God finished his works that he had made, and he left off on the seventh day from all his works that he had made.	2 And on the seventh day God finished the work that he had done, and he rested on the seventh day from all the work that he had done.
3 καὶ ηὐλόγησεν ὁ θεὸς τὴν ἡμέραν τὴν ἑβδόμην καὶ ἡγίασεν αὐτήν, ὅτι ἐν αὐτῇ κατέπαυσεν ἀπὸ πάντων τῶν ἔργων αὐτοῦ, ὧν ἤρξατο ὁ θεὸς ποιῆσαι.	3 And God blessed the seventh day and hallowed it, because on it he left off from all his works that God had begun to make.	3 So God blessed the seventh day and hallowed it, because on it God rested from all the work that he had done in creation.
4 Αὕτη ἡ βίβλος γενέσεως οὐρανοῦ καὶ γῆς, ὅτε ἐγένετο, ᾗ ἡμέρᾳ ἐποίησεν ὁ θεὸς τὸν οὐρανὸν καὶ τὴν γῆν	4 This is the book of the origin of heaven and earth, when it originated, on the day that God made the heaven and the earth	4 These are the generations of the heavens and the earth when they were created. In the day that the LORD God made the earth and the heavens,
5 καὶ πᾶν χλωρὸν ἀγροῦ πρὸ τοῦ γενέσθαι ἐπὶ τῆς γῆς καὶ πάντα χόρτον ἀγροῦ πρὸ τοῦ ἀνατεῖλαι· οὐ γὰρ ἔβρεξεν ὁ θεὸς ἐπὶ τὴν γῆν, καὶ **ἄνθρωπος** οὐκ ἦν ἐργάζεσθαι τὴν γῆν,	5 and all verdure of the field before it came to be upon the earth and all herbage of the field before it sprang up; for God had not sent rain upon the earth, and there was not a **human** to till the earth,	5 when no plant of the field was yet in the earth and no herb of the field had yet sprung up—for the LORD God had not caused it to rain upon the earth, and there was no **one** to till the ground;
6 πηγὴ δὲ ἀνέβαινεν ἐκ τῆς γῆς καὶ ἐπότιζεν πᾶν τὸ πρόσωπον τῆς γῆς.	6 yet a spring would rise from the earth and water the whole face of the earth.	6 but a stream would rise from the earth, and water the whole face of the ground—

LXX Greek	LXX English (NETS)	NRSV
7 καὶ ἔπλασεν ὁ θεὸς τὸν ἄνθρωπον χοῦν ἀπὸ τῆς γῆς καὶ ἐνεφύσησεν εἰς τὸ πρόσωπον αὐτοῦ πνοὴν ζωῆς, καὶ ἐγένετο ὁ ἄνθρωπος εἰς ψυχὴν ζῶσαν.	7 And God formed **man**, dust from the earth, and breathed into his face the breath of life, and the man became a living being.	7 then the LORD God formed **man** from the dust of the ground, and breathed into his nostrils the breath of life; and the man became a living being.
8 Καὶ ἐφύτευσεν κύριος ὁ θεὸς παράδεισον ἐν Εδεμ κατὰ ἀνατολὰς καὶ ἔθετο ἐκεῖ τὸν ἄνθρωπον, ὃν ἔπλασεν.	8 And the Lord God planted an orchard in Edem toward the east and there he put **the man** whom he had formed.	8 And the LORD God planted a garden in Eden, in the east; and there he put **the man** whom he had formed.
9 καὶ ἐξανέτειλεν ὁ θεὸς ἔτι ἐκ τῆς γῆς πᾶν ξύλον ὡραῖον εἰς ὅρασιν καὶ καλὸν εἰς βρῶσιν καὶ τὸ ξύλον τῆς ζωῆς ἐν μέσῳ τῷ παραδείσῳ καὶ τὸ ξύλον τοῦ εἰδέναι γνωστὸν καλοῦ καὶ πονηροῦ.	9 And out of the earth God furthermore made to grow every tree that is beautiful to the sight and good for food, the tree of life also in the orchard's midst and the tree for knowing what is knowable of good and evil.	9 Out of the ground the LORD God made to grow every tree that is pleasant to the sight and good for food, the tree of life also in the midst of the garden, and the tree of the knowledge of good and evil.
10 ποταμὸς δὲ ἐκπορεύεται ἐξ Εδεμ ποτίζειν τὸν παράδεισον· ἐκεῖθεν ἀφορίζεται εἰς τέσσαρας ἀρχάς.	10 Now a river goes out of Edem to water the orchard; from there it divides into four sources.	10 A river flows out of Eden to water the garden, and from there it divides and becomes four branches.
11 ὄνομα τῷ ἑνὶ Φισων· οὗτος ὁ κυκλῶν πᾶσαν τὴν γῆν Ευιλατ, ἐκεῖ οὗ ἔστιν τὸ χρυσίον·	11 The name of the one is Phison; it is the one that encircles the whole land of Heuilat, there where the gold is;	11 The name of the first is Pishon; it is the one that flows around the whole land of Havilah, where there is gold;
12 τὸ δὲ χρυσίον τῆς γῆς ἐκείνης καλόν· καὶ ἐκεῖ ἔστιν ὁ ἄνθραξ καὶ ὁ λίθος ὁ πράσινος.	12 now the gold of that land is good, and carbuncle and light green stone are there.	12 and the gold of that land is good; bdellium and onyx stone are there.
13 καὶ ὄνομα τῷ ποταμῷ τῷ δευτέρῳ Γηων· οὗτος ὁ κυκλῶν πᾶσαν τὴν γῆν Αἰθιοπίας.	13 And the second river's name is Geon; it is the one that encircles the whole land of Ethiopia.	13 The name of the second river is Gihon; it is the one that flows around the whole land of Cush.
14 καὶ ὁ ποταμὸς ὁ τρίτος Τίγρις· οὗτος ὁ πορευόμενος κατέναντι Ἀσσυρίων. ὁ δὲ ποταμὸς ὁ τέταρτος, οὗτος Εὐφράτης.	14 And the third river is the Tigris; it is the one that goes over against the Assyrians. As for the fourth river, it is the Euphrates.	14 The name of the third river is Tigris, which flows east of Assyria. And the fourth river is the Euphrates.

LXX Greek	LXX English (NETS)	NRSV
15 Καὶ ἔλαβεν κύριος ὁ θεὸς **τὸν ἄνθρωπον**, ὃν ἔπλασεν, καὶ ἔθετο αὐτὸν ἐν τῷ παραδείσῳ ἐργάζεσθαι αὐτὸν καὶ φυλάσσειν.	15 And the Lord God took the man whom he had formed and put him in the orchard to till and keep it.	15 The LORD God took the man and put him in the garden of Eden to till it and keep it.
16 καὶ ἐνετείλατο κύριος ὁ θεὸς **τῷ Αδαμ** λέγων Ἀπὸ παντὸς ξύλου τοῦ ἐν τῷ παραδείσῳ βρώσει φάγῃ,	16 And the Lord God commanded Adam, saying, "You shall eat for food of every tree that is in the orchard,	16 And the LORD God commanded the man, "You may freely eat of every tree of the garden;
17 ἀπὸ δὲ τοῦ ξύλου τοῦ γινώσκειν καλὸν καὶ πονηρόν, οὐ φάγεσθε ἀπ᾽ αὐτοῦ· ᾗ δ᾽ ἂν ἡμέρᾳ φάγητε ἀπ᾽ αὐτοῦ, θανάτῳ ἀποθανεῖσθε.	17 but of the tree for knowing good and evil, of it you shall not eat; on the day that you eat of it, you shall die by death."	17 but of the tree of the knowledge of good and evil you shall not eat, for in the day that you eat of it you shall die."
18 Καὶ εἶπεν κύριος ὁ θεός Οὐ καλὸν εἶναι **τὸν ἄνθρωπον** μόνον· ποιήσωμεν αὐτῷ βοηθὸν κατ᾽ αὐτόν.	18 Then the Lord God said, "It is not good that the man is alone; let us make him a helper corresponding to him."	18 Then the LORD God said, "It is not good that the man should be alone; I will make him a helper as his partner."
19 καὶ ἔπλασεν ὁ θεὸς ἔτι ἐκ τῆς γῆς πάντα τὰ θηρία τοῦ ἀγροῦ καὶ πάντα τὰ πετεινὰ τοῦ οὐρανοῦ καὶ ἤγαγεν αὐτὰ πρὸς **τὸν Αδαμ** ἰδεῖν, τί καλέσει αὐτά, καὶ πᾶν, ὃ ἐὰν ἐκάλεσεν αὐτὸ Αδαμ ψυχὴν ζῶσαν, τοῦτο ὄνομα αὐτοῦ.	19 And out of the earth God furthermore formed all the animals of the field and all the birds of the sky and brought them to Adam to see what he would call them, and anything, whatever Adam called it as living creature, this was its name.	19 So out of the ground the LORD God formed every animal of the field and every bird of the air, and brought them to the man to see what he would call them; and whatever the man called every living creature, that was its name.
20 Καὶ ἐκάλεσεν Αδαμ ὀνόματα πᾶσιν τοῖς κτήνεσιν καὶ πᾶσι τοῖς πετεινοῖς τοῦ οὐρανοῦ καὶ πᾶσι τοῖς θηρίοις τοῦ ἀγροῦ, τῷ δὲ Αδαμ οὐχ εὑρέθη βοηθὸς ὅμοιος αὐτῷ.—	20 And Adam gave names to all the cattle and to all the birds of the sky and to all the animals of the field, but for Adam there was not found a helper like him.	20 The man gave names to all cattle, and to the birds of the air, and to every animal of the field; but for the man there was not found a helper as his partner.
21 καὶ ἐπέβαλεν ὁ θεὸς ἔκστασιν ἐπὶ τὸν Αδαμ, καὶ ὕπνωσεν· καὶ ἔλαβεν μίαν τῶν πλευρῶν αὐτοῦ καὶ ἀνεπλήρωσεν σάρκα ἀντ᾽ αὐτῆς.	21 And God cast a trance upon Adam, and he slept, and he took one of his ribs and filled up flesh in its place.	21 So the LORD God caused a deep sleep to fall upon the man, and he slept; then he took one of his ribs and closed up its place with flesh.

LXX Greek	LXX English (NETS)	NRSV
22 καὶ ᾠκοδόμησεν κύριος ὁ θεὸς τὴν πλευράν, ἣν ἔλαβεν ἀπὸ τοῦ **Αδαμ**, εἰς γυναῖκα καὶ ἤγαγεν αὐτὴν πρὸς **τὸν Αδαμ**.	22 And the rib that he had taken from <u>Adam</u> the Lord God fashioned into a woman and brought her to <u>Adam</u>.	22 And the rib that the Lord God had taken from <u>the man</u> he made into a woman and brought her to <u>the man</u>.
23 καὶ εἶπεν **Αδαμ** Τοῦτο νῦν ὀστοῦν ἐκ τῶν ὀστέων μου καὶ σὰρξ ἐκ τῆς σαρκός μου· αὕτη κληθήσεται γυνή, ὅτι ἐκ τοῦ ἀνδρὸς αὐτῆς ἐλήμφθη αὕτη.	23 And <u>Adam</u> said, "This now is bone of my bones and flesh of my flesh; this one shall be called Woman, for out of her husband she was taken."	23 Then <u>the man</u> said, "This at last is bone of my bones and flesh of my flesh; this one shall be called Woman, for out of Man this one was taken."
24 ἕνεκεν τούτου καταλείψει ἄνθρωπος τὸν πατέρα αὐτοῦ καὶ τὴν μητέρα αὐτοῦ καὶ προσκολληθήσεται πρὸς τὴν γυναῖκα αὐτοῦ, καὶ ἔσονται οἱ δύο εἰς σάρκα μίαν.	24 Therefore a man will leave his father and mother and will be joined to his wife, and the two will become one flesh.	24 Therefore a man leaves his father and his mother and clings to his wife, and they become one flesh.
25 καὶ ἦσαν οἱ δύο γυμνοί, ὅ τε **Αδαμ** καὶ ἡ γυνὴ αὐτοῦ, καὶ οὐκ ᾐσχύνοντο.	25 And the two were naked, both <u>Adam</u> and his wife and were not ashamed.	25 And <u>the man</u> and his wife were both naked, and were not ashamed.

Chapter 3

LXX Greek	LXX English (NETS)	NRSV
1 Ὁ δὲ ὄφις ἦν φρονιμώτατος πάντων τῶν θηρίων τῶν ἐπὶ τῆς γῆς, ὧν ἐποίησεν κύριος ὁ θεός· καὶ εἶπεν ὁ ὄφις τῇ γυναικί Τί ὅτι εἶπεν ὁ θεός Οὐ μὴ φάγητε ἀπὸ παντὸς ξύλου τοῦ ἐν τῷ παραδείσῳ;	1 Now the snake was the most sagacious of all the wild animals that were upon the earth, which the Lord God had made. And the snake said to the woman, "Why is it that God said, 'You shall not eat from any tree that is in the orchard'?"	1 Now the serpent was more crafty than any other wild animal that the Lord God had made. He said to the woman, "Did God say, 'You shall not eat from any tree in the garden'?"
2 καὶ εἶπεν ἡ γυνὴ τῷ ὄφει Ἀπὸ καρποῦ ξύλου τοῦ παραδείσου φαγόμεθα,	2 And the woman said to the snake, "We shall eat of the fruit of the tree of the orchard,	2 The woman said to the serpent, "We may eat of the fruit of the trees in the garden;
3 ἀπὸ δὲ καρποῦ τοῦ ξύλου, ὅ ἐστιν ἐν μέσῳ τοῦ παραδείσου, εἶπεν ὁ θεός Οὐ φάγεσθε ἀπ' αὐτοῦ οὐδὲ μὴ ἅψησθε αὐτοῦ, ἵνα μὴ ἀποθάνητε.	3 but of the fruit of the tree that is in the middle of the orchard, God said, 'You shall not eat of it nor shall you even touch it, lest you die.'"	3 but God said, 'You shall not eat of the fruit of the tree that is in the middle of the garden, nor shall you touch it, or you shall die.'"

LXX Greek	LXX English (NETS)	NRSV
4 καὶ εἶπεν ὁ ὄφις τῇ γυναικί Οὐ θανάτῳ ἀποθανεῖσθε·	4 And the snake said to the woman, "You will not die by death;	4 But the serpent said to the woman, "You will not die;
5 ᾔδει γὰρ ὁ θεὸς ὅτι ἐν ᾗ ἂν ἡμέρᾳ φάγητε ἀπ᾽ αὐτοῦ, διανοιχθήσονται ὑμῶν οἱ ὀφθαλμοί, καὶ ἔσεσθε ὡς θεοὶ γινώσκοντες καλὸν καὶ πονηρόν.	5 for God knew that on the day you eat of it, your eyes would be opened, and you would be like gods knowing good and evil."	5 for God knows that when you eat of it your eyes will be opened, and you will be like God, knowing good and evil."
6 καὶ εἶδεν ἡ γυνὴ ὅτι καλὸν τὸ ξύλον εἰς βρῶσιν καὶ ὅτι ἀρεστὸν τοῖς ὀφθαλμοῖς ἰδεῖν καὶ ὡραῖόν ἐστιν τοῦ κατανοῆσαι, καὶ λαβοῦσα τοῦ καρποῦ αὐτοῦ ἔφαγεν· καὶ ἔδωκεν καὶ τῷ ἀνδρὶ αὐτῆς μετ᾽ αὐτῆς, καὶ ἔφαγον.	6 And the woman saw that the tree was good for food and that it was pleasing for the eyes to look at and it was beautiful to contemplate, and when she had taken of its fruit she ate, and she also gave some to her husband with her, and they ate.	6 So when the woman saw that the tree was good for food, and that it was a delight to the eyes, and that the tree was to be desired to make one wise, she took of its fruit and ate; and she also gave some to her husband, who was with her, and he ate.
7 καὶ διηνοίχθησαν οἱ ὀφθαλμοὶ τῶν δύο, καὶ ἔγνωσαν ὅτι γυμνοὶ ἦσαν, καὶ ἔρραψαν φύλλα συκῆς καὶ ἐποίησαν ἑαυτοῖς περιζώματα.	7 And the eyes of the two were opened, and they knew that they were naked, and they sewed fig leaves together and made loincloths for themselves.	7 Then the eyes of both were opened, and they knew that they were naked; and they sewed fig leaves together and made loincloths for themselves.
8 Καὶ ἤκουσαν τὴν φωνὴν κυρίου τοῦ θεοῦ περιπατοῦντος ἐν τῷ παραδείσῳ τὸ δειλινόν, καὶ ἐκρύβησαν ὅ τε **Αδαμ** καὶ ἡ γυνὴ αὐτοῦ ἀπὸ προσώπου κυρίου τοῦ θεοῦ ἐν μέσῳ τοῦ ξύλου τοῦ παραδείσου.	8 And they heard the sound of the Lord God walking about in the orchard in the evening, and both **Adam** and his wife hid themselves from the presence of the Lord God in the midst of the timber of the orchard.	8 They heard the sound of the LORD God walking in the garden at the time of the evening breeze, and **the man** and his wife hid themselves from the presence of the LORD God among the trees of the garden.
9 καὶ ἐκάλεσεν κύριος ὁ θεὸς **τὸν Αδαμ** καὶ εἶπεν αὐτῷ **Αδαμ**, ποῦ εἶ;	9 And the Lord God called **Adam** and said to him, "**Adam**, where are you?"	9 But the LORD God called to **the man**, and said to him, "Where are you?"
10 καὶ εἶπεν αὐτῷ Τὴν φωνήν σου ἤκουσα περιπατοῦντος ἐν τῷ παραδείσῳ καὶ ἐφοβήθην, ὅτι γυμνός εἰμι, καὶ ἐκρύβην.	10 And he said to him, "I heard the sound of you walking about in the orchard and I was afraid, because I am naked, and I hid myself."	10 He said, "I heard the sound of you in the garden, and I was afraid, because I was naked; and I hid myself."

LXX Greek	LXX English (NETS)	NRSV
11 καὶ εἶπεν αὐτῷ Τίς ἀνήγγειλέν σοι ὅτι γυμνὸς εἶ; μὴ ἀπὸ τοῦ ξύλου, οὗ ἐνετειλάμην σοι τούτου μόνου μὴ φαγεῖν ἀπ' αὐτοῦ, ἔφαγες;	11 And he said to him, "Who told you that you are naked, unless you have eaten from the tree of which I commanded you, of this one alone, not to eat from it?"	11 He said, "Who told you that you were naked? Have you eaten from the tree of which I commanded you not to eat?"
12 καὶ εἶπεν ὁ Αδαμ Ἡ γυνή, ἣν ἔδωκας μετ' ἐμοῦ, αὕτη μοι ἔδωκεν ἀπὸ τοῦ ξύλου, καὶ ἔφαγον.	12 And **Adam** said, "The woman, whom you gave to be with me, she gave me of the tree, and I ate."	12 The man said, "The woman whom you gave to be with me, she gave me fruit from the tree, and I ate."
13 καὶ εἶπεν κύριος ὁ θεὸς τῇ γυναικί Τί τοῦτο ἐποίησας; καὶ εἶπεν ἡ γυνή Ὁ ὄφις ἠπάτησέν με, καὶ ἔφαγον.	13 And God said to the woman, "What is this you have done?" And the woman said, "The snake tricked me, and I ate."	13 Then the LORD God said to the woman, "What is this that you have done?" The woman said, "The serpent tricked me, and I ate."
14 καὶ εἶπεν κύριος ὁ θεὸς τῷ ὄφει Ὅτι ἐποίησας τοῦτο, ἐπικατάρατος σὺ ἀπὸ πάντων τῶν κτηνῶν καὶ ἀπὸ πάντων τῶν θηρίων τῆς γῆς· ἐπὶ τῷ στήθει σου καὶ τῇ κοιλίᾳ πορεύσῃ καὶ γῆν φάγῃ πάσας τὰς ἡμέρας τῆς ζωῆς σου.	14 And the Lord God said to the snake, "Because you have done this, cursed are you from all the domestic animals and from all the wild animals of the earth; upon your chest and belly you shall go and earth you shall eat all the days of your life.	14 The LORD God said to the serpent, "Because you have done this, cursed are you among all animals and among all wild creatures; upon your belly you shall go, and dust you shall eat all the days of your life.
15 καὶ ἔχθραν θήσω ἀνὰ μέσον σου καὶ ἀνὰ μέσον τῆς γυναικὸς καὶ ἀνὰ μέσον τοῦ σπέρματός σου καὶ ἀνὰ μέσον τοῦ σπέρματος αὐτῆς· αὐτός σου τηρήσει κεφαλήν, καὶ σὺ τηρήσεις αὐτοῦ πτέρναν.	15 And I will put enmity between you and between the woman and between your offspring and between her offspring; he will watch your head, and you will watch his heel."	15 I will put enmity between you and the woman, and between your offspring and hers; he will strike your head, and you will strike his heel."
16 καὶ τῇ γυναικὶ εἶπεν Πληθύνων πληθυνῶ τὰς λύπας σου καὶ τὸν στεναγμόν σου, ἐν λύπαις τέξῃ τέκνα· καὶ πρὸς τὸν ἄνδρα σου ἡ ἀποστροφή σου, καὶ αὐτός σου κυριεύσει.	16 And to the woman he said, "I will increasingly increase your pains and your groaning; with pains you will bring forth children. And your recourse [or "return"] will be to your husband, and he will dominate you."	16 To the woman he said, "I will greatly increase your pangs in childbearing; in pain you shall bring forth children, yet your desire shall be for your husband, and he shall rule over you."

LXX Greek	LXX English (NETS)	NRSV
17 τῷ δὲ **Αδαμ** εἶπεν Ὅτι ἤκουσας τῆς φωνῆς τῆς γυναικός σου καὶ ἔφαγες ἀπὸ τοῦ ξύλου, οὗ ἐνετειλάμην σοι τούτου μόνου μὴ φαγεῖν ἀπ' αὐτοῦ, ἐπικατάρατος ἡ γῆ ἐν τοῖς ἔργοις σου· ἐν λύπαις φάγη αὐτὴν πάσας τὰς ἡμέρας τῆς ζωῆς σου·	17 Then <u>to Adam</u> he said, "Because you have listened to the voice of your wife and have eaten from the tree of which I commanded you, of this one alone, not to eat from it, cursed is the earth in your labors; with pains you will eat it all the days of your life;	17 And <u>to the man</u> he said, "Because you have listened to the voice of your wife, and have eaten of the tree about which I commanded you, 'You shall not eat of it,' cursed is the ground because of you; in toil you shall eat of it all the days of your life;
18 ἀκάνθας καὶ τριβόλους ἀνατελεῖ σοι, καὶ φάγῃ τὸν χόρτον τοῦ ἀγροῦ.	18 thorns and thistles it shall cause to grow up for you, and you will eat the herbage of the field.	18 thorns and thistles it shall bring forth for you; and you shall eat the plants of the field.
19 ἐν ἱδρῶτι τοῦ προσώπου σου φάγῃ τὸν ἄρτον σου ἕως τοῦ ἀποστρέψαι σε εἰς τὴν γῆν, ἐξ ἧς ἐλήμφθης· ὅτι γῆ εἶ καὶ εἰς γῆν ἀπελεύσῃ. —	19 By the sweat of your face you will eat your bread until you return to the earth from which you were taken, for you are earth and to earth you will depart."	19 By the sweat of your face you shall eat bread until you return to the ground, for out of it you were taken; you are dust, and to dust you shall return."
20 καὶ ἐκάλεσεν **Αδαμ** τὸ ὄνομα τῆς γυναικὸς αὐτοῦ Ζωή, ὅτι αὕτη μήτηρ πάντων τῶν ζώντων.	20 And **Adam** called the name of his wife Life, because she is the mother of all the living.	20 **The man** named his wife Eve, because she was the mother of all living.
21 Καὶ ἐποίησεν κύριος ὁ θεὸς **τῷ Αδαμ** καὶ τῇ γυναικὶ αὐτοῦ χιτῶνας δερματίνους καὶ ἐνέδυσεν αὐτούς. —	21 And the Lord God made leather tunics for **Adam** and for his wife and clothed them.	21 And the LORD God made garments of skins for **the man** and for his wife, and clothed them.
22 καὶ εἶπεν ὁ θεός Ἰδοὺ **Αδαμ** γέγονεν ὡς εἷς ἐξ ἡμῶν τοῦ γινώσκειν καλὸν καὶ πονηρόν, καὶ νῦν μήποτε ἐκτείνῃ τὴν χεῖρα καὶ λάβῃ τοῦ ξύλου τῆς ζωῆς καὶ φάγῃ καὶ ζήσεται εἰς τὸν αἰῶνα.	22 Then God said, "See, **Adam** has become like one of us, knowing good and evil, and now perhaps he might reach out his hand and take of the tree of life and eat, and he will live forever."	22 Then the LORD God said, "See, **the man** has become like one of us, knowing good and evil; and now, he might reach out his hand and take also from the tree of life, and eat, and live forever"—
23 καὶ ἐξαπέστειλεν αὐτὸν κύριος ὁ θεὸς ἐκ τοῦ παραδείσου τῆς τρυφῆς ἐργάζεσθαι τὴν γῆν, ἐξ ἧς ἐλήμφθη.	23 And the Lord God sent him forth from the orchard of delight to till the earth from which he was taken.	23 therefore the LORD God sent him forth from the garden of Eden, to till the ground from which he was taken.

LXX Greek	LXX English (NETS)	NRSV
24 καὶ ἐξέβαλεν <u>τὸν Αδαμ</u> καὶ κατῴκισεν αὐτὸν ἀπέναντι τοῦ παραδείσου τῆς τρυφῆς καὶ ἔταξεν τὰ χερουβιμ καὶ τὴν φλογίνην ῥομφαίαν τὴν στρεφομένην φυλάσσειν τὴν ὁδὸν τοῦ ξύλου τῆς ζωῆς.	24 And he drove <u>Adam</u> out and caused him to dwell opposite the orchard of delight, and he stationed the cheroubim and the flaming sword that turns, to guard the way of the tree of life.	24 He drove out <u>the man;</u> and at the east of the garden of Eden he placed the cherubim, and a sword flaming and turning to guard the way to the tree of life.

Chapter 5

1 Αὕτη ἡ βίβλος γενέσεως <u>ἀνθρώπων·</u> ᾗ ἡμέρα ἐποίησεν ὁ θεὸς τὸν <u>Αδαμ,</u> κατ᾽ εἰκόνα θεοῦ ἐποίησεν αὐτόν·	1 This is the book of the origin of <u>human beings</u>. On the day that God made <u>Adam</u>, he made him according to the divine image;	1 This is the list of the descendants of <u>Adam</u>. When God created <u>humankind,</u> he made them in the likeness of God.
2 ἄρσεν καὶ θῆλυ ἐποίησεν αὐτοὺς καὶ εὐλόγησεν αὐτούς. καὶ ἐπωνόμασεν τὸ ὄνομα αὐτῶν <u>Αδαμ,</u> ᾗ ἡμέρα ἐποίησεν αὐτούς.	2 male and female he made them and he blessed them. And he named their name "<u>Adam</u>" on the day that he made them.	2 Male and female he created them, and he blessed them and named them '<u>Humankind</u>' when they were created.
3 ἔζησεν δὲ <u>Αδαμ</u> διακόσια καὶ τριάκοντα ἔτη καὶ ἐγέννησεν κατὰ τὴν ἰδέαν αὐτοῦ καὶ κατὰ τὴν εἰκόνα αὐτοῦ καὶ ἐπωνόμασεν τὸ ὄνομα αὐτοῦ Σηθ.	3 Now <u>Adam</u> lived two hundred thirty years and became a father, according to his form and according to his image and named his name Seth.	3 When <u>Adam</u> had lived for one hundred thirty years, he became the father of a son in his likeness, according to his image, and named him Seth.
4 ἐγένοντο δὲ αἱ ἡμέραι <u>Αδαμ</u> μετὰ τὸ γεννῆσαι αὐτὸν τὸν Σηθ ἑπτακόσια ἔτη, καὶ ἐγέννησεν υἱοὺς καὶ θυγατέρας.	4 And the days of <u>Adam</u> after he became the father of Seth amounted to seven hundred years, and he had sons and daughters.	4 The days of <u>Adam</u> after he became the father of Seth were eight hundred years; and he had other sons and daughters.
5 καὶ ἐγένοντο πᾶσαι αἱ ἡμέραι <u>Αδαμ,</u> ἃς ἔζησεν, ἐννακόσια καὶ τριάκοντα ἔτη, καὶ ἀπέθανεν.	5 And all the days of <u>Adam</u>, that he lived, amounted to nine hundred thirty years, and he died.	5 Thus all the days that <u>Adam</u> lived were nine hundred thirty years; and he died.

List of Abbreviations

AB	Anchor Bible
ACW	Ancient Christian Writers
ANF	*The Ante-Nicene Fathers.* Edited by A. Roberts and J. Donaldson. 10 vols. Edinburgh: T&T Clark, 1867. Repr. Grand Rapids: Eerdmans, 1985–87.
2 Bar.	*2 Baruch (Syriac Apocalypse)*
Barn.	*Barnabas*
BCE	before the Common Era
BJS	Brown Judaic Studies
CE	Common Era
CRINT	Compendia rerum iudaicarum ad Novum Testamentum
CWS	Classics of Western Spirituality
ECF	Early Christian Fathers
FC	Fathers of the Church
FCT	Formation of Christian Theology
GCS	Die griechische christliche Schriftsteller der ersten [drei] Jahrhunderte
GNO	Gregorii Nysseni Opera
J	Jahwist or Yahwist source (of the Pentateuch)
JECS	*Journal of Early Christian Studies*
JSPSup	Journal for the Study of the Pseudepigrapha: Supplement Series
JTS	*Journal of Theological Studies*
Jub.	*Jubilees*
LCC	Library of Christian Classics
LCL	Loeb Classical Library
LXX	Septuagint
MS	manuscript
NETS	New English Translation of the Septuagint
NIV	New International Version
NovTSup	Novum Testamentum Supplements
NPNF¹	*A Select Library of Nicene and Post-Nicene Fathers of the Christian Church*, Series 1. Edited by Philip Schaff et al. 14 vols. New York: Christian Literature, 1886–90. Repr. Grand Rapids: Eerdmans, 1974–78

NPNF[2]	*A Select Library of Nicene and Post-Nicene Fathers of the Christian Church*, Series 2. Edited by Philip Schaff and Henry Wace. 14 vols. Oxford: Parker, 1890–1900. Repr. Grand Rapids: Eerdmans, 1978–79
NRSV	New Revised Standard Version
NS	new series
NT	New Testament
OECT	Oxford Early Christian Texts
OT	Old Testament
OTM	Oxford Theological Monographs
P	Priestly source (of the Pentateuch)
PG	Patrologia graeca [= Patrologiae cursus completus: Series graeca]. Edited by J.-P. Migne. 162 vols. Paris, 1857–66
PL	Patrologia latina [= Patrologiae cursus completus: Series latina]. Edited by J.-P. Migne. 217 vols. Paris, 1844–64
RechSR	*Recherches de science religieuse*
RSV	Revised Standard Version
SC	Sources chrétiennes
StudPat	Studia patristica
SupVC	Supplements to Vigiliae christianae
SVTQ	*St. Vladimir's Theological Quarterly*
TU	Texte und Untersuchungen zur Geschichte der altchristlichen Literatur
VC	*Vigiliae christianae*

Bibliography

Primary sources: critical texts and translations

References to the LXX are from Alfred Rahlfs, ed., *Septuaginta* (Stuttgart: Deutsche Bibelgesellschaft, 1979). For the Hebrew Bible, see R. Kittel, ed., *Biblia hebraica*, 4th ed. (Stuttgart: Privilegierte Württembergische Bibelanstalt, 1949). For the Greek New Testament, see E. Nestle, ed., *Novum Testamentum graece*, 25th ed. (London: United Bible Societies, 1963). This study refers to the texts of the early Christian writers by their English-language names; abbreviations for references, however, are based on the commonly accepted Latin abbreviations of the same texts.

Ambrose of Milan

Hex.: The Six Days of Creation. PL 14. Trans. John J. Savage, *Saint Ambrose: Hexaemeron, Paradise, and Cain and Abel*, FC 42 (Washington, DC: Catholic University of America Press, 1961).

Athanasius of Alexandria

CA: Orations against the Arians. Ed. Karin Metzler, Dirk U. Hansen, and Kyriakos Savvidis, *Orationes I et II contra Arianos*, fascicle 2 of *Die dogmatischen Schriften*, vol. 1.1 of *Athanasius Werke* (Berlin: de Gruyter, 1998); ed. K. Savvidis and K. Metzler, *Oratio III contra Arianos*, fascicle 3 of *Die dogmatischen Schriften* (Berlin: de Gruyter, 2000). Also ed. William Bright, *The Orations of St. Athanasius against the Arians* (Oxford: Clarendon, 1884). Trans. Archibald Robertson, *NPNF*[2] 4:303–447.

CG: Against the Pagans. Ed. and trans. Robert W. Thomson, *Contra gentes and De incarnatione* (Oxford: Clarendon, 1971).

Decr.: *Defense of the Nicene Definition.* Ed. H. G. Opitz, *Athanasius Werke,* vol. 2.1, *Die Apologien* (Berlin: de Gruyter, 1935), 1–45. Trans. Khaled Anatolios, *Athanasius,* ECF (London: Routledge, 2004), 176–211.

DI: *On the Incarnation.* Ed. and trans. Robert W. Thomson, *Contra gentes and De incarnatione* (Oxford: Clarendon, 1971), 134–277. Also ed. Charles Kannengiesser, *Sur l'incarnation du Verbe,* SC 199 (Paris: Cerf, 1973).

Basil of Caesarea

C. *Eun.: Against Eunomius.* Ed. B. Sesboüé, with G.-M. Durand and L. Doutreleau, *Basile de Césarée: Contre Eunome,* SC 299, 305 (Paris: Cerf, 1982, 1983).

De creat.: *On the Origin of Humanity.* Ed. Alexis Smets and Michel van Esbroeck, *Sur l'origine de l'homme,* SC 160 (Paris: Cerf, 1970). Trans. Nonna Verna Harrison, *St. Basil the Great: On the Human Condition,* Popular Patristics (Crestwood, NY: St. Vladimir's Seminary Press, 2005), 31–64.

DSS: *On the Holy Spirit.* Ed. Benoît Pruche, *Sur le Saint-Esprit,* SC 17 bis, 2nd ed. (Paris: Cerf, 1968). Trans. David Anderson, *St. Basil the Great: On the Holy Spirit,* Popular Patristics (Crestwood, NY: St. Vladimir's Seminary Press, 1980).

Ep.: *Letters.* Ed. and trans. Roy Joseph Deferrari, *Saint Basil: The Letters,* 4 vols., LCL (New York: G. P. Putnam's Sons, 1926–34). Also ed. Yves Courtonne, *Saint Basile: Lettres,* 3 vols., Collection des universités de France (Paris: Belles Lettres, 1957–66).

Hom.: *Homilies.*[1]

> Hom. 336 (*Homilia quod Deus non est auctor malorum*). PG 31:329–53. Trans. Nonna Verna Harrison, *St. Basil the Great: On the Human Condition,* Popular Patristics (Crestwood, NY: St. Vladimir's Seminary Press, 2005), 65–80.

> Hom. 350 (*Homilia in Psalmum 32*): PG 29:324–49. Trans. Agnes Clare Way, *Saint Basil: Exegetic Homilies,* FC 46 (Washington, DC: Catholic University of America Press, 1963), 227–46.

In Hex.: *Homilies on the Hexaemeron.* Ed. Stanislas Giet, *Homélies sur l'Hexaéméron,* SC 26 bis (Paris: Cerf, 1968). Trans. Agnes Clare Way, *Saint Basil: Exegetic Homilies,* FC 46 (Washington, DC: Catholic University of America Press, 1963), 3–150.

In Isa.: *Commentary on the Prophet Isaiah.* PG 30:117–668. Trans. Nikolai A. Lipatov, *St. Basil the Great: Commentary on the Prophet Isaiah,* Texts and Studies in the History of Theology (Mandelbachtal, Germany; Cambridge, UK: Cicero, 2001).

Lit.: *The Divine Liturgy of St. Basil the Great.* Ed. Stefano Parenti and Elena Velkovska, *L'Eucologio Barberini Gr. 336 (ff. 1–263),* Bibliotheca "Ephemerides liturgicae": Subsidia (Rome: Edizioni Liturgiche, 1995). Trans. *The Divine Liturgy according to St. John Chrysostom: With Appendices* (New York: Russian Orthodox Greek Catholic Church in America, 1967).

---

1. I adopt the homily numbering system employed by P. J. Fedwick (cf. *Basil of Caesarea,* 1:xxvii–xxviii) and also by P. Rousseau (*Basil of Caesarea*).

Clement of Alexandria

Protr.: Protrepticus. Ed. Claude Mondésert, rev. André Plassart, *Le protreptique*, SC 2, 4th ed. (Paris: Cerf, 1976).

Strom.: Stromata. Ed. Otto Stählin, *Clemens Alexandrinus*, vol. 2, *Stromata, Buch I–VI*, 3rd ed., GCS 52 (Berlin: Akademie, 1960). Trans. *ANF* 2:299–567. Also trans. John Ferguson, *Clement of Alexandria: Stromateis, Books One to Three*, FC 85 (Washington, DC: Catholic University of America Press, 1991).

Cyril of Jerusalem

Cat.: Catechetical Lectures. Ed. Wilhelm Karl Reischl and Joseph Rupp, *Cyrilli Hierosolymarum archiepiscopi Opera quae supersunt omnia*, 2 vols. (Munich, 1848–60; repr. Hildesheim: Georg Olms, 1967), 1:28–320, 2:2–342. Trans. Edwin H. Gifford, *NPNF*[2] 7:1–157. Also trans. William Telfer, in *Cyril of Jerusalem and Nemesius of Emesa*, LCC 4 (Philadelphia: Westminster, 1955), 64–192 (selections). Also trans. Edward Yarnold, *Cyril of Jerusalem*, ECF (London: Routledge, 2000), 79–171 (selections).

Didymus the Blind

In Gen.: Commentary on Genesis. Ed. Pierre Nautin and Louis Doutreleau, *Sur la Genèse*, 2 vols., SC 233, 244 (Paris: Cerf, 1976–78).

Epiphanius of Salamis

Ancoratus: Ed. Karl Holl, *Epiphanius*, GCS 25, 3 vols. (Berlin: Akademie, 1915), 1:1–149.

Panarion: Ed. Karl Holl, *Epiphanius*, GCS 25, 3 vols. (Berlin: Akademie, 1915), vol. 1. Ed. Karl Holl, rev. Jürgen Dummer, *Epiphanius*, 2nd ed., GCS 31, 37 (Berlin: Akademie, 1980–85), vols. 2–3. Trans. Frank Williams, *The Panarion of Epiphanius of Salamis*, 2 vols. (Leiden: Brill, 1987–94). Also trans. Philip R. Amidon, *The Panarion of St. Epiphanius of Salamis: Selected Passages* (Oxford: Oxford University Press, 1990) (selections).

Gregory of Nazianzus

Epistulae: Ed. Paul Gallay, *Lettres*, 2 vols. (Paris: Belles Lettres, 1964–67). Also ed. Paul Gallay, *Lettres théologiques*, SC 208 (Paris: Cerf, 1974) (*Ep.* 101–2, 202). Trans. Frederick Williams and Lionel Wickham, *On God and Christ: The Five Theological Orations and Two Letters to Cledonius*, Popular Patristics (Crestwood, NY: St. Vladimir's Seminary Press, 2002).

Or.: Orations

  Or. 1–5. Ed. Jean Bernardi, *Discours 1–3*, SC 247 (Paris: Cerf, 1978); *Discours 4–5*, SC 309 (Paris: Cerf, 1983).

Or. 6–12. Ed. Marie-Ange Calvet-Sebasti, *Discours 6–12,* SC 405 (Paris: Cerf, 1995).

Or. 20–23. Ed. J. Mossay, *Discours 20–23,* SC 270 (Paris: Cerf, 1980).

Or. 24–26. Ed. J. Mossay, *Discours 24–26,* SC 284 (Paris: Cerf, 1981).

Or. 27–31. Ed. Paul Gallay, *Discours 27–31,* SC 250 (Paris: Cerf, 1978). Also ed. Arthur James Mason, *The Five Theological Orations of Gregory Nazianzus* (Cambridge: Cambridge University Press, 1899). Trans. Lionel Wickham and Frederick Williams, *Faith Gives Fullness to Reasoning: The Five Theological Orations of Gregory Nazianzen,* ed. Frederick W. Norris (Leiden: Brill, 1991); these translations also published in F. Williams and L. Wickham, *On God and Christ: The Five Theological Orations and Two Letters to Cledonius,* Popular Patristics (Crestwood, NY: St. Vladimir's Seminary Press, 2002), 25–147.

Or. 32–37. Ed. Claudio Moreschini, *Discours 32–37,* SC 318 (Paris: Cerf, 1985).

Or. 38–41. Ed. Claudio Moreschini, *Discours 38–41,* SC 358 (Paris: Cerf, 1990).

Or. 42–43. Ed. Jean Bernardi, *Discours 42–43,* SC 384 (Paris: Cerf, 1992).

Or. 14, 19, 44, 45. PG 35–36. Trans. Charles Gordon Browne and James Edward Swallow, *NPNF²* 7 (selected orations).

Or. 8, 14, 20, 26, 38, 39, 42, 44. Trans. Brian Edward Daley, *Gregory of Nazianzus,* ECF (London: Routledge, 2006), 63–161.

Carm.: Poetica. PG 37–38. Trans. Peter Gilbert, *On God and Man: The Theological Poetry of St. Gregory of Nazianzus,* Popular Patristics (Crestwood, NY: St. Vladimir's Seminary Press, 2001) (selections). Also trans. Denis Molaise Meehan, *Saint Gregory of Nazianzus—Three Poems: Concerning His Own Affairs; Concerning Himself and the Bishops; Concerning His Own Life,* FC 75 (Washington, DC: Catholic University of America Press, 1987). Also trans. D. A. Sykes, *Gregory of Nazianzus: Poemata arcana,* ed. Claudio Moreschini, OTM (Oxford: Clarendon, 1997).

Gregory of Nyssa

C. Eun.: Against Eunomius. Ed. Werner Jaeger, *Contra Eunomium libri,* 2 vols., GNO 1–2 (Leiden: Brill, 1960). English trans. Stuart George Hall, in *El "Contra Eunomium I" en la producción literaria de Gregorio de Nisa: VI Coloquio internacional sobre Gregorio de Nisa,* ed. Lucas Francisco Mateo-Seco and Juan L. Bastero (Pamplona: Universidad de Navarra, 1988), 35–135 (*C. Eun.* 1). Also trans. Henry Austin Wilson, *NPNF²* 5:33–248.

C. Fatum: Against Fate. Ed. James A. McDonough, *Opera dogmatica minora,* GNO 3.2 (Leiden: Brill, 1987): 29–63. Trans. Casimir McCambley, "*Against Fate* by Gregory of Nyssa," *Greek Orthodox Theological Review* 37 (1992): 320–32.

DAR: On the Soul and the Resurrection. PG 46:12–160. Also ed. Johann Georg Krabinger, *De anima et resurrection cum sorore sua Macrina dialogus* (Leipzig: Gustav Wuttig, 1837). Trans. Catharine P. Roth, *St. Gregory of Nyssa: On the Soul and the Resurrection,* Popular Patristics (Crestwood, NY: St. Vladimir's Seminary Press, 1993).

De beat.: The Beatitudes. Ed. John Francis Callahan, *De Oratione dominica, De beatitudinibus,* GNO 7.2 (Leiden: Brill, 1992). Trans. Hilda C. Graef, *St. Gregory of Nyssa: The Lord's Prayer, The Beatitudes,* ACW 18 (Westminster, MD: Newman, 1954).

De inf.: On the Premature Death of Infants. Ed. Hadwig Hörner, *Dogmatica minora,* GNO 3.2 (Leiden, New York, Copenhagen, and Cologne: Brill, 1987), 65–97. Trans. William Moore, *NPNF*[2] 5:372–81.

De virg.: On Virginity. Ed. John Peter Cavarnos, *Sermones,* GNO 8.1 (Leiden: Brill, 1962), 247–343. Also ed. Michel Aubinau, *Traité de la virginité,* SC 119 (Paris: Cerf, 1966). Trans. Virginia Woods Callahan, *Gregory of Nyssa: Ascetical Works,* FC 58 (Washington, DC: Catholic University of America Press, 1967), 6–75.

De vita Moys.: On the Life of Moses. Ed. Herbert Musurillo, *De vita Moysis,* GNO 7.1 (Leiden: Brill, 1964). Trans. Abraham J. Malherbe and Everett Ferguson, *Gregory of Nyssa: The Life of Moses,* CWS (New York: Paulist, 1978).

DHO: On the Making of Humanity. PG 44:124–256. Also ed. G. Forbes, *Sancti patris nostri Gregorii Nysseni (Basilii Magni fratris) Quae supersunt omnia* (Burntisland, UK, 1855), vol. 1. Trans. Henry Austin Wilson, *NPNF*[2] 5:387–427.

In Cant.: On the Song of Songs. Ed. Hermann Langerbeck, *In Canticum canticorum,* GNO 6 (Leiden: Brill, 1960). Trans. Casimir McCambley, *Saint Gregory of Nyssa: Commentary on the Song of Songs,* Archbishop Iakovos Library of Ecclesiastical and Historical Sources (Brookline, MA: Hellenic College Press, 1987).

In Hex.: On the Hexaemeron. PG 44:61–124. Trans. Casimir McCambley, at www.sage.edu/faculty/salomd/nyssa/hex.html (accessed February, 2008).

In inscript.: On the Inscriptions of the Psalms. Ed. James McDonough, *In inscriptiones Psalmorum, In sextum Psalmum, In Ecclesiasten homiliae,* GNO 5 (Leiden: Brill, 1962), 24–175. Also ed. Jean Reynard, *Sur les titres des Psaumes,* SC 466 (Paris: Cerf, 2002). Trans. Ronald E. Heine, *Gregory of Nyssa's Treatise on the Inscriptions of the Psalms,* Oxford Early Christian Studies (Oxford: Clarendon, 1995).

Or. cat.: Catechetical Oration. Ed. Raymond Winling, *Discours catéchétique,* SC 453 (Paris: Cerf, 2000). Trans. Edward Rochie Hardy, *Christology of the Later Fathers,* LCC 3 (Philadelphia: Westminster, 1954), 268–325.

Ref. conf. Eun.: Refutation of Eunomius's Confession. Ed. Werner Jaeger, *Contra Eunomium libri,* 2 vols., GNO 1–2 (Leiden: Brill, 1960), 2:312–410. Trans. Henry Austin Wilson, *NPNF*[2] 5:250–314.

Gregory Palamas

Tri.: Triads (In Defense of the Holy Hesychasts). Ed. John Meyendorff, *Défense des saints hésychastes,* 2nd rev. ed., 2 vols., Spicilegium sacrum lovaniense: Études et documents 30 (Louvain: Université Catholique, 1973).

Ignatius of Antioch

Ep.: Epistles. Ed. Thomas Camelot, *Ignace d'Antioch [et] Polycarpe de Smyrne: Lettres, Martyre de Polycarpe,* 2nd ed., SC 10 (Paris: Cerf, 1951). Trans. Maxwell

Staniforth, *Early Christian Writings: The Apostolic Fathers* (New York: Dorset, 1968), 61–131.

Irenaeus of Lyons

AH: Against the Heresies. Ed. Adelin Rousseau, Louis Doutreleau, and Charles A. Mercier, *Contre les hérésies, livres I–V*, 10 vols., SC 100, 152–53, 210–11, 263–64, 293–94 (Paris: Cerf, 1965–82). Trans. Dominic J. Unger, *St. Irenaeus of Lyons: Against the Heresies, Book 1*, ACW 55 (New York: Paulist, 1992). Also (books 2–5) trans. *ANF* 1:359–567. Also trans. Robert M. Grant, *Irenaeus of Lyons*, ECF (London: Routledge, 1997) (selections).

Dem.: Demonstration of the Apostolic Preaching. Ed. Adelin Rousseau, *Démonstration de la prédication apostolique*, SC 406 (Paris: Cerf, 1995). Trans. John Behr, *St. Irenaeus of Lyons: On the Apostolic Preaching*, Popular Patristics (Crestwood, NY: St. Vladimir's Seminary Press, 1997).

Justin Martyr

Apol.: Apology 1 and 2. Ed. André Wartelle, *I, II Apologiae* (Paris: Études Augustiniennes, 1987). Trans. Leslie William Barnard, *St. Justin Martyr: The First and Second Apologies*, ACW 56 (New York: Paulist, 1997).

Dial.: Dialogue with Trypho. Ed. Edgar J. Goodspeed, *Die ältesten Apologeten: Texte mit kurzen Einleitungen* (Göttingen: Vandenhoeck & Ruprecht, 1914; repr. 1984), 90–265. Trans. Thomas B. Falls, *Writings of Saint Justin Martyr*, FC 6 (New York: Christian Heritage, 1948), 147–366.

Melito of Sardis

PP: On Pascha; Fragments. Ed. and trans. Stuart George Hall, *Melito of Sardis: On Pascha and Fragments*, OECT (Oxford: Oxford University Press, 1979). Also trans. Alistair Stewart-Sykes, *Melito of Sardis: On Pascha, with the Fragments of Melito and Other Material Related to the Quartodecimans*, Popular Patristics (Crestwood, NY: St. Vladimir's Seminary Press, 2001) (a freer, more flowing translation).

Origen

C. Cels.: Against Celsus. Ed. Marcel Borret, *Contre Celse*, 5 vols., SC 132, 136, 147, 150, 227 (Paris: Cerf, 1967–76). Trans. H. Chadwick, *Origen: Contra Celsum* (Cambridge: Cambridge University Press, 1965).

Comm. in Gen.: Commentary on Genesis. Ed. Eric Junod, *Philocalie 21–27*, SC 226 (Paris: Cerf, 1976) (fragments). Also PG 12:45–145. Trans. Joseph Trigg, *Origen*, ECF (London: Routledge 1998), 86–102 (selections).

De orat.: On Prayer. PG 11:416–561. Trans. Rowan A. Greer, *Origen*, CWS (New York: Paulist, 1979), 81–170.

DP: On First Principles. Ed. H. Görgemanns and H. Karpp, *Vier Bücher von den Prinzipien*, Texte zur Forschung 24 (Darmstadt: Wissenschaftliche Buchgesellschaft, 1976). Also ed. H. Crouzel and M. Simonetti, *Traité des principes*, 5 vols., SC 252–53, 268–69, 312 (Paris: Cerf, 1978–84). Trans. G. W. Butterworth, *On First Principles* (Gloucester, MA: P. Smith, 1973). Also (book 4) trans. Rowan A. Greer, *Origen*, CWS (New York: Paulist, 1979), 171–216.

Hom. in Gen.: Homilies on Genesis. Ed. H. de Lubac and L. Doutreleau, *Homélies sur la Genèse*, 2nd ed., SC 7 (Paris: Cerf, 2003). Trans. Ronald E. Heine, *Homilies on Genesis and Exodus*, FC 71 (Washington, DC: Catholic University of America Press, 1982), 47–224.

In Cant.: Commentary on the Song of Songs. Ed. P. Marcel Borret, Luc Brésard, and Henri Crouzel, *Commentaire sur le Cantique des cantiques*, 2 vols., SC 375–76 (Paris: Cerf, 1991–92). Trans. R. P. Lawson, *Origen: The Song of Songs—Commentary and Homilies*, ACW 26 (Westminster, MD: Newman, 1957), 21–263.

In Jer.: Commentary on Jeremiah. Ed. Pierre Nautin, *Homélies sur Jérémie*, SC 232, 238 (Paris: Cerf, 1976–77).

In Jo.: Commentary on John. Ed. C. Blanc, *Commentaire sur saint Jean*, 5 vols., SC 120, 157, 222, 290, 385 (Paris: Cerf, 1966–92). Trans. Ronald E. Heine, *Commentary on the Gospel according to John*, 2 vols., FC 80, 89 (Washington, DC: Catholic University of America Press, 1989–93).

In Lev.: Homilies on Leviticus. Ed. Marcel Borret, *Homélies sur le Lévitique*, 2 vols., SC 286–87 (Paris: Cerf, 1981).

In Matt.: Commentary on Matthew. Ed. E. Benz and E. Klostermann, *Matthäuserklärung*, 3 vols., GCS 38, 40–41 (Leipzig: Hinrich, 1935–55). Trans. John Patrick, *ANF* 9:413–512 (selections).

In Num.: Homilies on Numbers. Ed. L. Doutreleau, *Homélies sur les Nombres*, 3 vols., SC 415, 442, 461 (Paris: Cerf, 1996–2001).

In Rom.: Commentary on Romans. Ed. Caroline P. Hammond Bammel, *Der Römerbriefkommentar des Origenes: Kritische Ausgabe der Übersetzung Rufins*, 3 vols. (Freiburg: Herder, 1990–98). Trans. Thomas P. Scheck, *Commentary on the Epistle to the Romans*, 2 vols., FC 103–4 (Washington, DC: Catholic University of America Press, 2001–2).

Phil.: Philocalia of Origen. Ed. J. Armitage Robinson, *The Philocalia of Origen* (Cambridge: Cambridge University Press, 1893). Also ed. Eric Junod, *Philocalie 21–27: Sur le libre arbitre*, SC 226 (Paris: Cerf, 1976). Also ed. Marguérite Harl, *Philocalie 1–20: Sur les Écritures*, SC 302 (Paris: Cerf, 1983). Trans. George Lewis, *The Philocalia of Origen* (Edinburgh: T&T Clark, 1911).

Sel. in Gen.: Selections from the Commentaries on Genesis. PG 12:91–146.

Philo

Leg.: On the Laws of Allegory. Greek text and trans. Francis Henry Colson and George Herbert Whitaker, *Philo*, LCL (Cambridge, MA: Harvard University Press, 1956), 1:146–472.

Opif.: On the Creation of the World. Trans. David T. Runia, *Philo of Alexandria: On the Creation of the Cosmos according to Moses*, Philo of Alexandria Commentary Series 1 (Leiden and Boston: Brill, 2001).

Quaest.: Questions on Genesis. Greek text and trans. Ralph Marcus, *Philo Supplement I: Questions and Answers on Genesis: Translated from the Ancient Armenian Version of the Original Greek*, LCL (Cambridge, MA: Harvard University Press, 1923).

Tertullian

Adv. Marc.: Against Marcion. Ed. and trans. Ernest Evans, *Tertullian: Adversus Marcionem*, 2 vols. (Oxford: Clarendon, 1972).

De anima: On the Soul. Ed. Jan Hendrik Waszink, *De anima* (Amsterdam: J. M. Meuhlenhoff, 1947).

De res.: On the Resurrection of the Flesh. Ed. and trans. Ernest Evans, *Tertullian's Treatise on the Resurrection* (London: SPCK, 1960).

De spect.: On the Spectacles. Ed. Marie Turcan, *Les spectacles (De spectaculis)*, SC 332 (Paris: Cerf, 1986).

Herm.: Against Hermogenes. Ed. Frédéric Chapot, SC 439 (Paris: Cerf, 1999). Trans. Jan Hendrik Waszink, *Tertullian: The Treatise against Hermogenes*, ACW 24 (Westminster, MD: Newman, 1956).

Prax.: Against Praxeas. Ed. and trans. Ernest Evans, *Tertullian's Treatise against Praxeas* (London: SPCK, 1948).

Prescr.: On the Prescriptions of Heretics. Ed. R. F. Refoule, French trans. P. de Labriolle, *Traité de la prescription contre les hérétiques*, SC 46 (Paris: Cerf, 1957).

Theophilus of Antioch

Autol.: To Autolycus. Ed. and trans. Robert M. Grant, *Theophilus of Antioch: Ad Autolycum*, OECT (Oxford: Clarendon, 1970).

Secondary Sources

Alexandre, Monique. *Le commencement du livre Genèse I–V: La version grecque de la Septante et sa réception.* Christianisme antique 3. Paris: Beauchesne, 1988.

——— "L'exégèse de Gen. 1, 1–2a dans l'*In Hexaemeron* de Grégoire de Nysse: Deux approches du problème de la matière." In *Gregor von Nyssa und die Philosophie*, edited by Heinrich Dörrie, Margarete Altenburger, and Uta Schramm, 159–86. Leiden: Brill, 1976.

———. "La théorie de l'exégèse dans le *De hominis opficio* et l'*In Hexaemeron*." In *Écriture et culture philosophique dans la pensée de Grégoire de Nysse*, edited by Marguerite Harl, 87–110. Leiden: Brill, 1971.

Amand de Mendieta, Emmanuel. *L'ascèse monastique de saint Basile: Essai historique.* Maredsous, Belgium: Maredsous, 1949.

Anatolios, Khaled. *Athanasius: The Coherence of His Thought*. London: Routledge, 1998.

Andersen, Francis I., and David Noel Freedman. *Hosea: A New Translation with Introduction and Commentary*. AB. Garden City, NY: Doubleday, 1980.

Anderson, Gary A. "The Cosmic Mountain: Eden and Its Early Interpreters in Syriac Christianity." In *Genesis 1–3 in the History of Exegesis: Intrigue in the Garden*, edited by Gregory Allen Robbins, 187–224. Lewiston, NY, and Queenston, ON: Edwin Mellen, 1988.

———. "Ezekiel 28, the Fall of Satan, and the Adam Books." In *Literature on Adam and Eve: Collected Essays*, edited by Gary A. Anderson, Michael E. Stone, and Johannes Tromp, 133–47. Leiden and Boston: Brill, 2000.

———. *The Genesis of Perfection: Adam and Eve in Jewish and Christian Imagination*. Louisville: Westminster John Knox, 2001.

Anderson, Gary A., Michael E. Stone, and Johannes Tromp, eds. *Literature on Adam and Eve: Collected Essays*. Studia in Veteris Testamenti pseudepigrapha. Leiden and Boston: Brill, 2000.

Armstrong, A. H. "The Theory of Non-existence of Matter in Plotinus and the Cappadocians." In *Papers Presented to the Third International Conference on Patristic Studies Held at Christ Church, Oxford, 1959*, edited by F. L. Cross, 427–29. StudPat 3. TU 80. Berlin: Akademie, 1962.

Balthasar, Hans Urs von. *Presence and Thought: An Essay on the Religious Philosophy of Gregory of Nyssa*. San Francisco: Ignatius, 1995. Originally published as *Présence et pensée: Essai sur la philosophie religieuse de Grégoire de Nysse*. Paris: G. Beauchesne et Ses Fils, 1942.

Bammel, Caroline P. Hammond. "Adam in Origen." In *The Making of Orthodoxy: Essays in Honour of Henry Chadwick*, edited by Rowan Williams, 62–93. Cambridge: Cambridge University Press, 1989.

Barnes, Timothy David. *Tertullian: A Historical and Literary Study*. Revised edition. Oxford: Clarendon; New York: Oxford University Press, 1985.

Barr, James. "The Authority of Scripture: The Book of Genesis and the Origin of Evil in Jewish and Christian Tradition." In *Christian Authority: Essays in Honour of Henry Chadwick*, edited by G. R. Evans, 59–75. Oxford: Oxford University Press, 1988.

———. *The Garden of Eden and the Hope of Immortality*. Minneapolis: Fortress, 1993.

———. "Is God a Liar? (Genesis 2–3)—and Related Matters." *JTS* NS 57 (2006): 1–22.

Barth, Karl. *Christ and Adam: Man and Humanity in Romans 5*. New York: Collier, 1962. Originally published as *Christus und Adam nach Römer 5*. Zollikon-Zurich: Evangelischer Verlag, 1952.

———. *Church Dogmatics*. Vol. 3.2, *The Doctrine of Creation*. Translated by J. W. Edwards et al. Edinburgh: T&T Clark, 1948.

———. *Church Dogmatics*. Vol. 4.1, *The Doctrine of Reconciliation*. Translated by G. W. Bromiley and T. F. Torrance. Edinburgh: T&T Clark, 1956.

Bassler, Jouette. *1 Timothy, 2 Timothy, Titus*. Abingdon New Testament Commentaries. Nashville: Abingdon, 1996.

———. "Adam, Eve, and the Pastor: The Use of Genesis 2–3 in the Pastoral Epistles." In *Genesis 1–3 in the History of Exegesis: Intrigue in the Garden*, edited by Gregory Allen Robbins, 43–65. Lewiston, NY, and Queenston, ON: Edwin Mellen, 1988.

Batto, Bernard F. *Slaying the Dragon: Mythmaking in the Biblical Tradition*. Louisville: Westminster John Knox, 1992.

Bauckham, Richard. "The Early Jerusalem Church, Qumran, and the Essenes." In *The Dead Sea Scrolls as Background to Postbiblical Judaism and Early Christianity*, edited by James R. Davila, 63–89. Leiden and Boston: Brill, 2003.

Behr, John. *Asceticism and Anthropology in Irenaeus and Clement*. Oxford: Oxford University Press, 2000.

———. *The Mystery of Christ: Life in Death*. Crestwood, NY: St. Vladimir's Seminary Press, 2006.

———. *The Nicene Faith*. FCT 2. Crestwood, NY: St. Vladimir's Seminary Press, 2004.

———. "The Rational Animal: A Rereading of Gregory of Nyssa's *De hominis opificio*." *JECS* 7 (1999): 219–47.

———. *St. Irenaeus of Lyons: On the Apostolic Preaching*. Popular Patristics. Crestwood, NY: St. Vladimir's Seminary Press, 1997.

———. *The Way to Nicaea*. FCT 1. Crestwood, NY: St. Vladimir's Seminary Press, 2001.

Biram, A. "Ma'aseh Bereshit; Ma'aseh Merkabah." In *The Jewish Encyclopedia*, 8:235–36. New York: Funk & Wagnalls, 1901–6.

Blenkinsopp, Joseph. *Isaiah 40–55*. AB. New York: Doubleday, 2002.

Blowers, Paul M. "The *regula fidei* and the Narrative Character of Early Christian Faith." *Pro ecclesia* 6 (1997): 199–228.

Bogaert, Pierre. *Apocalypse de Baruch*. SC 144–45. Paris: Cerf, 1969.

Bolle, Kees W. "Myth: An Overview." In *Encyclopedia of Religion*, edited by Mircea Eliade et al., 10:261–73. New York: Macmillan, 1987.

Bonner, Campbell, ed. *The Homily on the Passion by Melito Bishop of Sardis and Some Fragments of the Apocryphal Ezekiel*. Studies and Documents 12. Philadelphia: Christophers, 1940.

Borgen, Peder. *Early Christianity and Hellenistic Judaism*. Edinburgh: T&T Clark, 1996.

———. "Philo of Alexandria." In *Jewish Writings of the Second Temple Period*, edited by Michael E. Stone, 233–82. Philadelphia: Fortress, 1984.

———. *Philo of Alexandria: An Exegete for His Time*. NovTSup. Leiden and Boston: Brill, 1997.

Bouteneff, Peter C. "All Creation in United Thanksgiving: Gregory of Nyssa and the Wesleys on Salvation." In *Orthodox and Wesleyan Spirituality*, edited by S T Kimbrough, 189–201. Crestwood, NY: St. Vladimir's Seminary Press, 2002.

————. "Essential or Existential: The Problem of the Body in the Anthropology of St. Gregory of Nyssa." In *Gregory of Nyssa: Homilies on the Beatitudes—an English Version with Commentary and Supporting Studies*, edited by H. R. Drobner and A. Viciano, 409–19. Leiden and Boston: Brill, 2000.

————. "The Mystery of Union: Elements in an Orthodox Sacramental Theology." In *Gestures of God: Explorations in Sacramental Theology*, edited by Geoffrey Rowell and Christine Hall, 91–107. New York: Continuum, 2004.

————. "St. Gregory Nazianzen and Two-Nature Christology." *SVTQ* 38 (1994): 255–70.

————. *Sweeter Than Honey: Orthodox Thinking on Dogma and Truth*. Crestwood, NY: St. Vladimir's Seminary Press, 2006.

Brown, Raymond E. *The Gospel according to John (I–XII)*. AB. New York: Doubleday, 1966.

Bruggemann, Walter. *Genesis*. Interpretation: A Bible Commentary for Teaching and Preaching. Atlanta: John Knox, 1982.

Burkert, Walter. "The Logic of Cosmogony." In *From Myth to Reason? Studies in the Development of Greek Thought*, edited by Richard Buxton, 87–106. Oxford: Oxford University Press, 1999.

Calame, Claude. *Myth and History in Ancient Greece: The Symbolic Creation of a Colony*. Translated by Daniel W. Berman. Princeton: Princeton University Press, 2003.

Canévet, Mariette. *Grégoire de Nysse et l'herméneutique biblique: Étude des rapports entre le langage et la connaissance de Dieu*. Paris: Études Augustiniennes, 1983.

Carmichael, Calum M. *The Story of Creation: Its Origin and Its Interpretation in Philo and the Fourth Gospel*. Ithaca, NY: Cornell University Press, 1996.

Carr, David. *Reading the Fractures of Genesis: Historical and Literary Approaches*. Louisville: Westminster John Knox, 1996.

Chadwick, Henry. "St. Paul and Philo of Alexandria." *Bulletin of the John Rylands Library* 48.2 (1966): 286–307.

Charles, R. H. *The Apocrypha and Pseudepigrapha of the Old Testament in English*. 2 vols. Oxford: Oxford University Press, 1913.

————. *The Book of Jubilees; or, The Little Genesis*. London: Adam & Charles Black, 1902.

Clark, Elizabeth. *The Origenist Controversy: The Cultural Construction of an Early Christian Debate*. Princeton, NJ: Princeton University Press, 1992.

Clifford, Richard J. "The Hebrew Scriptures and the Theology of Creation." *Theological Studies* 46 (1985): 507–23.

Cohick, Lynn H. *The* Peri pascha *Attributed to Melito of Sardis: Setting, Purpose, and Sources*. BJS 327. Providence: Brown Judaic Studies, 2000.

Collins, John J. *Jewish Wisdom in the Hellenistic Age*. Old Testament Library. Louisville: Westminster John Knox, 1997.

Crouzel, Henri. *Origen*. 1985. Translated by A. S. Worrall. San Francisco: Harper & Row, 1989.

Dahood, Mitchell. *Psalms II (51–100)*. AB. Garden City, NY: Doubleday, 1968.

Daley, Brian E. *Gregory of Nazianzus*. ECF. London and New York: Routledge, 2006.

———. "Origen's 'De principiis': A Guide to the 'Principles' of Christian Scriptural Interpretation." In *Nova et Vetera: Patristic Studies in Honor of Thomas Patrick Halton*, edited by John F. Petruccione, 3–21. Washington, DC: Catholic University of America Press, 1998.

D'Angelo, Mary Rose. "The Garden: Once and Not Again. Traditional Interpretations of Genesis 1:26–27 in 1 Corinthians 11:7–12." In *Genesis 1–3 in the History of Exegesis: Intrigue in the Garden*, edited by Gregory Allen Robbins, 1–41. Lewiston, NY, and Queenston, ON: Edwin Mellen, 1988.

Daniélou, Jean. "La chronologie des oeuvres de Grégoire de Nysse." In *Papers Presented to the Fourth International Conference on Patristic Studies Held at Christ Church, Oxford, 1963*, edited by F. L. Cross, 159–69. StudPat 7.1. TU 92 (Berlin: Akademie, 1966).

———. *From Shadows to Reality: Studies in the Biblical Typology of the Fathers*. London: Burns & Oates, 1960.

———. *Origen*. Translated by Walter Mitchell. New York: Sheed & Ward, 1955. Originally published as *Origène* (Paris: La Table Ronde, 1948).

Davidson, Richard M. *Typology in Scripture: A Study of Hermeneutical τύπος Structures*. Andrews University Seminary Doctoral Dissertations 2. Berrien Springs, MI: Andrews University Press, 1981.

Davila, James R., ed. *The Dead Sea Scrolls as Background to Postbiblical Judaism and Early Christianity*. Leiden and Boston: Brill, 2003.

Dawson, David. *Allegorical Readers and Cultural Revision in Ancient Alexandria*. Berkeley: University of California Press, 1992.

Dechow, Jon F. *Dogma and Mysticism in Early Christianity: Epiphanius of Cyprus and the Legacy of Origen*. Patristic Monograph Series. Macon, GA: Mercer University Press, 1988.

———. "The Heresy Charges against Origen." In *Origeniana quarta*, edited by Lothar Lies, 112–22. Innsbruck: Tyrolia, 1987.

———. "Origen's 'Heresy': From Eustathius to Epiphanius." In *Origeniana quarta*, edited by Lothar Lies, 405–9. Innsbruck: Tyrolia, 1987.

Dibelius, Martin, and Hans Conzelmann. *The Pastoral Epistles*. Translated by P. Buttolph and A. Yarbro. 4th revised edition. Hermeneia. Philadelphia: Fortress, 1972.

Dines, Jennifer M. *The Septuagint*. New York: T&T Clark, 2004.

Dively Lauro, Elizabeth Ann. *The Soul and Spirit of Scripture within Origen's Exegesis*. Leiden and Boston: Brill, 2005.

Donovan, Mary Ann. *One Right Reading? A Guide to Irenaeus*. Collegeville, MN: Liturgical Press, 1997.

Droge, Arthur J. *Homer or Moses? Early Christian Interpretations of the History of Culture*. Tübingen: Mohr, 1989.

Dundes, Alan, ed. *The Flood Myth*. Berkeley: University of California Press, 1988.

———. *Holy Writ as Oral Lit: The Bible as Folklore.* New York: Rowman & Little-field, 1999.

Dunn, Geoffrey D. *Tertullian.* ECF. London: Routledge, 2004.

Dunn, James D. G. *Christology in the Making: An Inquiry into the Origins of the Doctrine of the Incarnation.* London: SCM, 1980.

———. *The Theology of Paul the Apostle.* Grand Rapids: Eerdmans, 1998.

Edwards, Mark. "Justin's Logos and the Word of God." *JECS* 3 (1995): 261–80.

———. "On the Platonic Schooling of Justin Martyr." *JTS* NS 42 (1991): 17–34.

Ellis, E. Earle. *Paul's Use of the Old Testament.* Edinburgh and London: Oliver & Boyd, 1957.

Ernest, James D. *The Bible in Athanasius of Alexandria.* Bible in Ancient Christianity. Leiden and Boston: Brill, 2004.

Fantino, Jacques. *L'homme image de Dieu chez saint Irénée de Lyon.* Thèses. Paris: Cerf, 1986.

———. *La théologie d'Irénée: Lecture des Écritures en réponse à l'exégèse gnostique—une approche trinitaire.* Cogitatio fidei. Paris: Cerf, 1994.

Farges, Jacques. *Les idées morales et religieuses de méthode d'Olympe: Contribution à l'étude des rapports du christianisme et de l'hellénisme à la fin du troisième siècle.* Paris: Beauchesne, 1929.

Fedwick, Paul Jonathan, ed. *Basil of Caesarea: Christian, Humanist, Ascetic,* 2 vols. Toronto: Pontifical Institute of Medieval Studies, 1981.

———. "A Chronology of the Life and Works of Basil of Caesarea." In *Basil of Caesarea: Christian, Humanist, Ascetic,* edited by Paul Jonathan Fedwick, 1:3–19. Toronto: Pontifical Institute of Medieval Studies, 1981.

Fenwick, John R. K. *The Anaphoras of St. Basil and St. James: An Investigation into Their Common Origin.* Orientalia christiana analecta. Rome: Pontificium Insti-tutum Orientale, 1992.

Fitzmyer, Joseph A. *Romans.* AB. New York: Doubleday, 1992.

Floyd, W. E. G. *Clement of Alexandria's Treatment of the Problem of Evil.* OTM. Oxford: Oxford University Press, 1971.

Frye, Northrop. *The Great Code: The Bible and Literature.* New York and London: Harcourt Brace Jovanovich, 1981.

Gerhardsson, Birger. *Memory and Manuscript: Oral Tradition and Written Trans-mission in Rabbinic Judaism and Early Christianity.* Translated by Eric J. Sharpe. Lund, Sweden: C. W. K. Gleerup, 1961. Reprinted, with a new preface, in combined edition with *Tradition and Transmission in Early Christianity.* Grand Rapids: Eerdmans, 1998.

———. *The Origins of the Gospel Traditions.* Philadelphia: Fortress, 1979.

Golitzin, Alexander. "Recovering 'The Glory of Adam': 'Divine Light' Traditions in the Dead Sea Scrolls and the Christian Ascetical Literature of Fourth-Century Syro-Mesopotamia." In *The Dead Sea Scrolls as Background to Postbiblical Judaism and Early Christianity,* edited by James R. Davila, 275–308. Leiden and Boston: Brill, 2003.

Goodenough, E. R., with A. Thomas Kraabel. "Paul and the Hellenization of Christianity." In *Religions in Antiquity: Essays in Memory of Erwin Ramsdell Goodenough*, edited by Jacob Neusner, 23–68. Studies in the History of Religions (supplement to *Numen*) 14. Leiden: Brill, 1968.

Goppelt, Leonhard. *Typos: The Typological Interpretation of the Old Testament in the New*. Grand Rapids: Eerdmans, 1982. Originally published as *Typos: Die typologische Deutung des Alten Testaments im Neuen*. Gütersloh: C. Bertelsmann, 1939.

Grant, Robert M. *Greek Apologists of the Second Century*. Philadelphia: Westminster, 1988.

———. *Irenaeus of Lyons*. ECF. London: Routledge, 1997.

Greenberg, Moshe. *Ezekiel 21–37*. AB. New York: Doubleday, 1997.

Greene-McCreight, Kathryn. *Ad litteram: How Augustine, Calvin, and Barth Read the "Plain Sense" of Genesis 1–3*. Issues in Systematic Theology 5. Berlin: Peter Lang, 1999.

Gribomont, Jean. "Notes biographiques sur s. Basile le Grand." In *Basil of Caesarea: Christian, Humanist, Ascetic*, edited by Paul Jonathan Fedwick, 1:21–48. Toronto: Pontifical Institute for Medieval Studies, 1981.

———. "L'origénisme de saint Basile." In *L'homme devant Dieu: Mélanges offerts au père Henri de Lubac*, Marie-Thérèse d'Alverny, 1:281–94. Paris: Aubier, 1963.

Gunkel, Hermann. *Legends of Genesis: The Biblical Saga and History*. New York: Schocken, 1964. Originally published as *Genesis, übersetzt und erklärt*. Göttingen: Vandenhoeck & Ruprecht, 1901.

Hainsworth, John. "The Force of the Mystery: Anamnesis and Exegesis in Melito's *Peri pascha*." *SVTQ* 46 (2002): 107–46.

Halliwell, S. "The Subjection of Muthos to Logos: Plato's Citations of the Poets." *Classical Quarterly* 50 (2000): 94–112.

Hanson, R. P. C. *Allegory and Event: A Study of the Sources and Significance of Origen's Interpretation of Scripture*. Louisville: Westminster John Knox, 2002.

Harl, Marguerite. "La préexistence des âmes dans l'oeuvre d'Origène." In *Origeniana quarta*, edited by Lothar Lies, 238–58. Innsbruck: Tyrolia, 1987.

Harrison, Nonna Verna. "Male and Female in Cappadocian Theology." *JTS* NS 41 (1990): 441–71.

———. "The Maleness of Christ." *SVTQ* 42 (1998): 111–51.

Hasan-Rokem, Galit. "And God Created the Proverb . . . Inter-generic and Inter-textual Aspects of Biblical Paremiology—or the Longest Way to the Shortest Text." In *Text and Tradition: The Hebrew Bible and Folklore*, edited by Susan Niditch, 107–20. Atlanta: Scholars Press, 1990.

Havelock, Eric A. *The Muse Learns to Write: Reflections on Orality and Literacy from Antiquity to the Present*. New Haven: Yale, 1986.

Heine, Ronald E. "Origen's Alexandrian *Commentary on Genesis*." In *Origeniana octava: Origen and the Alexandrian Tradition*, edited by L. Perrone, 63–73. Leuven: Leuven University Press, 2003.

———. "The Testimonia and Fragments Related to Origen's Commentary on Genesis." *Zeitschrift für Antikes Christentum* 9 (2005): 122–42.

Heinrichs, Albert. "Demythologizing the Past, Mythicizing the Present: Myth, History, and the Supernatural at the Dawn of the Hellenistic Period." In *From Myth to Reason? Studies in the Development of Greek Thought*, edited by Richard Buxton, 223–48. Oxford: Oxford University Press, 1999.

Hill, Robert C. "His Master's Voice: Theodore of Mopsuestia on the Psalms." *Heythrop Journal* 45 (2004): 40–53.

Jaki, Stanley L. *Genesis 1 through the Ages*. London: Thomas More, 1992.

Jellicoe, Sidney. *The Septuagint and Modern Study*. Oxford: Oxford University Press, 1968.

Johnson, Luke Timothy. *The First and Second Letters to Timothy*. AB. New York: Doubleday, 2001.

Junod, Éric. "Remarques sur la composition de la Philocalie d'Origène par Basile de Césarée et Grégoire de Nazianze." *Revue d'histoire et de philosophie religieuses* 52 (1972): 149–56.

Kannengiesser, Charles. *Handbook of Patristic Exegesis*. Bible in Ancient Christianity. Leiden and Boston: Brill, 2006.

———. "Philon et les Pères sur la double création de l'homme." In *Philon d'Alexandrie, Lyon, 11–15 Septembre 1966*, 277–97. Paris: Centre National de la Recherche Scientifique, 1967.

Kelly, J. N. D. *A Commentary on the Pastoral Epistles*. New York: Harper & Row, 1963.

Kirk, G. S. *Myth: Its Meaning and Functions in Ancient and Other Cultures*. Cambridge: Cambridge University Press, 1970.

Knapp, Henry. "Melito's Use of Scripture in *Peri pascha*: Second-Century Typology." *VC* 54 (2000): 343–74.

Knibb, Michael A. "Life and Death in the Old Testament." In *The World of Ancient Israel: Social, Anthropological, and Political Perspectives*, edited by R. E. Clements, 395–415. Cambridge: Cambridge University Press, 1989.

Kugel, James L. *The Bible as It Was*. Cambridge, MA: Belknap Press of Harvard University Press, 1997.

Lampe, G. W. H. "The Exposition and Exegesis of Scripture to Gregory the Great." In *The Cambridge History of the Bible*. Vol. 2, *The West from the Fathers to the Reformation*, edited by G. W. H. Lampe, 155–83. Cambridge: Cambridge University Press, 1969.

Lange, N. R. M. de. *Origen and the Jews: Studies in Jewish-Christian Relations in Third-Century Palestine*. Cambridge: Cambridge University Press, 1976.

Lengsfeld, Peter. *Adam und Christus: Die Adam-Christus-Typologie im Neuen Testament und ihre dogmatische Verwendung bei M. J. Scheeben und K. Barth*. Essen: Ludgerus, 1965.

Levison, John R. *Portraits of Adam in Early Judaism*. JSPSup 1. Sheffield: Sheffield Academic Press, 1988.

Lewis, Jack P. "The Days of Creation: An Historical Survey of Interpretation." *Journal of the Evangelical Theological Society* 32 (1989): 433–55.

Lim, Richard. "The Politics of Interpretation in Basil of Caesarea's Hexaemeron." VC 44 (1990): 351–70.

Lim, Timothy H. "Studying the Qumran Scrolls and Paul in Their Historical Context." In The Dead Sea Scrolls as Background to Postbiblical Judaism and Early Christianity, edited by James R. Davila, 135–56. Leiden and Boston: Brill, 2003.

Lipatov, Nikolai A., trans. St. Basil the Great: Commentary on the Prophet Isaiah. Texts and Studies in the History of Theology. Mandelbachtal, Germany, and Cambridge, UK: Cicero, 2001.

Loader, William. The Septuagint, Sexuality, and the New Testament: Case Studies on the Impact of the LXX in Philo and the New Testament. Grand Rapids: Eerdmans, 2004.

Longenecker, Richard N. Biblical Exegesis in the Apostolic Period. 2nd edition. Grand Rapids: Eerdmans, 1999.

Lossky, Vladimir. In the Image and Likeness of God. Crestwood, NY: St. Vladimir's Seminary Press, 1974. Originally published as À l'image et à la ressemblance de Dieu (Paris: Aubier-Montaigne, 1967).

Louth, Andrew. Discerning the Mystery: An Essay on the Nature of Theology. Oxford: Oxford University Press, 1983.

Lubac, Henri de. "'Typologie' et 'allégorisme.'" RechSR 34 (1947): 180–226.

Mackenzie, Ian M. Irenaeus's Demonstration of the Apostolic Preaching: A Theological Commentary and Translation. Burlington, VT: Ashgate, 2002.

May, Gerhard. "Die Chronologie des Lebens und der Werke des Gregor von Nyssa." In Écriture et culture philosophique dans la pensée de Grégoire de Nysse, edited by Marguerite Harl, 51–66. Leiden: Brill, 1971.

McCarthy, Carmel, and William Riley. The Old Testament Short Story: Explorations into Narrative Spirituality. Wilmington, DE: Michael Glazier, 1986.

McGuckin, John. "Patterns of Biblical Exegesis in the Cappadocian Fathers: Basil the Great, Gregory the Theologian, and Gregory of Nyssa." In Orthodox and Wesleyan Scriptural Understanding and Practice, edited by S T Kimbrough, 37–54. Crestwood, NY: St. Vladimir's Seminary Press, 2005.

———. St. Gregory of Nazianzus: An Intellectual Biography. Crestwood, NY: St. Vladimir's Seminary Press, 2001.

McKenzie, John L. Second Isaiah. AB. Garden City, NY: Doubleday, 1968.

Milgrom, Jacob. Leviticus 1–16: A New Translation with Introduction and Commentary. AB. New York: Doubleday, 1991.

Momigliano, Arnaldo. "Pagan and Christian Historiography in the Fourth Century A.D." In Paganism and Christianity in the Fourth Century, edited by Arnaldo Momigliano, 79–99. Oxford: Oxford University Press, 1963.

Moore, G. F. Judaism in the First Centuries of the Christian Era: The Age of the Tannaim. 3 vols. Cambridge, MA: Harvard University Press, 1927.

Most, Glenn. "From Logos to Mythos." In From Myth to Reason? Studies in the Development of Greek Thought, edited by Richard Buxton, 25–47. Oxford: Oxford University Press, 1999.

Murray, Gilbert. Five Stages of Greek Religion. Garden City, NY: Doubleday, 1951.

Murray, Penelope. "What Is a *muthos* for Plato?" In *From Myth to Reason? Studies in the Development of Greek Thought*, edited by Richard Buxton, 251–62. Oxford: Oxford University Press, 1999.

Myers, Jacob M. *I and II Esdras*. AB. Garden City, NY: Doubleday, 1974.

Nautin, Pierre. *Origène: Sa vie et son oeuvre*. Christianisme antique. Paris: Beauchesne, 1977.

Nicholson, Ernest. *The Pentateuch in the Twentieth Century: The Legacy of Julius Wellhausen*. Oxford: Clarendon, 1998.

Nickelsburg, George W. E. "The Bible Rewritten and Expanded." In *Jewish Writings of the Second Temple Period*, edited by Michael E. Stone, 89–156. Philadelphia: Fortress, 1984.

Niditch, Susan. *Chaos to Cosmos: Studies in Biblical Patterns of Creation*. Chico, CA: Scholars Press, 1985.

———. *Folklore and the Hebrew Bible*. Minneapolis: Fortress, 1993.

———. *Oral World and Written Word: Ancient Israelite Literature*. Louisville: Westminster John Knox, 1996.

Nielsen, J. T. *Adam and Christ in the Theology of Irenaeus of Lyons*. Assen: Van Gorcum, 1968.

Oliver, Harold H. "Relational Ontology and Hermeneutics." In *Myth, Symbol, and Reality*, edited by Alan M. Olson, 69–85. Notre Dame, IN: University of Notre Dame Press, 1980.

Olson, Alan M. "Myth, Symbol, and Metaphorical Truth." In *Myth, Symbol, and Reality*, edited by Alan M. Olson, 99–125. Notre Dame, IN: University of Notre Dame Press, 1980.

O'Malley, T. P. *Tertullian and the Bible: Language, Imagery, Exegesis*. Latinitas Christianorum primaeva. Utrecht: Dekker & Van de Vegt, 1967.

Ong, Walter J. *Orality and Literacy: The Technologizing of the Word*. New York: Routledge, 1988.

Orr, William F., and James Arthur Walther. *1 Corinthians*. AB. Garden City, NY: Doubleday, 1976.

Osborn, Eric. *Irenaeus of Lyons*. Cambridge: Cambridge University Press, 2001.

———. "Origen: The Twentieth Century Quarrel and Its Recovery." In *Origeniana quinta*, edited by Robert J. Daly, 26–39. Leuven: Leuven University Press, 1992.

———. "Reason and the Rule of Faith in the Second Century AD." In *The Making of Orthodoxy: Essays in Honour of Henry Chadwick*, edited by Rowan Williams, 40–61. Cambridge: Cambridge University Press, 1989.

———. *Tertullian, First Theologian of the West*. Cambridge: Cambridge University Press, 1997.

Pagels, Elaine. *Adam, Eve, and the Serpent*. New York: Random House, 1988.

Patterson, L. G. *Methodius of Olympus: Divine Sovereignty, Human Freedom, and Life in Christ*. Washington, DC: Catholic University of America Press, 1997.

Pearson, Birger. *The pneumatikos-psychikos Terminology in 1 Corinthians: A Study in the Theology of the Corinthian Opponents of Paul and Its Relation to Gnosticism*.

Society of Biblical Literature Dissertation Series 12. Missoula, MT: Scholars Press, 1973.

Pelikan, Jaroslav. "The 'Spiritual Sense' of Scripture: The Exegetical Basis for St. Basil's Doctrine of the Holy Spirit." In *Basil of Caesarea: Christian, Humanist, Ascetic*, edited by Paul Jonathan Fedwick, 2:337–60. Toronto: Pontifical Institute of Medieval Studies, 1981.

Phipps, William E. *Genesis and Gender: Biblical Myths of Sexuality and Their Cultural Impact*. New York: Praeger, 1989.

Pope, Marvin H. *Job*. AB. Garden City, NY: Doubleday, 1965.

Prigent, Pierre. *Justin et l'Ancien Testament*. Études bibliques. Paris: Lecoffre, 1964.

Rad, Gerhard von. *Genesis: A Commentary*. Revised edition. Old Testament Library. Philadelphia: Westminster, 1973.

———. "The Theological Problem of the Old Testament Doctrine of Creation." Translated by E. W. Truman Dicken. In *The Problem of the Hexateuch and Other Essays*, edited by Gerhard von Rad, 131–43. Edinburgh and London: Oliver & Boyd, 1966.

Rajak, Tessa. "Talking at Trypho: Christian Apologetic as Anti-Judaism in Justin's *Dialogue with Trypho the Jew*." In *Apologetics in the Roman Empire: Pagans, Jews, and Christians*, edited by Mark Edwards, Martin Goodman, and Simon Price, 59–80. Oxford: Oxford University Press, 1999.

Reese, James M. *Hellenistic Influence on the Book of Wisdom and Its Consequences*. Analecta biblica 41. Rome: Biblical Institute, 1970.

Rendsburg, Gary A. *The Redaction of Genesis*. Winona Lake, IN: Eisenbrauns, 1986.

Ricoeur, Paul. "Myth and History." In *Encyclopedia of Religion*, edited by Mircea Eliade et al., 10:273–82. New York: Macmillan, 1987.

———. *The Rule of Metaphor*. Toronto: University of Toronto Press, 1977. Originally published as *La métaphore vive*. Paris: Seuil, 1975.

Ricoeur, Paul, and André LaCocque. *Thinking Biblically: Exegetical and Hermeneutical Studies*. Chicago: University of Chicago Press, 2003.

Robbins, Gregory Allen, ed. *Genesis 1–3 in the History of Exegesis: Intrigue in the Garden*. Studies in Women and Religion 27. Lewiston, NY, and Queenston, ON: Edwin Mellen, 1988.

Roberts, C. H. "Books in the Greco-Roman World and in the New Testament." In *The Cambridge History of the Bible*, edited by P. Ackroyd and C. F. Evans, 1:48–66. Cambridge: Cambridge University Press, 1970.

Rogers, Rick. *Theophilus of Antioch: The Life and Thought of a Second-Century Bishop*. New York: Lexington, 2000.

Rokéah, David. *Justin Martyr and the Jews*. Jewish and Christian Perspectives. Leiden and Boston: Brill, 2002.

Rose, Seraphim. *Genesis, Creation, and Early Man: The Orthodox Christian Vision*. Platina, CA: St. Herman of Alaska Brotherhood, 2000.

Rousseau, Philip. *Basil of Caesarea*. Berkeley: University of California Press, 1994.

Runia, David T. "Philo, Alexandrian and Jew." In *Exegesis and Philosophy: Studies on Philo of Alexandria*, 1–18. Aldershot, UK: Variorum; Brookville, VT: Gower, 1990.

———. *Philo and the Church Fathers*. SupVC 32. Leiden and Boston: Brill, 1995.

———. *Philo in Early Christian Literature: A Survey*. CRINT. Minneapolis: Fortress, 1993.

———. "References to Philo from Josephus up to 1000 AD." *Studia philonica* 6 (1994): 111–21.

Russell, D. A. *Criticism in Antiquity*. 2nd edition. Bristol, UK: Bristol Classical Press, 1995.

Sanchez, Sylvain Jean Gabriel. *Justin apologiste chrétien*. Cahiers de la Revue biblique. Paris: Gabalda, 2000.

Sanders, E. P. *Paul and Palestinian Judaism: A Comparison of Patterns of Religion*. Philadelphia: Fortress, 1977.

———. *Paul, the Law, and the Jewish People*. Philadelphia: Fortress, 1983.

Sandmel, Samuel. *The Genius of Paul: A Study in History*. New York: Schocken Books, 1970.

———. *Philo of Alexandria: An Introduction*. Oxford: Oxford University Press, 1979.

Sarna, Nahum. *Understanding Genesis*. Heritage of Biblical Israel 1. New York: Jewish Theological Seminary of America Press, 1966.

Schüssler Fiorenza, Elisabeth. *In Memory of Her: A Feminist Theological Reconstruction of Christian Origins*. New York: Crossroad, 1983.

Scott, Alan. *Origen and the Life of the Stars: A History of an Idea*. Oxford Early Christian Studies. Oxford: Oxford University Press, 1991.

Segal, Robert A. *Theorizing about Myth*. Amherst: University of Massachusetts Press, 1999.

Sesboüé, Bernard. *Tout récapituler dans le Christ: Christologie et sotériologie d'Irénée de Lyon*. Jésus et Jésus-Christ. Paris: Desclée, 2000.

Shotwell, Willis A. *The Biblical Exegesis of Justin Martyr*. London: SPCK, 1965.

Skarsaune, Oskar. *The Proof from Prophecy: A Study in Justin Martyr's Proof-Text Tradition: Text-Type, Provenance, Theological Profile*. Supplements to Novum Testamentum. Leiden: Brill, 1987.

Skehan, Patrick W., and Alexander DiLella. *The Wisdom of Ben Sira: A New Translation with Notes*. AB. New York: Doubleday, 1987.

Smith, J. Warren. *Passion and Paradise: Human and Divine Emotion in the Thought of Gregory of Nyssa*. New York: Herder & Herder, 2004.

Soskice, Janet Martin. *Metaphor and Religious Language*. Oxford: Oxford University Press, 1985.

Sowers, Sidney G. *The Hermeneutics of Philo and Hebrews: A Comparison of the Interpretation of the Old Testament in Philo Judaeus and the Epistle to the Hebrews*. Basel Studies of Theology. Richmond, VA: John Knox, 1965.

Sparks, Kenton L. "The Problem of Myth in Ancient Historiography." In *Rethinking the Foundations—Historiography in the Ancient World and in the Bible: Essays in Honour of John Van Seters*, edited by S. L. McKenzie and T. Römer, 269–80. New York: de Gruyter, 2000.

Speiser, E. A. *Genesis*. AB. Doubleday: New York, 1964.

Stewart-Sykes, Alistair. *The Lamb's High Feast: Melito, Peri pascha, and the Quarto-deciman Paschal Liturgy at Sardis*. SupVC. Leiden and Boston: Brill, 1998.

Stone, Michael E. *A Commentary on the Book of Fourth Ezra*. Hermeneia. Minneapolis: Fortress, 1990.

———. *A History of the Literature of Adam and Eve*. Society of Biblical Literature Early Judaism and Its Literature. Atlanta: Scholars Press, 1992.

———, ed. *Jewish Writings of the Second Temple Period*. CRINT. Philadelphia: Fortress, 1984.

Stowers, Stanley K. *A Rereading of Romans: Justice, Jews, and Gentiles*. New Haven: Yale University Press, 1994.

Tarazi, Paul Nadim. *The Old Testament: An Introduction*. Vol. 1, *Historical Traditions*. Crestwood, NY: St. Vladimir's Seminary Press, 1991.

Testuz, Michel. *Les idées religieuses du livre des Jubilés*. Geneva: E. Droz, 1960.

Tobin, Thomas H. *The Creation of Man: Philo and the History of Interpretation*. Catholic Biblical Quarterly Monograph Series 14. Washington, DC: Catholic Biblical Association of America, 1983.

———. "The Jewish Context of Rom 5:12–14." In *In the Spirit of Faith: Studies in Philo and Early Christianity in Honor of David Hay*, edited by David T. Runia and Gregory E. Sterling, 159–75. Studia philonica Annual: Studies in Hellenistic Judaism 13. Providence: Brown Judaic Studies, 2001.

Torjesen, Karen Jo. *Hermeneutical Procedure and Theological Method in Origen's Exegesis*. Patristische Texte und Studien. New York: de Gruyter, 1986.

———. "Hermeneutics and Soteriology in Origen's *Peri archon*." *JTS* NS 21 (1989): 333–48.

Torrance, Thomas F. *Divine Meaning: Studies in Patristic Hermeneutics*. Edinburgh: T&T Clark, 1995.

Tov, Emanuel. "The Septuagint." In *Mikra: Text, Translation, Reading and Interpretation of the Hebrew Bible in Ancient Judaism and Early Christianity*, edited by Martin Jan Mulder, 161–88. CRINT. Philadelphia: Fortress, 1988.

VanderKam, J. *Textual and Historical Studies in the Book of Jubilees*. Harvard Semitic Monographs 14. Missoula, MT: Scholars Press, 1977.

Van Seters, John. *In Search of History: Historiography in the Ancient World and the Origins of Biblical History*. New Haven: Yale University Press, 1983.

———. *Prologue to History: The Yahwist as Historian in Genesis*. Louisville: Westminster John Knox, 1992.

Van Winden, J. C. M. "The World of Ideas in Philo of Alexandria: An Interpretation of *De opificio mundi* 24–25." *VC* 37 (1983): 209–17.

Ware, Timothy. *The Orthodox Church*. Revised edition. New York: Penguin, 1993.

Watson, Gerard. "Origen and the Literal Interpretation of Scripture." In *Scriptural Interpretation in the Fathers: Letter and Spirit*, edited by Thomas Finan and Vincent Twomey, 75–84. Portland, OR, and Dublin: Four Courts, 1995.

Weigle, Luther A., ed. *The Genesis Octapla: Eight Versions of the Book of Genesis in the Tyndale–King James Tradition*. New York: Thomas Nelson and Sons, 1965.

Wellhausen, Julius. *Prolegomena to the History of Ancient Israel*. New York: Meridian, 1957. Originally published as *Prolegomena zur Geschichte Israels*. 6th edition. Berlin: Georg Reimer, 1905.

Westerholm, Stephen. *Perspectives Old and New on Paul: The "Lutheran" Paul and His Critics*. Grand Rapids: Eerdmans, 2004.

Westermann, Claus. *Creation*. Translated by John J. Scullion. Philadelphia: Fortress, 1974.

———. *Genesis 1–11: A Commentary*. Minneapolis: Augsburg, 1984. Originally published as *Genesis 1–11*. 2nd edition. Darmstadt: Wissenschaftliche Buchgesellschaft, 1976.

Wevers, John William. *Notes on the Greek Text of Genesis*. Atlanta: Scholars Press, 1993.

Wheeldon, M. J. "'True Stories': The Reception of Historiography in Antiquity." In *History as Text: The Writing of History in the Ancient World*, edited by Averil Cameron, 33–62. London: Duckworth, 1989.

White, Hugh C. *Narration and Discourse in the Book of Genesis*. Cambridge: Cambridge University Press, 1991.

Whybray, Roger Norman. *The Making of the Pentateuch: A Methodological Study*. Journal for the Study of the Old Testament: Supplement Series 53. Sheffield: Sheffield Academic Press, 1987.

Williams, Rowan. "Historical Criticism and Sacred Text." In *Reading Texts, Seeking Wisdom: Scripture and Theology*, edited by David Ford and Graham Stanton, 217–28. Grand Rapids: Eerdmans, 2003.

———. "Macrina's Deathbed Revisited: Gregory of Nyssa on Mind and Passion." In *Christian Faith and Greek Philosophy in Late Antiquity: Essays in Tribute to George Christopher Stead*, edited by L. R. Wickham and Caroline P. Hammond Bammel, 227–46. Leiden and New York: Brill, 1993.

Williamson, Ronald. *Philo and the Epistle to the Hebrews*. Arbeiten zur Literatur und Geschichte des hellenistischen Judentums 4. Leiden: Brill, 1970.

Winston, David. *The Wisdom of Solomon: A New Translation with Introduction and Commentary*. AB. Garden City, NY: Doubleday, 1979.

Wolfson, Elliot R. *Language, Eros, Being: Kabbalistic Hermeneutics and Poetic Imagination*. New York: Fordham University Press, 2005.

Young, Frances. "Adam and Anthropos: A Study in the Interaction of Science and the Bible in Two Anthropological Treatises of the Fourth Century." VC 37 (1983): 110–40.

———. *Biblical Exegesis and the Formation of Christian Culture*. Cambridge: Cambridge University Press, 1997.

————. "Greek Apologists of the Second Century." In *Apologetics in the Roman Empire: Pagans, Jews, and Christians*, edited by Mark Edwards, Martin Goodman, and Simon Price, 81–104. Oxford: Oxford University Press, 1999.

————. "The Rhetorical Schools and Their Influence on Patristic Exegesis." In *The Making of Orthodoxy*, edited by Rowan Williams, 182–99. Cambridge: Cambridge University Press, 1989.

————. *Virtuoso Theology: The Bible and Interpretation*. Cleveland: Pilgrim, 1993. Originally published as *The Art of Performance: Towards a Theology of Holy Scripture*. London: Darton, Longman & Todd, 1990.

Zachhuber, Johannes. *Human Nature in Gregory of Nyssa: Philosophical Background and Theological Significance*. SupVC. Leiden and Boston: Brill, 2000.

————. "Once Again: Gregory of Nyssa on Universals." *JTS* NS 56 (2005): 75–98.

Zimmerli, Walther. *Ezekiel: A Commentary on the Book of the Prophet Ezekiel*. Vol. 1. Translated by Ronald E. Clements. Hermeneia. Philadelphia: Fortress, 1979.

Modern Author Index

Scripture and Ancient Sources Index

Subject Index

Lightning Source UK Ltd.
Milton Keynes UK
UKHW020623140322
400024UK00005B/149